Praise for *Still Moving: How to Lead Mindful Change*

Still Moving is groundbreaking in this time of increasing complexity and ongoing disruption. Rowland's work in the field is 10 years ahead of the industry and she speaks into our deepest need right now. This book is an essential companion for CEOs and anyone leading large, complex change and those who advise them. Let the book speak to you, consume the wisdom, and put that wisdom into practice. You, your family, customers, employees, business and the planet will all be the benefactors.

Bill Adams, *CEO, The Leadership Circle and Full Circle Group, co-author of Mastering Leadership and The Whole Systems Approach*

It is now commonplace to talk about the constancy of change in the business world as a backdrop for the latest best approach to its leadership. This book sets its ambitions far higher: the increasingly intractable and bewildering dilemmas we all see and face, not only in business, but related to issues such as migration, climate change, inequality and terrorism.

Rowland meets this burning need for a profoundly different and more effective leadership with real insight into what this needs to look like – no magic formulas but deep exploration of our own role as leaders. These insights need to be heard and adopted in all walks of life.

Ruth Cairnie, *Non-executive Director, Rolls-Royce Holdings, Associated British Foods and Keller Group*

Deborah Rowland has written a truly groundbreaking book. Based on sound research, she shows for the first time that success in leading large-scale change depends not only on what a leader does but, crucially, on how they are – on their inner states and capacities.

How strange that it has taken so long for us to wake up to the fact that the inner states and capacities of leaders really matter. And how wonderful that Deborah has so convincingly been able to open our eyes to that deep truth.

Michael Chaskalson, *Professor of Practice, Ashridge Business School*

More traditional ways of managing change in this fast, disruptive and increasingly uncertain world are no longer enough. Transformational change requires purposeful leadership with a deep awareness of self and the needs of others.

Still Moving provides the perfect blend of a rigorous analytical study coupled with powerful real-life stories of successful transformation. If you are about to lead change, this is a must have companion.

Steven Cooper, *CEO, Personal Banking and Executive Director, Barclays Bank plc*

I read this book because I have long admired Deborah's innate gift to look well past the obvious and to illuminate the parts of leadership and change simply not visible to most of us. With *Still Moving*, she provides a series of insights into one of the great ironies of leadership in this decade: the most effective way to lead through the dynamic, distracting minefields of chaos we face in our lives is to nurture the inner space that enables us to lead from a place of profound mindfulness. *Still Moving* provides the proof of concept, the motivation and the instruction to begin a leader's most important journey.

Kevin Cox, *Chief Human Resources Officer, American Express Company*

A powerful exposition on the need to first look within ourselves to find the leadership skills required for our fast changing and dislocated world, *Still Moving* is a welcome and much-needed contribution on how to lead for positive social change in an era when leaders need to be in a continual state of adaptation.

Within this world Rowland convincingly shows us why a thoughtful, mindful and purpose-driven approach to leading change is the one most likely to endure.

Paul Polman, *CEO, Unilever*

Still Moving is a compelling and practical guide to the leadership of change. By sharing her self-reflection and brave journey into her past, Deborah inspires us all to become more conscious and embracing of our own life narratives – a key underpinning of her framework to help us become more effective leaders and agents of change in our organisations and in society today.

Ann Sarnoff, *President, BBC Worldwide North America*

An inspiring, practical and provocative take on the power of mindful leadership to reshape our world

Otto Scharmer, *Senior Lecturer, MIT and co-founder of the Presencing Institute*

Still Moving is an inspiring, practical and well-researched treatise on how to navigate change in this fast-moving world. It is a wake up call to more mindful leadership, and Rowland's writing style took my own mind on a heartfelt and enriching journey. For all leaders of any change, this book could be your most valuable guide.

Mimi Tang, *Founder and CEO, Wing's Share (and former President, Kering Asia Pacific)*

In *Still Moving* Deborah Rowland comprehensively describes how fundamental change can only be achieved when leaders combine their own capacity for mindfulness with business transformation. What's more, she pulled this off in my company, where she successfully guided us through a large, complex transformation – she has been in the field, and felt it and shaped it. I can think of no one with greater passion, wisdom and authority on the subject – and who, at the same time, exposes her own vulnerability and learning.

Peter Terium, *CEO, RWE (now innogy)*

Rowland's book *Still Moving* is an exciting breakthrough in thinking on leading change and is an invaluable guide for anyone leading major change in business, or in society, today. She uniquely has recognised that the massive scope and rapid speed of today's changes require new approaches, and that leaders must focus on *how* change is led not just on *what* change needs to be implemented. And with change a constant part of today's business landscape, Rowland convincingly sets out the four key inner capacities needed to enhance a leader's effectiveness in such a fast-paced world.

Mike White, *former Chairman and CEO, DirecTV*

Still Moving

How to Lead Mindful Change

Deborah Rowland

This edition first published 2017
© 2017 John Wiley & Sons Ltd

Registered Office
John Wiley & Sons Ltd, The Atrium, Southern Gate, Chichester, West Sussex,
PO19 8SQ, UK

Editorial Offices
350 Main Street, Malden, MA 02148-5020, USA
9600 Garsington Road, Oxford, OX4 2DQ, UK
The Atrium, Southern Gate, Chichester, West Sussex, PO19 8SQ, UK

For details of our global editorial offices, for customer services, and for information about
how to apply for permission to reuse the copyright material in this book please see our
website at www.wiley.com/wiley-blackwell.

The right of Deborah Rowland to be identified as the author of this work has been
asserted in accordance with the UK Copyright, Designs and Patents Act 1988.

Library of Congress Cataloging-in-Publication Data

Name: Rowland, Deborah, author.
Title: Still moving : how to lead mindful change / Deborah Rowland.
Description: Chichester, West Sussex, UK : John Wiley & Sons, 2017. |
    Includes bibliographical references and index.
Identifiers: LCCN 2016040291 (print) | LCCN 2016054026 (ebook) |
    ISBN 9781119164920 (cloth) | ISBN 9781119164890 (pdf) |
    ISBN 9781119164906 (epub)
Subjects: LCSH: Organizational change. | Leadership. | Mindfulness (Psychology)
Classification: LCC HD58.8 .R6937 2017 (print) | LCC HD58.8 (ebook) |
    DDC 658.4/06—dc23
LC record available at https://lccn.loc.gov/2016040291

A catalogue record for this book is available from the British Library.

Cover image: Courtesy of the author
Cover design: Wiley

Set in 10/12pt Warnock by SPi Global, Pondicherry, India

10 9 8 7 6 5 4 3 2 1

To Mum and Dad

Contents

Foreword

There are many books that have been described as 'waiting to be written'. *Still Moving* was not so much waiting to be written, as *needing* to be written.

Over the past 20 years and more, so much has been written on the question of effective leadership. And so much has been invested by large organisations in leadership development. It is a puzzle that organisations, and indeed societies, still suffer from major failures in leadership. It is incredible that leaders in one of the world's most successful car companies thought it acceptable to 'cheat' both the regulatory authorities, and more significantly, its customers – a move that is already costing the company many billions of dollars. It is equally extraordinary that a bank which had partnered with one of the world's leading business schools in developing its leaders could make a major acquisition that triggered its collapse and bail out by its national government.

Readers of *Still Moving* may be aware of many other instances of such failures of leadership (either from direct personal experience, or from the media), both large and small. It cannot be argued, therefore, that these are individual and isolated cases.

I have spent much of the past 20 years trying to address this puzzle. The potential benefit not only to business organisations, but to societies and the world, from the array of leadership insights is vast. Some of the puzzle is explained by misdirected leadership development. We have expended too much effort in trying to develop leaders simply to inspire and engage their people. In saying this, I am not suggesting that this is not vital. But it is not enough. Most organisations create or destroy value through the major strategic decisions they make. The process, culture and behaviours through which such decisions are taken, and the engagement – or otherwise – of the external environment is at least of equal importance. Yet leadership competency frameworks and engagement processes rarely embrace this.

It is also true that too much of the delivery mechanism for leadership development programmes has been 'offline'. The intellectual capacity to understand what leadership works in a classroom, or decision-making conducted in an outdoor team event, is not the same as making it work under the relentless day-to-day pressure that comes with leading organisations in today's massively complex and changing environment.

There have, of course, been significant benefits from this investment in leadership. But, the reality is that most organisations have not seen the expected return. The above reasons only provide a small part of the answer.

In *Still Moving*, Deborah Rowland provides compelling insights and practical responses to this leadership puzzle that many others and I have encountered.

In her original research along with Malcolm Higgs – *Sustaining Change: Leadership that Works* (2008, Wiley) – Deborah set out a cogent and coherent framework for leading complex change. Moreover, this framework was validated by empirical research.

Still Moving, again based on thorough and robust research, not only validates the original proposition, but takes it to another level, revealing not only the external practices but also the inner state needed to lead change well.

In recent years, much has been written on the subject of 'mindfulness' and what is described as 'mindful leadership'. Deborah Rowland argues that, while mindfulness is an essential *starting point* for the inner state of effective and successful leadership, it is only part of the process of leading change. The breakthrough element is the combination of mindfulness with the *systemic capacity* that makes up the leader's inner state. In this context, systemic capacity means much more than 'Systems Thinking'. It embraces not only the personal ability to tune into the feelings and emotions of others, but also the wisdom to understand and appreciate that patterns of events are somehow 'meant to happen', and give the leader true insight into what actually needs to, and is waiting to, change.

The explicit connection between the inner capacities and external exhibited practices forms the basis of a new way of understanding leadership. The research demonstrates the vital importance of the inner state as the foundation of what leaders actually practise on a day-to-day basis. Moreover, this applies across the range of tasks undertaken by leaders. As well as inspiring followership among colleagues, the idea of combining an inner state with external practice applies across engagement with the external environment and stakeholders, setting strategic direction and strategic decision-making, building the organisation's capacity to execute and delivering ongoing performance.

This is not dry theory leavened with obscure academic research. Deborah brings it to life with a wealth of real leadership stories. Stories drawn from multiple sectors, profit and not for profit, national and transnational, provide a rich tapestry of real experience that allows the reader to readily relate the content to their own experience. Moreover, Deborah has brought her personal experience of leadership into every chapter, relating her own triumphs and struggles that must surely connect to every reader's reality. This is leading change as we know and experience it, explained and understood.

However, Deborah has brought more than her own extensive leadership experience to *Still Moving*. What is remarkable is the way in which she has used the peaks and the troughs, the joy and the anxiety of her own personal journey of experiencing change. It is this more than anything else that makes the book intensely readable, it brings her own inner state out into the open for us all to see – and to connect with what that has meant to her – and in so doing illuminates what it means and could mean for each of us.

Like all important books, *Still Moving* needs and deserves to be read 'mindfully'; to be read with curiosity rather than judgement; to be absorbed with an open heart and open mind. In this way, each one of us who reads this book will have the opportunity to adjust our own leadership, to the benefit of ourselves, those around us and society as a whole.

Roger Bellis
London, May 2016

Roger Bellis has over 25 years' direct experience of leading change on a national and transnational scale – as a FTSE 100 Human Resources Director, as a Director of Talent and Leadership in large, global organisations and as a consultant working with CEOs and their leadership teams.

Acknowledgements

This book stands on many people's shoulders. I first wish to thank its three closest companions and indispensable guides: Jackie Gittins, Roger Bellis and Ron Rowland. Jackie provided me with wise reflection and counsel throughout the writing process, each chapter's first draft would inevitably return to me from her with insight, encouragement, challenge and inspiration. Roger acted as a hugely supportive thinking partner as I embarked on each chapter and an ever-patient on-the-spot helpline for those inevitable moments when I became stuck. Like Jackie and Roger, my father Ron reviewed each chapter as it came off the press and notwithstanding the familial tie would give me just the right amount of gentle challenge when needed – and, of course, heaps of encouragement to his daughter.

The book also rests on the outputs of the research team, who gathered together to undertake my second large study into the nature of change and its leadership. I have already acknowledged Roger Bellis. In addition I particularly wish to thank Anjet van Linge, Professor Malcolm Higgs, Michael Chaskalson and Katie Jones. Anjet – aside from creating the beautiful painting for the book's front cover – provided much depth of critical insight and spirit-level wisdom into the *Still Moving* leadership construct as it emerged from the study. Without the objective research wizardry and clear-minded guidance of Malcolm this study would have lacked the empirical rigour I wished to bring to a subject that can be so confusing for practising leaders. As a lifelong mindfulness practitioner Michael's subject matter expertise, intellectual curiosity and kindly compassion brought both depth and spirit to our team. And without the indefatigable Katie Jones we would never have been able to organise and administer such a comprehensive research project in the first place. For assistance in the interviewing process I would also like to express gratitude to Helen Bellis, Barbara Mastoroudes, Anne Behringer and Nicole Brauckmann.

Of course, the research team needed its subjects. So I also wish to acknowledge the 65 leaders from around the world who so generously gave of their time to be interviewed for our study. Their open, honest and in-depth stories of change fuel this book, making *Still Moving* very much a 'book by leaders for leaders'.

One organisation in particular stands out for me as an inspiration for *Still Moving*. And that is RWE, the Germany-based energy producer, trader and supplier. In my role as change coach to them and their CEO, Peter Terium, over the past 3 years I have packed in enough leadership lessons about how to take a large system through big change to last the remainder of my lifetime. I am deeply grateful for the experience, and wish to thank all of their 360 most senior leaders whom I have had the privilege to intimately support and learn from. Critically, I could not have accomplished this assignment without the world class, tireless and loving support of a Faculty Team who came together to facilitate the leadership development programme I talk of in Chapter 9. I wish to single out Nicole Brauckmann for her courageous and dedicated partnership with me on the programme, but also acknowledge Roger Bellis, John Briffa, Paul Byrne, Sytske Casimir, Michael Chaskalson, Anke Geber, Judith Hemming, Anja Leao, Paul Pivcevic, Barbara Roscher, Peter Stoppelenburg, Anjet van Linge and Nicola Wreford-Howard. Petra Rutz too, for how she helped inspire the original programme concept, and Ruud Wilgenkamp and Arndt Brandenberg for their business sponsorship.

This book is not just about others' leadership. You will discover this book gets personal. I will share with you some key elements of my own leadership journey and how that has been influenced by early life experience. For inspiring me to have the courage to do this – in addition to helping with the editing process – I wish to thank the challenging minds and warm-hearted support of Stuart Crainer and Des Dearlove. They, together with the editorial team at Wiley, have made book writing a pleasurable process. Within this context I also wish to express my deep gratitude to the residents of the village of Portloe, in Cornwall, UK, where I wrote this book. They looked with curiosity and kindness on this strange new neighbour who had arrived from London to write in their midst. Their ongoing encouragement has meant a lot.

If I look back over my past decade of personal growth certain guides feature strongly. Be that Chris Robertson at Spiral Consulting, Judith Hemming at Moving Constellations or Susan Nordhaal, my therapist in Bath, they have all helped me drop into a deeper level of consciousness, a truly perspective altering level from which I now look on myself with more insight and kindness and the world around me with more respectful and systemic eyes. As a species it is natural for us to be well defended and unwilling to be vulnerable. But that doesn't help us learn and grow.

I thank all of my guides and colleagues, who have helped me to open my defences and endanger myself to growth. I hope this book can inspire you likewise.

Last, I wish to acknowledge the loving and supportive embrace of my adopted Rowland family. Their embrace healed my early fractured soul and generously supported me through life. This crib of good values is something I will be eternally grateful for. Mum and Dad, I'm glad you made the right choice.

Moved by Stillness

I sat on the edge of the balcony, my door open, tuning into the sea I saw before me. I sat and watched for a long time. What I saw changed every second and the more I tried to paint it all, the less I was able to. And I realised I did not want to capture the detail. I wanted to find a way to frame what I experienced. The broad bands of grey sky, the sea, the breakers, wet sand, dry sand. And when I painted only that, the stillness and the movement of all that sky, of all the water and the solid sand landed itself on paper.

Anjet van Linge, artist and painter of
Still Moving's front cover work, 'Texel'

1

Introduction

Stillness is what creates love,
Movement is what creates life,
To be still,
Yet still moving –
That is everything!

Do Hyun Choe, Japanese Master

My life began in change, the ultimate change, when I was handed over at 6 weeks old and adopted into the welcome and hugely loving embrace of the Rowland family. I had experienced an ending, with my biological mother, at the very start of life. An in-between time, floating without family, in a Lancashire mother-and-babies home. And then here was a new beginning with my adopted family. Born Wendy Juliet, I was renamed Deborah Anne. Since that cataclysmic time, no change has ever seemed insurmountable.

It meant that I learned to live life on a boundary. As an adopted child I grew up with detached curiosity, an outsider in my own life. Seeking to belong yet hard-wired not to trust, I cautiously put one foot into my new family, and, at the same time, carefully kept one foot out, just in case I had to leave – or be left – again. Perhaps I was always on the look out for a bond, for intimacy. However, it seemed I both tumbled into it and ran away from it almost at the same time. The edge, for me, felt the safest place.

Yet this detachment, this instinct to be *alongside* rather than *inside* gave me a helpful vantage point to observe and notice. I was intensely curious about people, in particular how they related to each other and formed systems. I could make good use of my fate.

My earliest companion – detached curiosity – set my life on its course. Holding Mum and Dad's hands as a wondrous wide-eyed 10-year-old, I was transfixed by the blockbuster Tutankhamun exhibition in London

Still Moving: How to Lead Mindful Change, First Edition. Deborah Rowland.
© 2017 John Wiley & Sons Ltd. Published 2017 by John Wiley & Sons Ltd.

in 1972, the treasure trove of royal Egyptian artefacts unearthed by the archaeologist Howard Carter. And when in 1977 Desmond Morris published *Manwatching: A Field Guide to Human Behaviour*, I knew I had found my field.

And so I read archaeology and anthropology at university. From the Trobrianders of New Guinea to the Nuer of the Nile, their ethnographies provided many hours of absorbing reading and reflection in the university library. The anthropological discipline of acute unbiased observation enhanced my sensitivity to diversity and to context. All thought and action, however seemingly strange, make perfect sense when you can see the system within which they are situated. I also spent many hours on my hands and knees in deep Neolithic trenches, using a tiny trowel to gently scrape away and reveal history's previously unearthed layers. I felt both strengthened and humbled when I stood in that deep messy line of time.

As compelling as the experience was, I put down my trowel and continued my personal line out of those trenches. And I did so because a single memory from just one anthropology lecture had already awakened my purpose. A purpose that has guided the intervening 30 years I have spent in business – and that still guides me today. Indeed, it is the reason why I write this book.

The memory came from a grainy black and white film shown in that fateful lecture. Shot at the turn of the last century, it falteringly documented how a group of British Christian missionaries entered a native tribe in Africa with the aim of 'civilising' its seemingly primitive culture. This was the *change goal*. As a result of inter-village warfare, this native culture was thought to be on the verge of extinction. What caught my attention, beyond the misguided arrogance of the change goal, was the *change approach*.

The missionaries decided to introduce the villagers to the game of cricket. Believing they would channel their aggression into this edifying game, the missionaries looked on aghast as the African warriors picked up the cricket stumps as javelins, and the cricket balls as missiles. Far from reducing the inter-village warfare, the change approach amplified it. On entering a strange landscape the missionaries had sought new results by importing old routines. Big mistake.

Worryingly those lessons of over a century ago still need heeding today. There remain plenty of well-intended missionaries with antique approaches to change. History repeats.

But the lessons from the missionaries pointed me to my (professional) fate. I have spent 30 years exploring what it truly takes to lead change in new and uncertain environments, where past solutions no longer work and in fact become a dangerous liability.

I believe I have found some of the answers, and offer them to you in *Still Moving*.

Leading Change Starts Inside Yourself

Here's my primary insight – start by becoming *still* and examining the source of your thinking and action.

The missionaries leapt into their habitual routines without first questioning the deeper beliefs shaping them. Unaware of these biased lenses they could not clearly see the system they were seeking to change. Blind to their own impulses and ignorant of context, all they could do was reactively shape – and not resourcefully respond – to the escalating fray.

Now, I can hear you thinking, 'I would never have done anything like that!' Really?

We all grow up in our stories, our personal histories. Like my adoption story, the narratives of our lives lay down deep deposits in the layers of our being – deposits of emotional instinct, felt security or insecurity, self-identity, adaptive coping behaviour. And we take those deposits and we import those routines into our adult life: our relationships and our leadership. They are the source of our repeating patterns and impulses in the present – particularly in stressful and challenging situations. In these circumstances we naturally get anxious, and can resort to primitive self-limiting patterns of thinking and acting that lead to the very opposite of the results we are trying to create.

The dual capacity to be aware of, and able to regulate our response to, experience guides the entire quality of our thinking, action and results. What's more, my new research has shown that this ability to tune into and regulate the self, within an evolving system, is the number one inner skill in being able to lead change well. If senior leaders stay stuck in habitual response, so do their organisations.

Once you are able to come off autopilot and hold your default impulses lightly, you are freed of their attachment and can intentionally and less habitually respond. You see what shows up in experience with systemic perception not just personal projection. Easy to say, much harder to do!

I am grateful for how my instinctive preference to be on the observational edge of human systems has enabled me to have a rewarding career in the field of leadership and change. Yet, even today when guiding leadership groups, and the two seats on either side of me remain empty, I can easily tip into my default story: 'Here we go again, I am left alone, abandoned!' Rather than hold the systemic insight: 'My distance from others has given me the necessary detachment for leadership'.

It's a wafer-thin line between impulsive, anxious reaction, and mindful, perceptive response, especially when the world feels threatening and disruptive.

Aha, the 'M word' has made its first appearance. Let's go there now.

The Mindfulness Explosion

In my first book with Malcolm Higgs, *Sustaining Change: Leadership That Works* (2008), we set out the four leadership practices, or exhibited behaviours, that our research showed in combination were highly correlated with successful change outcomes.

These were: *Attractor* – creating an emotional pull in your organisation towards shared purpose; *Edge and Tension* – naming reality and amplifying disturbance in order to innovate; *Container* – channelling anxiety and uncertainty into productive energy by being calm, confident and affirming; and *Transforming Space* – taking actions that create deep change in the here-and-now experience.

At that time we also drew attention to what we surmised were two critical *inner conditions* behind these practices: self-awareness and ego-less intention.[1]

Yet in that round of research we did not empirically test the relationship between this inner state and a leader's successful practice. It remained a hypothesis. We focused on what leaders *did*, the four practices above. And this was largely because we had not found a single coherent framework that could describe this inner state.

In the decade since we wrote *Sustaining Change* there has been an explosion of interest in so-called 'mindfulness'.[2,3] While newly arrived on the public scene mindfulness has in fact been in existence for almost 2,500 years. Originally derived from ancient Buddhist contemplative tradition, and more recently adopted into western settings through the fields of medicine, social psychology, education and general work place productivity, the practice of mindfulness – classically trained via meditation – has now found its way into leadership.

Mindfulness is, in essence, the cultivation of a deeper awareness of the self, others and the world through focused, non-judgemental and intentional attention on the present moment.[4] This is a radical shift in how we show up in our lives, where research shows that our attention is only on the present moment for half of the time.[5] Our uncontained minds naturally wander. The promise of mindfulness is that by bringing our attention intentionally and non-judgementally to what we are experiencing, in the present moment, we will be more able to regulate our emotional and cognitive response to experience leading to calmer and more resourceful lives.

You can imagine how this capacity to approach all of experience – and in particular difficulty – with greater equilibrium could be important in leading change. I define change as the disturbance of repeating patterns – a task that by definition is fraught with difficulty. Patterns are stable constructs that are hard to break – especially human mindset and behaviour. As a living species our brains are hard-wired for survival and that tends to mean repeating the coping patterns of the past. Disturbing these patterns is not only difficult to do, it comes at a price for those disturbing them, as it requires breaking previous commitments and loyalties. Ouch.

It's hardly surprising then that in the past 2 years alone circa 50 books purporting to associate mindfulness with leadership success have been launched onto the virtual Amazon bookshelf. But while tested in clinical settings and personality disciplines, mindfulness has not yet been empirically proven to relate to management or success in top leadership. Studies to date have been limited to examining personal benefits to the leader; for example, stress reduction, enhanced task performance and general well-being.[6,7,8] They have not looked into broader organisational outcomes. There is a paucity of research into the relationship between mindfulness, leader effectiveness and successful change outcomes.[9,10,11]

I wanted to change that, and address what I saw as the somewhat *mindless* take up of mindfulness, fast in danger of becoming a fad rather than a deeply understood discipline.

Does Mindfulness Matter?

As I got more acquainted with the field of mindfulness, I sensed that it could hold a key to unlocking the meaning of the inner state we wrote of in *Sustaining Change*. Just after publishing that book, and partly inspired by the wishful thought that I could put my own research into action, I had left consulting and returned to the corporate world. In the two executive roles that followed, both of which entailed leading major restructurings, I certainly learned about what *not* to do as well as what *to* do when leading change. But more than that, I came to a stark and vital realisation that proved a further ignition point for this book.

My realisation was that change does indeed start on the inside. I had always claimed that 'change starts with self', however I had not quite comprehended that this did *not* mean having to change yourself. It meant accessing your highest and most conscious self.

What do I mean by that? In my corporate roles it became very clear that I had to be in the right place personally before I could skilfully lead or do anything. *Being* at ease with all of experience felt as important as what I *did* in experience. And for that ease to be with me it required that I cultivated a point of inner spaciousness, or stillness. From this place, and only this place, could I gain the courage, resilience and wisdom to tackle the most stressful and complex of changes.

I was starting to see why those four leadership practices we set out in *Sustaining Change* were theoretically sound yet dastardly hard to practise. I had had to do it to get it.

With my personal experience in the corporate world and the burgeoning field of mindfulness entering into leadership, I wanted to investigate more fully the relationship between a leader's ability to mindfully regulate their inner state and their ability to lead change. The workings of destiny continued in that I was then offered the chance to act as change coach to the Executive Board of a large European energy company going through a major transition. The CEO, my client, wished mindfulness to be the cornerstone new skill for his leaders. This experience was the final tap on the shoulder that I needed to return to the drawing board of research.

And here, in summary, is what my research team and I found.

After the forensic examination of evidence coming from coding 88 different stories of leading change, we can say, *yes*, mindfulness does make a difference to a leader's ability to lead big change. Staying calm, connected and resourceful in challenging conditions was a hallmark of the most successful change leaders. And yet we found that mindfulness, while the starting point, is not the only component to a leader's inner state.

We found that a leader's ability to be mindful needs to be supplemented by a deep capacity to perceive the world through a systemic lens. And it was this deeper interpretative capacity that proved the biggest differentiator between high and low success in leading large complex change.

This systemic capacity, the *perceiving skill* of being able to look beneath visible experience and see its deeper governing structures, was a clear differentiator between leaders who could lead big change well, and those who could not. It led them to create movement – and not just busy action.

It makes sense. When you rise to a senior leadership position, such a role requires you to understand and influence a large complex interconnected system that seems to have its own life and intentionality (if only we could simply pull a lever at the top of an organisation to change it!). In times of major change, systemic capacities enable leaders to sustainably and more effortlessly move this wider and deeper field.

Still Moving – a Call to Leadership

We found that when mindfulness and systemic skills were combined, this inner capacity led to highly successful change outcomes. To be mindful and systemic at the same time requires you to stop and find an inner place of stillness. Just as the Hindu concept of *Madhya* describes that still point of pure present-moment awareness, like the momentary pause between your in breath and your out breath, so does a leader need to find that place of deep consciousness from which they can clearly perceive and respond to experience. This inner still capacity is a quality of *being*.

Successful change leadership is also about moving the world around you, and for this task the four external leadership practices combine. With a nuance here or there, our new research re-validated the vital role that Attractor, Edge and Tension, Container and Transforming Space leadership play in leading change well. This external moving capacity is a quality of *doing*.

This combination of being and doing – at the same time – is the concept behind Still Moving. Our research found that this combination of skills explained 52% of the reason why leaders can lead big change well. Put another way, if you can't practice Still Moving leadership, you reduce your chances of successfully leading change by half.

To be still, yet still moving, that is (almost) everything.

Who is This Book For?

Still Moving is a book for leaders wishing to approach the challenges of changing their institutions, or society at large, in a more skilful and humane way. This is not a book for leaders wishing only to increase shareholder value. But it will appeal to leaders who desire to bring about big change in ways that increase productivity *and* achieve those desired outcomes in ways that leave the world in a stronger place.

The concept of Still Moving has, of course, a double meaning. It not only encompasses putting two skill sets together to describe a certain way to move a system. The concept also means the ability to achieve ongoing, longer lasting and more sustainable change that replenishes the world and our leadership more than it takes away. Still is an adverb as well as an adjective.

The book is also aimed at leadership coaches and change consultants who wish to create a deeper capacity for leading change in the systems of their clients – be they individuals, top teams, whole organisations or multistakeholder societal groups. To cultivate both being and doing requires a certain kind of development experience, one that is grounded in lived moments rather than taught models. (If this were followed through it would call into question the vast bulk of the €45bn spent on leadership development and training every year.[12] That might also help the world a little.)

If you already feel this book speaks to you then I welcome you on its journey. To help you *mindfully* navigate that journey, here's an overview of what to expect.

Chapter 2: Is Change Changing?

In this chapter I set out what I see as the bigger picture context within which today's leadership is exercised – the major societal trends that both challenge and disrupt how today's businesses and institutions are run. This presents an adaptive change challenge requiring an adaptive leadership response such as greater agility, shorter planning cycles, working more collaboratively across multistakeholder groups, and upturning conventional hierarchies and control systems. At its core, it requires that we operate from a new mode of perception about the world and our place in it.

Chapter 3: Still Moving – The Inner and Outer Skills

In this chapter I describe in more detail our research and the Still Moving framework. I reiterate the four external leadership practices set out in *Sustaining Change*, including how I have now refined these through the lessons of experience. And I will introduce you to the four inner mindfulness and systemic capacities, which we found to be essential antecedents and enhancers of these practices. A story of business transformation illustrates these throughout.

Chapter 4: It All Starts in Mindfulness

In more detail I set out in this chapter the two inner mindfulness capacities that we found to be most associated with success in leading big change: *Staying Present*, the ability to pay close attention to the present moment without getting caught up in it; and *Curious and Intentional Responding*, consciously choosing how to be with what you have noticed is present. I draw from the research and my experience to illustrate these capacities and share an in-depth case study of how they can be used to lead big change well.

Chapter 5: The Power of the Systemic

Two systemic capacities significantly differentiate the most successful change leaders: *Tuning into the System* and *Acknowledging the Whole*. These two inner capacities place the mindful self within a wider context and in this chapter I show how a leader can not just notice and regulate what is going on for them, but use this inner awareness as a valuable source of data about the system – in particular tuning into the emotional climate of their organisation and giving a place to difficulty, the two greatest sources of movement and change.

Chapter 6: Make Disturbance Your Friend

This leads me to illustrate the leadership skill of *Edge and Tension*. Our research showed that this was the external practice that made the biggest single difference to a leader achieving successful change. Yet despite its power, it is the practice most feared, avoided or clumsily done. In a revealing case study, I show how Edge and Tension can be combined with the inner capacities to enable a leader to disturb repeating patterns using great poise and empathy, without causing resistance and defensive routines in others.

Chapter 7: Holding the Fire

Our research found that top leaders in high magnitude change need to combine Edge and Tension with *Container* leadership practice – the ability to channel the fierce energy stirred up through Edge and Tension without anxiety. I describe how Container leadership can build ownership, trust and psychological safety across a system in turbulence, and, in the case study, show again how this practice must be combined with certain inner capacities so that the human dynamics of change are skilfully handled.

Chapter 8: The Time for Emergence

This chapter steps away from your personal leadership capability to show how you can architect an overall approach to change that fits today's dynamic and increasingly uncertain context. It is around 15 years since the notion of *emergent change* hit the world of organisational theory and management practice. I show in a story of radical performance improvement how this more bottom-up, step-by-step and giving-up-of-control change approach is more suited to today's world.

Chapter 9: A Tale of Still Moving and Business Transformation

Our research found that leaders who had been exposed to a Still Moving type leadership development experience displayed greater change leadership skill. In this chapter I tell the story of how I partnered with a courageous CEO and a strong faculty team to deliver a pioneering and innovative developmental experience that helped an entire organisation face major disruptive change.

Chapter 10: Still Moving and Your Leadership

In this chapter I set out the key principles for how to cultivate your own Still Moving leadership skills. Much traditionally delivered *offline* leadership development programmes are not worth their investment, and a more *online* experiential form of leadership development could yield far greater return. This chapter will take you along what I hope is a rich personal learning journey.

Chapter 11: The Sense of an Ending

Finally, I summarise the main messages and provocatively place them into a wider societal context. Still Moving is a style of leadership that allows us to be part of something bigger. How can the insights be applied to the wider challenges of the world we live in? What deep shift in mindset is required and how might that come about, including how our institutions might need to be set up and governed differently?

I have been on a personal journey in the 10 years since I wrote *Sustaining Change*, which has proven challenging. It involved a deep look into my self and my repeating story. This was not always a pleasant experience. Yet what is a life unless it can be lived with full awareness?

I share some of my personal journey in this book. This is not without risk but it is with intention. And my intention is to help you look inside yourself too. I can stay very safe and comfortable in my old story of deficit. Yet it never brought me the prize of living my full life.

2

Is Change Changing?

At the still point of the turning world. Neither flesh
Nor fleshless;
Neither from nor towards; at the still point, there the
Dance is

T.S. Eliot, Burnt Norton, Four Quartets

When I completed my initial research into change and its leadership I would never have predicted that a decade later we would have a world where financial austerity still lingers after the biggest global economic crisis since World War II; an internet explosion that has blown apart traditional business models; digital democratisation with 2.6bn smartphone users and 6.1bn people (80% of the world's population) predicted to have one by 2020; 65 m refugees fleeing from their strife-torn homelands, an increase from 19.2 m in 2005; acts of brutal terrorism that have put fear onto the beaches of Egypt and the South of France and into the heart of cities such as Beirut, Baghdad, Istanbul, Mumbai, Orlando, Paris and Sydney; the UK dealing a seismic blow to cross-country collaboration and cooperation by voting in a referendum to exit the European Union after 43 years of membership; the deliberate deception of consumers, shareholders, employees and society by the second largest car manufacturer in the world, Volkswagen; and a −1.9 °C temperature at the North Pole in December 2015, approaching melting point for the first time in its history.

Such unpredictable, turbulent and dynamic conditions change the very nature of change.

Still Moving: How to Lead Mindful Change, First Edition. Deborah Rowland.
© 2017 John Wiley & Sons Ltd. Published 2017 by John Wiley & Sons Ltd.

Change is Changing

First and foremost, change moves from being a one-off episode that can be discretely managed, to an ongoing changing phenomenon. Survival now requires that you be in a continual state of adaptation to new contexts, a state novelist Douglas Coupland describes as the 'extreme present'. For sure there will still need to be set piece change, such as an acquisition, a new brand launch or an IT system change. Yet the emphasis has now shifted from viewing change as an event to acknowledging it as an endemic phenomenon. This switch from change to changing, from noun to gerund, *places a high premium on leaders who can build the capability of their institutions to remain in constant change.* In one sense, the primary task of top leaders is no longer to come up with the definitive grand plan for the future, but to create the capacity for ongoing innovation. Today's solution can – and almost inevitably will – look quickly outmoded.

Second, it is clear that we live in a world that is increasingly *interconnected.* Change no longer lies within our personal control. Be it a result of social media, technology innovation, global migration or geopolitical union, it is far less easy to isolate the cause of an event to a single location. Systemic and complex issues require a commensurate response, one that is rooted in our willingness to collaborate across traditional boundaries. Leading change demands a deep capacity to acknowledge a whole system over the selective promotion of certain parts, beliefs or interests.

Finally, today's disruptive and often worrying change sharpens our *attention to its process.* Given the increasingly high cost of failing to adapt to today's changing context – including our planet's very survival – it is no longer good enough for leaders to bring about change without equal consideration for how to implement it. Too often I see leaders only attending to *what* has to be done without any consideration of *how* to bring this about, for example, through top-down directives or collaborative design. It is irresponsible to be a leader if you are not prepared to examine and adapt your own response to these changing contexts. How you *do* change fundamentally determines where you end up.

So, change is now ongoing, endemic and not directly controllable, yet still an essential leadership capability as the price tag of failure becomes ever more expensive. I have consistently shown through my own research that high quality leadership is the single biggest determinant of successful change. Yet while the need to master it rises in importance, the inherent difficulties faced in implementing change are not only increasing they are changing in nature.

Within this perfect storm, can *we* find the still point in our turning world, where T.S. Eliot so eloquently tells us the dance is?

In the rest of this chapter I examine more deeply the societal and work-place forces that are changing the nature of change and its leadership. Put starkly, I believe people are increasingly fed up with how the world is being run and we are facing a crisis of leadership. So I also put forward my key messages about how to dance the dance in the still point of today's turbulent world, and close the chapter with a heartening story of how major change can be led well in this new era.

The Context For Leading Change Today

Many social, economic, geo-political and technological disrupters fundamentally challenge the traditional way of leading our institutions. But there are three that I believe have significant consequences for leading change: the collapse of confidence in the vertical hierarchy, or low trust in our institutions; the power of those on the ground; and a distracted and divided attention.

The Collapse of the Vertical, Low Trust in Our Institutions

I am not normally prone to pessimism, but in just one edition of the *Financial Times* I read that:

- An 8-year ban had secured the downfall of Fédération Internationale de Football Association (FIFA) president, Sepp Blatter, after 17 years at the pinnacle of football. He was banned for unethical behaviour and for abusing his position. Breathtakingly, even though Blatter was the most senior leader accountable for the institution under investigation for the most serious corruption committed in its history, he continued to insist he had done nothing wrong and should not be held responsible.
- In a report on the Spanish general election, the reason stated for a shift to younger, anti-austerity insurgent movements was not voter disillusionment with economic incompetence but 'disgust at perceived official corruption in a period of high unemployment and of widespread hardship'.
- Toshiba, the Japanese industrial group, had warned of losses of Y550bn (US$4.5bn) following the scandal of disclosure irregularities in its books. Shareholders had had to forego dividend payments and its employees suffered from 10,600 job cuts. CEO Masashi Muromachi was quoted as saying, 'If we had taken action earlier, we may not have had to suffer such enormous pain'.
- International investors were suing Portugal's Banco Espirito Santo for €105 m in damages after the value of its shares was wiped out within weeks of their subscribing to a €1bn capital increase. The former chief

executive is now a suspect in two police investigations and a defendant in numerous civil lawsuits arising from the 2014 collapse.

- JPMorgan Chase had settled a lawsuit stemming from the London Whale scandal, agreeing to pay $150m to a group of investors who claimed they were misled by statements that urged them not to worry about losses that topped $6.2bn. In what is now a legendary tale, the bank's boss Jamie Dimon had, in an analysts' call, dismissed their concerns as a 'tempest in a teapot'. Within less than a month he revealed losses of $2bn. To date, the bank has paid more than $1bn to settle US and British probes into losses, and has admitted flaws in its risk management.

- As the corporate mergers and acquisitions deals tally climbed to a record $4.6tn in 2015, surpassing 2007's peak, it was reported that this would be driven by more sensibly leveraged deals than those in the pre-financial crisis era. However, it was also reported, 'Too many of the $4.6tn total will have been motivated by big egos and poorly implemented, leaving both investors and employees worse off'.

- As the leaders of our countries tighten their borders against immigrants, this has led to rises in the number of smuggling gangs who prey on migrants. They take advantage of families desperate at any cost to find ways to cross borders. The price a family has to pay to cross the Turkish border had risen from $5 a person to $400 to $1000, depending on their family size. And as one Syrian lady with a family of seven was forced to give up the last $150 the family possessed to a smuggler, I read in another article that more than 60% of workers in the City of London are ready to quit their organisations if their year-end pay package falls short of expectations, the day after the European Banking Authority said it had delayed the full launch of new restrictions on bankers' pay.

- Finally, a columnist writing of Europe's decline maintained 'national governments and the EU apparatus in Brussels look increasingly as if they are not up to the numerous challenges bearing down simultaneously from every direction'. And efforts to bring more efficient and effective integration across the EU to tackle issues such as immigration, terrorism, homegrown political extremism and lacklustre economic growth are 'mere lip service to an ideal'. He even goes on to quote Jean-Claude Juncker, who noted with regards to defence collaboration, 'If I look at the common European defence policy, a bunch of chickens would be a more unified combat unit in contrast'.

Within this context it is hardly surprising that – contrary to all the facts and arguments from economic experts – 51.9% of the UK population voiced a protest against the political elite and big business by voting to exit a union that had held together decades of peace and prosperity. And when such stories above are supplemented by corporate tales such as the major deceit of Volkswagen in their car emissions testing scandal of 2015, and the world's largest digital companies, such as Google and Amazon, avoiding paying their fair share of tax while the ordinary citizen has no choice, it's hardly surprising that according to the latest 'trust barometer' produced by public relations company Edelman, the level of trust in business has declined in 16 out of the 27 countries surveyed.

One root cause for this decline in trust is attributed to the increasing imbalance in income and resurgence in inequality. For most of the twentieth century, income inequality fell. The top 10% had 30% of the world's income in 1939 and this had reduced to 20% by 1979. But that figure has now increased back to 30% and is still growing despite the global recession. Growing income and asset inequality is a big threat to economic stability and growth as well as geopolitical stability, and is not being tackled seriously.

Another barometer of the crumbling faith we have in our institutions comes from the Pew Research Center, which claims that just 24% of Americans say they trust government. In the late 1960s, this figure was nearly 75% and even at the start of the twenty-first century it was hovering around the 50% mark.[1] And surveys by Gallup show that faith in almost every major institution, from big business to the church, has fallen steadily in the past four decades in America.

With such a massive vote against the establishment, what have our leaders done (or not done) to bring about this deep disaffection and societal collapse in the trust we hold in our institutions?

In general I believe very well intentioned and smart people run the major institutions of the world. And in my career I have had the good fortune to work alongside many of them. Yet if the people who lead organisations can be loosely described as good, the obvious conclusion is that their brand of leadership is no longer the kind of leadership the world requires. It is extraordinarily hard to lead big change in a climate of low trust, when the elite are out of touch with those who elect them and are only seen to be feathering their own nest.

Alternatively, perhaps these leaders are overwhelmed by context. A whole range of systemic forces now puts pressure on leaders to fly close to the wire. Deregulation of markets, increased competition and pressure from investors to create short-term results are all broader contextual dynamics that play their part. For example, in the UK the average period of shareholding has fallen from 5 years in the 1960s to less than a year. These are not automatically pernicious forces, but they create contexts that now require a new kind of leadership response.

How heartening in this context was it to hear that Paul Polman, when newly appointed as Unilever CEO in 2009, took the bold step of loosening the shackles of quarterly reporting to shareholders, as he believed instead in a long-term value-creation model. Indeed, he went even further to say that short-term shareholders interested only in speculative profit would not be welcome in his company as he also had other stakeholders interests' at heart, including climate-change activists and consumers in the developing world.

The Power of the Ground

Just as society is losing trust in traditional vertical hierarchies, there is a converse trend to place more trust in devolved lateral networks, where technology and social media have been a major driver in placing information and hence power into the hands of the people. 'While trust in authority has declined, faith in our peer group seemingly remains high', argues the *Financial Times*' Gillian Tett.[2] She reports another Edelman Group survey finding which suggests that people now trust the views of a 'person like me' more than anything a business or political leader might say. She shares research from the Socialnomics blog that reveals that only 14% of people say they trust online advertising from the big companies, while 90% of consumers trust online recommendations from their peers.

The peer-to-peer based social media revolution is causing many industries to wake up to the need to implement radically different ways of connecting with consumers. Just witness the fashion industry migrating away from the exclusive preserves of cities such as Paris, Milan, London and New York to the blogger-rich, social media-savvy cities of Shanghai, Seoul and the Far East. British fashion power house Burberry launched the first ever fashion show on a live Twitter feed, taking advantage of the immediate, peer-to-peer influence power of social media. Indeed in response to the 'see now, buy now' society, Burberry is breaking with decades of fashion industry tradition to have two fashion shows a year, after which consumers can buy their merchandise in store immediately rather than waiting for several months.

Trust in the cyber crowd remains strong, and indeed is extended even further as the 'sharing economy' extends its reach. From sharing taxi rides on Uber to holiday rentals via Airbnb, from sharing camping pitches via Camp in My Garden to car rides on FlightVar, and from offering city tours on Trip4Real to sharing home-cooked meals via VizEat, the sharing economy has been heralded, perhaps more accurately, as a new era of 'dotcommunism'.

And all of these online peer-to-peer platforms, which offer not just financial reward to ground level providers like you and me, but also appeal to our growing motivation to consume things more efficiently for the planet, are a significant competitive threat to the traditional providers of such services. In the 1930s, a company in the Standard & Poor's (S&P) could expect to stay on the US blue-chip index for 75 years. Today, the average stay is about 15 years. And in half that time, a social network can go from zero to a billion active monthly users; a time span that will no doubt diminish even further as mobile technology and smartphone usage increases.

In *Peers Inc.*, Robin Chase (2015) claims that the collaboration of peers, offering myriad assets in different locations, gives social network companies phenomenal flexibility and explosive growth potential. This is a major competitive threat to old-style businesses, particularly those stuck in the quarterly reporting cycle, and those who wish to maintain ownership and control of the asset. Skype does not own any infrastructure, Airbnb has created a business out of other people's homes and Alibaba owns no inventory.

Of course, the canniest of these 'old-style' providers can take advantage of this ground-based, technology-led revolution, as long as they are sufficiently open-minded, adaptable and humble enough to work as just one player within an ecosystem. As an example, the major hotel chain Hyatt now provides investment for private home vacation rental firms such as OneFineStay.

From the consuming worlds of fashion, travel and dining through to even the protesting worlds of Arab uprisings and terrorising extremist religious cells, the rise of digital technology, the internet and social media have been an unquestionable force. These technologies are reshaping the nature of communication, collaboration, power and influence in today's society. They upturn society's hierarchical pyramid and place the person on the street on top.

So when we combine this *power of the ground* movement with that of *declining trust in the traditional vertical hierarchies*, fuelled by out-of-touch leaders caught up in their own hubris, and sometimes just plainly corrupt, there are powerful forces gathering that disrupt the nature of the ground upon which leaders walk: a move of influence from the vertical hierarchy to the horizontal network; impulses for change shifting from the previously unquestioned knowledge of the centre to the emerging intelligence of the periphery; and the locus of control slipping from an elite few into the command of the collective.

Given the increasing power of the ground, how should leaders in the upper echelons of society re-perceive their role in the collective? From whose reality do they now draw inspiration for influence, change and decision-making? What should be their response to the digitally native millennials generation who are swelling the workforces with a desire to work for purpose, and not pay? And what shifts in style do they need to require both of themselves, and of their organisations, in their wider relationship to society? The era in which big leaders in traditional institutions could unilaterally dictate to other members of society what was best for them, is over.

In tune with this, Paul Polman's move to shift the culture of Unilever from a short-term to a longer-term mindset was accompanied by a far greater outreach to groups in society, including non-governmental organisations (NGOs), governments and consumers. To help achieve his 10-year goal to both double revenue and reduce his organisation's carbon footprint by 50%, he has formed associations with activist groups such as Global Citizen and Live Earth. In a *Forbes* interview[3] he reflected on his decision-making process, noting that he always consciously monitors the fine line between making decisions that are a product of his own influencing experiences, which could tip into ego-led goals, and making decisions that are 'based on a solid foundation of wanting to serve society'.

A Distracted and Divided Attention

In addition to the loss of trust in vertical hierarchy, and the growing power of the ground, there is a third factor that shapes the context for today's leadership: a distracted and divided attention. To some extent, this represents the shadow, or unintended consequence that technology innovation, social media, people power and interconnectivity can bring. While they undoubtedly offer us greater information transparency, a feeling of an interconnected virtual community and enhanced personal choice, paradoxically, they also strengthen a sense of individual isolation.

Mobile technology grants us 'see now, buy now' power at the touch of a screen, and 24/7 connectivity with our virtual friends around the world, but it can also create self-centred non-human bubbles that separate us from meaningful, and perhaps more challenging or heartfelt discourse. It disconnects us from attending to the present moment, or engaging with our lived experience.

2015 research by Microsoft shows that our ability to focus on one thing at any one time now only lasts for 8 s, down from 12 s in their previous 2000 survey.[4] (We have even sunk below goldfish at 9 s...) Our minds increasingly wander. Eight seconds is not very long to be present in a conversation with someone, or attending to a complex task before our minds get distracted and we are no longer there, unavailable for what might arise in the present moment.

In *Reclaiming Conversation*, clinical psychologist and Massachusetts Institute of Technology (MIT) professor Sherry Turkle relates how smartphones have damaged spontaneous human interaction. Based on her interviews with young Americans, she claims that the current generation struggles to listen, make eye contact or read body language. 'Most teenagers send 100 texts a day, 44 per cent do not unplug, ever', she reports. This is the result of what Turkle calls 'continuous partial attention'.

I'm sure we recognise this trend not just in our teenagers but also among our work colleagues and ourselves as we struggle to put down that smartphone during meetings, heaven forbid leave it outside the room.

In 2015, there was a subtle shift against the seemingly unstoppable march of the digital algorithm. Aside from Silicon Valley (of all places) now introducing 'digital holidays', where people can put their mobile devices to one side, mega tech brands such as Google, Facebook, Amazon and eBay, which have made their billions by exploiting the power of their software, are also trying to bring back the human touch. Apple Music was launched with over 300 human editors, rather than algorithmically controlled curation. Jimmy Iovine its Director noted, 'Algorithms can't do that emotional task – you need a human touch'.

Aside from the impact of the internet and mobile devices in creating a divided and distracted and not just connected world, there are wider geopolitical and social forces that both separate and unite. Just as the world, via geopolitical integration, economic globalisation and common threats such as climate change and terrorism, is increasingly interconnected, there co-exists a countervailing force towards nationalism, self-identity, and a reassertion of local rights and independence. While this reclamation of local sovereignty represents a positive force for devolution and empowerment, it also risks a return to isolationism, self-protection at the expense of the other and the implementation of only local, partial solutions to what are commonly created systemic problems.

We see this self-sealing isolationism primarily in our political systems as the strains grow within the EU for country independence beyond the UK vote to exit the union, and as a US presidential candidate calls for a closure of its borders to Muslims and Mexicans. But this fearful-of-the-other force shows up in more subtle ways, even under the guise of political correctness. Take Oxford University Oriel College students, who considered removing a statue of Cecil Rhodes, the nineteenth-century imperialist politician and businessman who controlled the diamond mining industry in South Africa, or Cardiff University students, who signed a petition to block Germaine Greer from a talk because of her views on transsexuals.

This trend to exclude the other, to eliminate difference, or ban people whose views you don't like is not conducive to open inquiry and deeper systemic perception. When we stand in judgement of something, or of someone, it breeds wider division as we fail to see the system from which the target of our dislike originates. In the 4 days following the UK EU referendum vote to exit the Union police reported that hate crime against immigrants rose by over 50%. And when the other feels judged then their worldview only becomes stronger. Far from Nigel Farage, leader of the UK Independence Party (UKIP), enabling change when he launched his invective at the European Parliament in Brussels days after the referendum, such gloating proclamations only reinforce prejudicial thinking. This breeds what MIT's Otto Scharmer calls self-preserving ego-systems, as opposed to collaborative ecosystems.[5] This isolationism dangerously divides the world.

After the 2015 Paris attacks, the journalist Simon Kuper tells the story of coming across a homeless Guyanese man living outside on his street. This man had witnessed one of the terrorist attacks of men shooting at people on a café pavement. Kuper reports, 'He says he hid under a car, and lay there fearing the terrorists had seen him. I cannot be sure that his account is true. But I do know that he has asked the best question about the attacks. At the moment he saw the terrorists, he thought: "*With what perception must I perceive this?*"' (my emphasis).[6]

Kuper's point, that many people in the aftermath of the attacks seemed to proclaim only their own certainty about the problem (including political leaders, 'we are at war'), and that this certainty not only displayed ignorance about a wider context but also shaped dangerous and divisive acts that would only escalate the problem, highlights the central risk of not examining your own response to what is being experienced. *Not looking at the nature of your perceiving can lead to partial awareness, impulsive statements and reactive interventions that aim to show instant response but that fail to see the complexities of the situation and its multiple causes.*

The fact that there are no simple satisfying solutions to today's complex geopolitical challenges also holds true for our business leaders. In situations of market disruption, competitive threat, financial challenge and falling profits they are often under extreme pressure to instantly read the situation, swiftly implement a solution and then keep holding the same course even if signs call for adjustment. While bold and decisive action is sometimes necessary in change, and essential in crisis, it needs to spring from a wise holistic appraisal of the underlying and not just presenting issues of a situation. Otherwise, all we get are short-term fixes rather than sustainably effective longer-term solutions.

Leadership in Changing Times

So, in a world that is both more interconnected and straining for local identity, in a digital society with both a light and a dark side to resulting human interaction, on a planet and in markets requiring both longer-term collaborative solutions as well as short-term local measures, how does leadership need to show up?

Like Simon Kuper, I believe there is a need for a greater, more conscious attention to our perception. As the Christian missionaries in that anthropology lecture taught me over 30 years ago, our minds create the lens through which we perceive and interpret the world. I am hopeful that the earthquake of the UK's vote to exit from the EU will invite us all to raise our levels of consciousness. If we are not mindful, if we don't stop, pause and pay attention to the nature of this lens then we live our lives on blind autopilot, recreating the world in our own image, imposing our will on others, failing to see both the wider systemic causes for the situation and what a more creative response to that might be. When we intentionally give our mental process our attention, we are able to choose the nature of our response more wisely.

This interplay between systemic perceiving and leadership has already been recognised in ancient wisdom. The root of the Sanskrit word 'Ajna' (one of the seven chakras, or energy centres in the body, Ajna is the point between your eyebrows, otherwise known as your 'third eye') means both to perceive *and* to command. In this worldview perception and command are synonymous: comprehending *is* authority; seeing *is* direction giving. Perceiving wisely is therefore the first step in having mastery over experience and bringing forth what is most desired.

The rest of the book explores what is required to address today's contextual challenges, based on my personal leadership experience and research. In my interviews with leaders, it was striking how often they returned to how the nature of change is, itself, changing. I collected their most thought-provoking insights. As you read, register any impacts that their reflections have on you, start to notice any recurring themes. Create your own *still point* of awareness in this turning world we live in today.

CEO, Personal Banking Division – Taking People Through a Digital Revolution

This CEO transformed his retail bank from a high cost manual operation into a technology-led organisation, where branches are close again to the customer. He showed courageous personal leadership in committing to cost reduction and technology investment before knowing things would work. You might have been in this kind of situation yourself. Here's what he told us about what it feels like to lead change in today's world.

> I was on a panel recently with the deputy CEOs of BNP and Deutsche Bank. We were asked what is the biggest thing we're grappling with. One said regulation; one said capital, and I gave

both of those, and I said change. The scale of change I have on at the moment is huge and how I help a large number of people through that change is my biggest challenge.

And much of this is the first time that we've done this as an organisation, the first time we've done it actually as leaders. So we are finding our way through it but there's not one silver bullet in isolation, its lots and lots of bits of change all coming together.

Chief Human Resources Officer – Transforming his HR Organisation and also Healthcare for his Peer Group of Large Employers

This leader took a bold step to transform his human resources (HR) organisation to better serve the business. This entailed radical cost cutting, the establishment of four broad competency roles and new, globally interconnected ways of working. He had also noticed the impact of President Obama's healthcare law on all large employers, and galvanised inter-company support to positively engage with the changing environment. Here are his reflections.

> This industry has been in constant change, and this company has been in need to either lead that change or respond to that change. It seems like the change gets harder, but it's not for lack of practice.
>
> And it's coming out of the financial crisis. So the era is, we've sort of gotten through the worst of it, but I'm not convinced that the business model is going to ever snap back to where it was pre-crisis.
>
> The wisdom was actually the vision to say that we needed to do this and if we didn't get started on this, this was going to be a large problem. But it was not put upon us. It was anticipating that.
>
> We have put together a coalition, and that is going to be the best way to think about it, as a cooperative. We believe that by doing that, we are going to drive a great deal of change in the way that healthcare is actually delivered in the United States.

CEO, International Children's Charity – Transforming and Uniting a Country Organisation into a Global One

This leader built a US$2bn global charity organisation from what had previously been a loose confederation of 30 separate country organisations. In so doing she and her team dismantled 14 separate legal entities and united 25,000 staff across 120 countries behind a shared vision, strategy and governance structure. Here are her reflections on what it took.

> I realised pretty early on, in fact even before I joined, that this structure was not fit for the twenty-first century. We agreed that we were up for some radical change.
>
> We were on the stage, and those country directors could ask us questions, and I do recall the audience really pointing up to us and asking – virtually demanding – to know when we were going to get our act together as Chief Execs because we were all running separate organisations and, on the ground, they were feeling the brunt of that.
>
> These all were just little moments along the way. It wasn't a logical process. It wasn't 'A, then B, then C'. It was much more of a meandering kind of process with two steps forward, one step back, a step to the side.

CEO, Major US Cable TV Operator – Improving the Customer Experience Journey

In a fiercely competitive market driven by price and cost, and with disruptive threats coming from content streaming services, such as Netflix and YouTube, this CEO nonetheless dramatically improved the customer experience of his organisation. Here's how he saw the challenges facing him.

> For most CEOs in today's world, there are so many things coming at you. You need to try to sort out the things you're going to change, that will make a difference, and then be persistent enough to follow them through.
>
> I looked around at things like Uber and you could say the standard the customers expected for the service that they received in any industry was dramatically increasing, driven by Zappos for shoes, Amazon and how easy it is to order books, and other digital dotcom approaches to service. So my view was the world is changing, it's going to get tougher. So even though we're good, we need to change.
>
> I'm a big believer right now when everything is changing around you, we're at a moment in time where you better not keep doing the same old thing. But you also better not presume you have it all figured out because most people don't. And it's not clear. I would say change isn't always coherent. It's not moving in a consistent,

coherent direction. So you may want to place some small bets. And then you try some other things.

I think that in today's world where things are changing, you need to be constantly reflecting. So when I read a customer complaint or whatever, you're checking for a change in the winds, you're checking for priorities. So you're constantly trying to calibrate whether I need to kind of tack or not, in what I'm doing.

CEO, European Utility – Major Transformation of a 100-Year-Old Stable Company

This CEO we interviewed was at the head of a €32bn, 60,000 staff company, who, in a market place that was entering unprecedented disruptive change, in which no obvious strategy could be clearly articulated at the outset, nonetheless set about creating new capacities in his organisation to be open-minded and ready for whatever future path emerged. This involved putting a lot of his personal beliefs into the programme, which was risky and exposing. Ever been in a dramatically dynamic situation where you simply can't identify a strategy overnight, but nonetheless need to do something personally inspiring? You might recognise this CEO's take on the experience.

> To see that company in a liberalised market, in an environment where the whole competitiveness is shaking the grounds of the company, both in a sense of consolidations and takeovers, as well as in the sense of new entrants coming in, entrants like the telecom companies, entrants like the Googles of this world with Nest means that it drastically needs to change the way we do things around here.
>
> We already knew that a one off would not be sufficient because this market's going to stay very volatile and very demanding, so it needed to be a change with an immediate impact but with a sustainable character, and I think that was the very difficult thing to get realised.
>
> People say, 'You're the CEO; tell this joint where to go'. And it's tempting to step into that and say, 'I've given it some thought; here we go', but you need to be very careful as people have been used to working in a direct control environment. So very often I'm consciously not doing that in order to create the vacuum that people then are forced to start making their own ideas.
>
> Yes, I was nervous, there was an element of tension. It was most of all a feeling of making yourself vulnerable because the ingredients in the programme were not only professional ingredients.

They were giving people that immediate and direct insight into your personal history. I mean, there's a public me as a CEO. You always try to shield off something, which is private. You want to have something for your own, and if you have to open up the whole body shop it makes it for you very, very ... sensitive.

Summary – Implications of Today's World for Change and its Leadership

What does change mean for you? How do you deal with this new context? Did you *feel* and recognise yourself in these leaders' reflections? While the change goal was different in each of these cases, their approaches to the change hold similarities: stay alert and nimble; be open-minded and work step by step; expect messiness; collaborate across borders; and resist pressure to provide the answers yourself.

You might now be noticing patterns in how you currently lead change: your habitual tendencies when approaching novelty; how you deal with uncertainty; your approach to setting priorities and making decisions when there are no obvious solutions; your natural way of responding to the demands and projections of those around you.

Leading big change in today's world is not for the faint hearted. It is for the bold and big hearted. Our world is getting increasingly unpredictable, dynamic and interconnected. This makes change endemic, fast paced, systemic and complex. Leading such volatility requires a certain type of leadership, one that not only acts boldly, able to absorb personal risks and attack, but also holds humanity at its core.

In some ways, the new less monolithic world has many opportunities to improve the human condition. The potential exists for greater freedom, for example, a move away from office-based working or the tyranny of salaried working. Look at the explosion of self-employment in the UK. More information via the internet shifts power and influence to the person on the street. There is much goodness to bring forth.

To achieve this, though, demands a shift in consciousness from goal to process. Your overall approach to change needs to feature:

- Above all else, *the adoption of an emergent change approach* in which you set a loose overall intention, but within that frame tear up any thought of long-term plans, or finding a single silver bullet, and instead work in a step-by-step, experimental, trial and error way.
- Within this more iterative approach, continually *work to join up multiple stakeholders* in both the diagnosis of the issue and the creation

of the solution, and especially engage your beneficiaries in the change process (those for whom the change is ultimately intended).

- As this approach could create a flood of needs and ideas, *focus on a few ripe issues* to cut through the many competing priorities. And select these issues by your ability to tune into the 'power on the ground' – notice the changing winds at the periphery, not the centre, of your organisation.
- An *investment in cultivating the readiness and capacity of your organisation* to embrace change, consider multiple perspectives, collapse hierarchies, work across silos, reach out to society and continually adapt and innovate – even before the solution to today's issues is known.

And within this overall change approach, it seems your leadership can thrive and not just simply survive when you are able to:

- Above all else, *own your personal responsibility* for both creating today's situation and finding a new way through it. At the root of systemic perception is the ability to see how you are creating the very situation you wish to change.
- *Continually reflect on your own responses to experience*, including the projections of others' needs and issues onto you, not automatically being a hostage to these. Widen your perceptions to incorporate a bigger context – putting the wider good ahead of personal or immediate interests.
- *Not wait, but initiate*: have the courage to stand out from the crowd and try something new, even if that brings a touch of fear and a sense of personal vulnerability. ('Fear is wisdom in the face of danger', Sherlock Holmes sagely tells us in *The Abominable Bride*).
- *Halt the personal heroics*: hold the big picture and intention, but within that build trust, transparency, ownership and broad collaboration in the many stakeholder groups around you, especially encouraging peer-to-peer collaboration, networks and platforms.
- *Look after yourself*: in whatever way best works for you, make sure you have periods of time for space, stillness and silence, create regular opportunities to detach, reflect and restore the batteries – even if that is just a 30 min walk outdoors at lunchtime.

Despite my tinge of pessimism at the start of this chapter, I ended 2015 with an enormous sense of hope for how we lead change in today's world – not just for our own institutions but also for the planet we share. This was built upon the successful and historic outcome to the Paris climate talks, which will change the trajectory of growth of hydrocarbon consumption. While the agreement – to a goal of keeping global temperature rises well below 2 °C and even to 'pursue efforts' to keep them below 1.5 °C – was less than the world needs, it is far more than what could have been expected in the wake of the previous failed Copenhagen summit.

Almost 200 countries in Paris (and, subsequently, both the United States and China) signed up to act in the face of a shared danger; action that required each of them to participate in the effort, and in which the rich countries agreed to help the poor in the meeting of their decarbonisation objectives. This historic agreement represents an unprecedented acceptance of a whole over the promotion of national agendas.

This is leading change in today's world on a scale as big as it can get.

And what most gladdened me in this story, beyond its outcomes, is that commentators, who chose to be optimistic, reported both about the style in which the process was run and also the quality of leadership that it took, and how this was different to previous efforts. Change really had changed.

In other words it is the *how*, or change *process* of the agreement, that most brings confidence that its outcomes will be reached. The way in which change happens does get noticed. It makes a difference not only to the outcome but also to how people *feel* about the intended outcome. And how people feel – positively or negatively disposed – will significantly impact the commitment to and momentum of change implementation.

In particular for the Paris climate agreement, it is noted this time that the countries were able to set their own local targets for decarbonisation (power of the ground), whereas in Copenhagen imposed top-down targets failed. In addition, the ongoing mechanism to monitor progress towards implementation of those targets forces each country into a process of peer review. Every country will need to resubmit their plans every 5 years (peer-to-peer process).

What's more, the reporting and monitoring system is to be more transparent and comprehensive than ever before, and in particular the emerging and developing countries will be part of that system (engage the whole ecosystem). As everybody committed to producing a plan, it will now be far harder to argue that failure to meet its promises does not matter. This is an astonishing achievement on a global stage to operate a change process that is not doing things *to* people, but doing things *with* people.

And this change process required leadership. In the commentary on the achievement, skills and tireless commitment of the many involved in helping to secure the agreement, two individual leaders in particular have been singled out, namely Laurent Fabius, the French Foreign Minister, and Laurence Tubiana, the French climate envoy.

Fabius was the mastermind behind the decision to make the agreement a voluntary process. He recognised that governments are not prepared to give up their sovereignty and would respond better to a common direction and a broad range of steps (set the frame and then build ownership). He didn't need to nail people to the mast with imposed goals and detail (respect for difference within a connected whole). His second key to success has been reported as leading his team within the French Foreign Service to run a brilliant coordinated process across the world in the past 5 years (within boundaries, inspire a collaborative and collective effort). Their approach has been called global, inclusive and creative, which has strengthened resolve, spurred collective responsibility and promoted initiative.

Part of his leadership masterstroke was to get 'A players' into the key roles in his team. Enter Laurence Tubiana, the economist and environmental policy expert he chose to lead the French delegation. From her day job at New York's Columbia University she was lured away by Fabius to be his ambassador (inspire people to work beyond personal interest).

It was a brave decision to bring in an outsider to the French foreign office that felt this was its big moment (disrupt repeating patterns). But it was her unusual career, spanning the worlds of academic research, NGOs and the byzantine UN climate negotiations, that led Fabius to pick her for the job. A true ecosystem leader, it was reported that she had an incredible capacity to get people together to find a solution (collaborate across boundaries). Not an ambassador in the conventional sense, it has also been said that her straight talking candour and support of everyday activism were key ingredients in the design of the strategy that gave place to the importance of domestic policies (power of the ground), which ultimately helped secure the global agreement.

It. Can. Be. Done.

And so the world today needs bold leadership that can rise above self-interest, relinquish direct personal control over outcomes, and put in place structures and processes for ongoing, sustainable and empowered local innovation. Yet, the very challenging, disruptive and fast-moving nature of this new era also creates anxiety and its natural bedfellows – shaping heroics and knee-jerk responses. What a perfect storm. The next chapter offers a leadership solution to resolve this dilemma. If you wish to make the most of yourself as a leader, I invite you to read on.

3

Still Moving – The Inner and Outer Skills

Speed is often, ironically, a symptom of complete immobility.
David Whyte, Crossing the Unknown Sea

Each year I retreat from the hurly burly of work and life to seek a dedicated place of stillness and solitude – a place where I can listen to myself, reconnect with my source and get in contact with what is calling me next. And I find it helpful to do that towards the end of the year, when it seems like – at least in north-western Europe – the world is hunkering down for a while, finding its own *Madhya*, that pause point between the life and vitality of one year and that which is to come.

Most recently, I chose to attend a week's silent working retreat on the desolate yet savagely beautiful island of Texel, off the North Sea coast of the Netherlands. The week involved not complete solitude but being present, for the most part in silence, with a community of diverse yet like-minded people, each of us bringing some task for which a quiet and contemplative week would be beneficial.

Each morning before breakfast we gathered for a 45-min Qigong session. I had never encountered Qigong before. Yet as the week progressed, in the December dark and gale-battered room overlooking the awakening beach, I came to experience an intense inner energy that remains with me still.

Intellectually, I learned that Qigong is a holistic system of coordinated body posture, movement, breathing and meditation used for health, spirituality and martial arts training. Emotionally, it brought me glimpses of calmness, connectedness and deep purpose. At the physical level, it was an invigorating yet kind way to get my body moving for the day. But I also struggled. The sessions were demanding. I came to realise how hard it is to stay completely present, and coordinate your body through such simple movement. I kept finding myself wanting to *get going!*

Still Moving: How to Lead Mindful Change, First Edition. Deborah Rowland.
© 2017 John Wiley & Sons Ltd. Published 2017 by John Wiley & Sons Ltd.

Our teacher was one of those people who can command attention without the need to dominate. In his quiet yet strong manner, he perfectly tuned into our needs and gently guided us through the practice. On the second day I asked him what had led him into Qigong? His answer was very straightforward, 'I tried to learn Tai Chi, a more energetic form of martial arts, however my teacher told me, "Marc, you have to learn how to stand before you can learn how to move"'.

The Fine Line Between Movement and Action

His clear simple response to my question was one of the wisest sentences about leadership I had heard. You have to learn how to stand before you can learn how to move.

Yet when a troubling or difficult situation requires our response, we can move into impulsive action before attending to the quality of its source – how we are consciously standing in that action. We restructure our teams and organisations before acknowledging the energy needed to let go of previous affiliations. We bring in new information technology platforms before facing the emotional residue of dealing with the last. We launch multiple change initiatives before attending to the alignment of the human system necessary to implement these new demands.

Of course, we think we already know how to stand – we are two-legged *Homo sapiens* after all. But what is the *quality* of our standing? Are we even aware that all our action begins in thoughts, feelings, embodied sensations and ultimately a complex cocktail of chemical neural transmitters? Do we take time to examine our instinctive emotional patterns formed in childhood and life experience, and identify how they now guide the quality of the relationships we have as a leader today? Are we aware that the impact we have on others is not determined by our intention, but by our own inner feeling states and the mirror neurons in our brain that govern our quality of empathy? Do we pause to notice how we are responding to experience, and interpret that as an empathic and systemic clue about how our team might be responding to the change?

This examination of our inner world is not an everyday leadership practice. Yet if we do not cultivate this inner capacity we will be unaware of, and unable to attend to, the source from which our actions originate – how we are standing. This has consequences. We will stay on autopilot. We may busily repeat past patterns. By not getting in contact with our feeling states we will miss empathy with others. In our impulse to act we might not tune into wider system dynamics, and could exclude difficulty. We might be busily acting yet moving nowhere.

Conversely, if we *do* attend to our inner state, the place from which we stand, we pay attention to the source of our impulses and have the opportunity to regulate our response. Moving off autopilot. Becoming more conscious. Contacting our self in order to contact others. Opening our awareness to the surrounding system, and able to approach difficulty. Leadership requires not just skills, but more complex ways of understanding the self in a context. When we can cultivate this still inner state (which can and needs to happen *in the moment*), our outer practice will flow so much more effortlessly and be an inspiration for others.

As in Qigong and Tai Chi, leaders need to stand well in order to move. We have to be moving, but *still* moving.

This is not just wishful (martial arts-inspired) thinking on my part. I now have research findings that back this claim. In this chapter I share these findings, the *Still Moving* leadership framework it led to and, via a change story from our research, show how one leader put both his inner and outer skills superbly together.

The Change Leadership Research – Context and Big Messages

Ten years since conducting my first study into what leads to successful change, I found a very different, disruptive and more systemically interconnected world. By then I had also been in executive positions myself and experienced senior level change leadership – both major restructurings – first hand. I felt it was time to re-examine my original findings. Somehow, I felt that the leadership practices set out in *Sustaining Change* were not enough. They were special, yet they had to come from a deep place. What was that place?

I have related how I got in contact with the field of *mindfulness*. Inspired by seeing its impact in a major client assignment I now wished to rigorously and empirically examine the relationship between *mindfulness* and the leadership of change. So a 12-strong research team and I spent 9 months rigorously examining this relationship. The full methodology is set out in Appendix 1. In summary, we first created a new mindfulness and systemic leadership construct. We then used that, together with the *Sustaining Change* leadership practices, to code 88 change stories gleaned from Behavioural Event Interviews with 65 cross-industry leaders around the world. Finally, we subjected the coded data to both quantitative and qualitative analysis.

It was an intense yet inspiring effort and I am grateful to all who participated. What now follows – the key research messages and explanation of the whole Still Moving construct – stands on their shoulders.

Big Message One – We Created a Change Leadership Construct, Still Moving, That Accounts for Over Half the Reason why Leaders can Lead Change Well

Still Moving comprises the four external practices (i.e., exhibited behaviours) set out in *Sustaining Change,* combined with the four new internal capacities that we created in this research (see Figure 3.1). In high magnitude change contexts (i.e., change that was complex and impacting many people), leaders who put all of these skills together were significantly more successful than those who did not. This construct accounted for 52% of the variance between success and failure.

Big Message Two – The Inner Capacities Come First

We investigated how the inner capacities and external practices combined. What we found was that the inner skills need to antecede the outer skills. Leaders who were able to get in touch with their inner state first were more successful. The four inner capacities together significantly enhanced the impact that the four external practices had on successful change outcomes. That is why I portray the eight *Still Moving* skills in a spiral – the four inner capacities are like the inner mechanism of a fly wheel that when engaged can activate the four external practices on the perimeter. And, at its heart, leaders who could cultivate their inner capacities were closely in touch with their essential nature, or source. They had figured out who they were in the world and what their leadership was for.

Big Message Three – The Key Element of a Leader's External Practice is to Bring Purposeful Edge and Tension to Their System

All of the four leadership practices set out in *Sustaining Change* – Attractor, Edge and Tension, Container and Transforming Space – were again significantly correlated with success in implementing big complex change. But this time, the Edge and Tension leadership practice was shoulders above the rest – in today's context amplifying disturbance at the edge of a system helps you get the most transformation. Importantly, we also found that this practice needs to be anteceded by key inner skills, otherwise leaders shy away from it, or they are very good at doing it very badly.

Big Message Four – Top Leaders in Particular need to be able to Attend to Whole System Dynamics

We separated out organisational level in the analysis to see whether or not different skills were needed dependent on your place in the hierarchy. Overall, all of the capacities and practices were needed across the

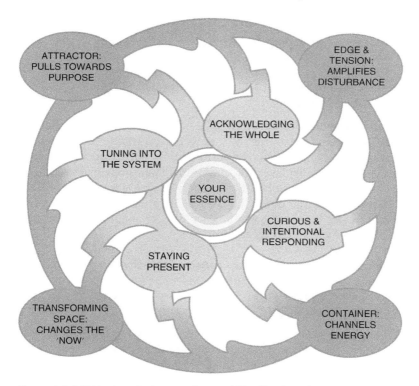

Figure 3.1 Still Moving: the inner and outer skills of leading change.

board. However, we found one clear distinguishing finding: the more senior you are as a leader, the more you have to be able to provide an affirming and non-anxious presence to your organisation, i.e., Container leadership, focusing on what brings strength to the whole system. Top leaders need to attend to whole-enterprise dynamics and not see their organisations as a set of disconnected parts.

Big Message Five – In Today's Uncertain and Disruptive World You can only Adopt an Emergent Step-by-Step Approach to Change

We also studied the overall approach to change, not just how the individual leader needs to show up. In our earlier research we found that more systemic and less programmatic approaches to change were most successful. This finding was revalidated. Change just cannot be approached in a simplistic way. Moreover, in today's dynamic and disruptive world an emergent approach to big complex change can be the quickest way to get results, and needs to be accompanied by Attractor leadership skill – building fresh purpose and meaning for people's daily work.

Big Message Six – Still Moving Skills can be Cultivated, But Not How We've Done it in the Past

Out of the 65 leaders we interviewed, eight came from an organisation that had implemented a highly innovative leadership development process as a key vehicle to achieve transformation. These leaders displayed a proportionately higher level of change leadership competence to others in the study. To cultivate Still Moving leadership an organisation needs to create the right cultural context, and deliver learning experiences that are less about taught training programmes and more about lived collective experiences in the change process itself.

Big Message Seven – Low Success in Change is Driven by a Leadership Style that is Non-Mindful (with Low Self-Awareness), Ego-Centric and Characterised by a Change Approach that is Top-Down and Directive

We found that a non-mindful inner state was highly negatively corre-lated with change success. Some leaders did not just have an absence of mindfulness; they had an inner state that was the *opposite* of being mindful. Key signs of this were low empathy, impulsive reactivity, overly judging of others or the situation and deploying tactical, not systemic solutions. The data also showed that being non-mindful was highly cor-related with a *Shaping* external leadership practice, whose controlling, pace-setting and ego-led style we had found in earlier research to be negatively correlated with leading change well. When non-mindfulness and Shaping leadership were combined, this explained over half of the reason why big change fails.

The data were clear. Still Moving leadership creates value. Busily acting leadership destroys value.

Moving Well: The External Practices – What Great Change Leaders *Do*

I start with describing the external practices of Still Moving as this pro-vides continuity with *Sustaining Change*. The four leadership practices of Attractor, Edge and Tension, Container and Transforming Space allow change to move forward with greater ease. Moreover, the most successful change leaders combine all four; they are an interconnected system

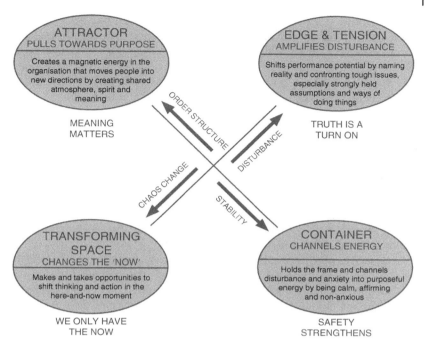

Figure 3.2 Still Moving: external practices – what to *do* to lead change.

combining both forces for stability and structure (Attractor and Container) and forces for disruption and movement (Edge and Tension and Transforming Space) (see Figure 3.2).

We know from research into complex adaptive systems,[1] which human communities certainly are, that an equal amount of structure and disruption allows for ongoing, self-directed innovation (more of which in Chapter 8, on emergent change). When leaders combine all four practices, they are able to create sustainable change *without having to personally shoulder all the effort.* The system can do its own changing, it can do the right things and move of its own accord.

Attractor: A Pull Towards Purpose – Meaning Matters

A 'strange attractor' is a force in the universe, gravity being a prime example, which exerts significant aligning pull on all matter. If organisations are to function as living systems, they need aligned purpose and shared meaning. Exceptional Attractor leadership has the power to build this, connecting us with forces wider and deeper than our immediate selves. Without such leadership, change feels aimless and unimportant. With Attractor leadership, change deeply matters. There are three primary levers through which you can exercise this practice: purpose, meaning and presence.

The Power of Purpose

In any change, people need to identify with the answer to the question, 'Why?' and in particular, 'Why us, and why now?' In big change we move two steps forward and one step back. There will be obstacles along the way. The initial solution is unlikely to be the final one. Disillusionment sets in. At times we might wonder why we ever embarked on the change in the first place. Without the pulling power of purpose, we might never embark, let alone persist, on a change journey.

And by purpose I do not mean the textbook case for change, which tends to be composed of rational logic – so-called 'burning platforms' – explaining why the sky will fall in if we don't change. What I have learned is that Attractor leadership at its most powerful is about having a compelling *emotional* purpose, as that is what keeps us going, even when the change path at the rational level looks a crazy one.

Importantly, the question of purpose starts with you. As a leader, what is your leadership, ultimately, for? It is nigh on impossible for you to inspire your teams behind a new collective intention unless you have addressed the question of *your* personal purpose. Change becomes compelling when people can see and feel that their leaders hold the entire purpose for the change effort as their own, it matters to them, and is in their hearts.

Meaning Makes Sense

Attractor leadership also builds deeper meaning behind day-to-day events, taking the purpose and sustaining it through an ability to interpret all of experience through its lens. Meaning modulates attentional selection, it determines both whether and how we notice things. This is important in change as the sense making of experience removes its ambiguity. I have found the best way to build compelling meaning for change is through the lens, or perspective, of the beneficiary. The beneficiary is the person, or stakeholder group, for whom the change is ultimately intended. He, she or they become the guiding North Star for your change effort. Who are they, what's going on in their world, what problems and needs do they have that your change can solve? Build your change purpose and narrative from this source.

What is Your Presence Signifying?

Together, purpose and meaning create a collective pulling power in the system, it has its own sustaining energy. Notwithstanding that, an important lever for Attractor leadership is your own presence. Have you reflected on what the change means for your own leadership, and do you actively seek to model that? Don't forget that people will watch you the leader like a hawk, and how you show up and where you show up will all have an influence on how people interpret the *real* intention and meaning of the change effort.

Attractor Leadership in Action

In this chapter I'd like to introduce you to Clark, a CEO of an international retail bank, who led his branch network, in just 2 years, through a significant digital revolution. With 20,000 staff serving 14 million customers, this was a tall order. Yet it proved an inspiring one. Clark knew that any change in how his bank staff served their local communities had the power to transform lives and livelihoods.

In a nutshell, he transformed his bank from operating as a high-cost manual operation into one that became a lower-cost, technology-led organisation, where branches and frontline staff were close once again to the customer. The tangible change outcomes: £0.5bn in savings; improved net promoter score (the degree to which customers recommended his bank to others); people far more engaged and involved in the business. You can see already the breadth of his intention.

At the outset Clark benchmarked and talked to people both within the business and to customers, all of which pointed to the single biggest ripe issue: his bank was far too manual and expensive. The driving force for the whole change could easily have been cost, or new technology. He chose instead to make the primary reason for the change the changing needs of the local communities his bank served. His mission was to align his entire organisation to these changing societal needs and, through new digital technology, free his staff from the drudgery of mind-numbing manual operations. He wanted them to 'use their hearts and minds to engage with others'. Clearly, Clark's leadership had a compelling emotional task.

And his Attractor leadership helped inspire a pull towards this radically new purpose. His leadership team members were used to running a branch network organised into product silos, not one that was built around local customers and communities. Their whole mindset had been about selling an existing product range, not tuning into and serving the lives of their local communities. Clark asked them to imagine they were serving just one particular community.

> 'The way that I'm looking at it, you are the leader for Newcastle, someone who lives in Newcastle doesn't think about whether you're the retail bank, or the corporate bank, or the investment bank. They just look at you as "X" (name of company) and they look to you to solve any issues they have with us. So I need you to start thinking about our bank as a whole and I also want you to start thinking about you as a leader.' And they'd never, ever thought about this before.

Clark also knew he had to translate this overarching purpose into daily reality so that everything lined up to this radical new intent. And the creation of day-to-day meaning was going to be tricky as digitising his branches effectively meant removing the role of the cashiers and back office processing. And so he paid special attention to the language, or the narrative for the change, which could easily have become 'technology replacing people'. Instead, he created a beneficiary-led story that came to be known as 'automating the counter, turning the counter round so that the customer is in control of the transaction'. Removing people from stamping cheques behind counters to walking around the branch with their iPads, engaging customers, brought this new story to life.

His organisation was getting a completely new gravitational pull.

Edge and Tension: The Amplification of Disturbance – Truth is a Turn On

I've already described change as *the disturbance of repeating patterns.* So let's now take a look at the *disturbance* part. Innovation happens when we are on our edge, a place outside of our comfort zone, and it is only natural that we will find the non-familiar a challenging place to be. The brain is always busy with what it knows, so its automatic response to the unknown sends out neurochemical defence signals so that you are ready to respond to a perceived threat (the fight, flight, freeze syndrome). Yet it is only by encountering the new that change can occur: leaders need to learn to escape their biology and help others to do so too.

So, a key leadership task in any change is to cultivate and amplify disturbance. Not for the sake of it, but to enable a system to face that which is most holding back its ability to adapt. Edge and Tension leadership can be best exercised in three ways: acknowledging reality; challenging assumptions; and stretching the art of what's possible.

Acknowledge Reality

It is a systemic law of the universe that when reality is truthfully faced, a system gains strength. Far from causing collapse, reality helps systems relax and become resourceful. When reality is denied, troubling issues get passed on. We know this in our family systems when in the interests of protecting others and ourselves we will not rock the boat. We stay quiet about a difficult issue out of embarrassment. We sense that a family member is going through a hard time yet feel ill equipped to have a conversation about it.

And the same holds true in our work life. When the senior boss comes to visit our location we clean it all up and present a shiny reality. When a team member is continually underperforming we shunt them into a new 'special project role' without telling them the real reason why. And when it is clear that a part of our organisation is facing terminal decline due to changed market conditions, we tell them not to worry, as society still needs them. Difficulty gets denied and buried.

Yet by doing what we feel is most safe in the circumstances, i.e., not raising alarm bells, it paradoxically only makes things worse. And when contexts have so radically changed, it could be the most unsafe thing to do. Parking the problem only delays the inevitable, if not for your tenure, certainly for the next. On the other hand, I have seen time and time again the power of a leader who can cleanly and crisply 'tell it as it is'. Put reality on the table. Name and own the difficulty. And when disturbance is named and given a place, any fear it might have generated when not acknowledged loses its grip on people. Truth is a turn on.

Challenge Assumptions

The second key dimension of Edge and Tension is being able to hold up existing ways of thinking to question, and by redirecting thinking disrupt habitual routines. In Chapter 6 I will demonstrate how this needs to be complemented by certain inner capacities such as empathy, as otherwise this practice can easily become intimidation and even bullying. But, it is an important change leadership skill because if you don't surface the underlying ways in which reality is being perceived, you might fix the immediate problem but not have changed the source from which today's thinking occurs, and today's patterns will keep repeating.

Stretch What's Possible

Finally, Edge and Tension leadership is about moving an organisation towards its highest performance potential. And this is why the ability to spot and challenge assumptions is a key leadership practice. When we are not stretched, we limit discovering just how far we can go. Edge and Tension is about continually challenging your team, and yourself, to go that little bit further, setting an even higher quality standard, or performance goal. So, call on your team's ingenuity, keep asking questions about 'what will it take' to go beyond today, keep standards high, focus on the few things that matter, and take your people to places where they can see excellence in practice and ask them, 'why not us?'

Edge and Tension Leadership in Action

Clark amplified his team's discomfort in moving from selling long established products to collaboratively serving local communities, by: against the advice of consultants, removing any financial incentives to selling products – in fact, removing divisive branch manager targets all together; delayering the organisation to get more roles in contact with the front office; and requiring his leaders to change their job titles in order to transform how they perceived their primary task. 'What I want to do is call you community leaders', he told his people.

> They didn't like that so I said, 'Okay, tell me what you don't like about the word leader? That's what you do, your job is to lead.' It's position, it's status and it's recognition. I said, 'It might be recognition in terms of how you thought about it. But ultimately you lead; that's what I want you to do and I want the role to describe what you do and I want people to think differently going forward.'
>
> And then I said, 'Tell me what you think about the word community, what's wrong with the word community?' And in their mind it was not sophisticated. So I said, 'Okay, here's what we're going to do, there's two words in "community leader"; I'm going to choose one word and you can choose one word. And I'm choosing the word "leader"; you can decide the other one.'

Notice how Clark wove a complementary leadership quality into his straight talking Edge and Tension: he stayed present with his team, he tuned into their issues and he created co-ownership for the solution. Choice encourages mindfulness in others.

Container: The Channelling of Anxiety into Purposeful Energy – Safety Strengthens

A combination of Attractor and Edge and Tension leadership stokes up the energy and passion for transforming today's reality. It can also result in confusion and anxiety, especially when the initial flush of enthusiasm dissipates, and people remain foggy as to precisely *how* to get to the new future. Or they see leaders not aligned at the top, or unreceptive to hearing feedback about progress. All of which are a sure sign of a lack of Container leadership. Without its secure and guiding hand, any intention established through Attractor becomes groundless, and any anxiety generated in Edge and Tension becomes paralysing.

Container leadership helps people move through difficult transition. There are three primary ways through which it can be exercised: clarity of the contract; a well-held process; and non-anxious affirming leadership.

A Clear Contract

At its most basic, Container leadership is about establishing clearly framed boundaries, expectations and hard rules as to *what* has to be done and *how*. Boundaries enable people to know the scope – what is in, and what is out of the change. Expectations clarify what the leader is asking of the organisation, and what the organisation can expect from them. Ground rules establish the kind of behaviour that is expected and valued in the change. This contract, once clear and in place, helps people navigate their day-to-day activities and gives them the freedom to act on their own without leader control. Far from constraining, leaders who can give clear boundaries, expectations and ground rules liberate people to take initiative.

A Well-Held Process

Another key element of Container leadership is the design and implementation of well-held change processes. In particular, spaces for engagement and quality dialogue in which people can voice difficult issues, name anxiety, and build trust and new capabilities – important in any big change, where there is by definition ambiguity and uncertainty.

Very often leaders feel that this slows change down, as they want to get on with the main business. Rather than spend time investing in the set up of a new team, a leader might feel compelled to rush into task and early results. Instead of putting effort into setting up cross-departmental task forces to work on a restructuring, a leader will ask in an external consultant to coordinate action. And in place of creating powerful leadership development experiences to create cultural shift, it is very tempting to rely on rolling out 1-day briefing workshops on the new set of values.

None of these latter scenarios really cut it. I have seen them only create a false sense of security and progress. Whereas the former – investing in team development, establishing cross-company networks, providing well-moderated leadership development experiences – provides channels that make the change go so much more effortlessly.

Non-Anxious Leadership in a Sea of Anxiety

Above all, we found that the most differentiating element of Container practice is the leader's intra- and inter-personal ability to stay non-anxious, even if they are personally experiencing difficulty. Throughout the unnerving times of change, a key differentiator between success and low success is your ability to be calm, confident and un-thrown by experience.

I emphasise this does not mean the absence of fear and anxiety. It means the leader being secure *in* their anxiety, being able to express doubt *in* difficulty. I show in Chapter 7 the importance of combining Container leadership with key inner skills to enable you to remain strong and composed in troubling experiences. It is a vital practice for two reasons. First, it enables others around you to voice their own difficulties, which has a cathartic effect, as the discharge of painful emotion is a vital precursor to movement. Second, it makes others feel secure and resourceful, as your emotions as a leader are contagious.

A leader's ability to provide affirming and confidence building signals to people around them is a significant differentiator. The most successful leaders in our research spent an inordinate amount of time ensuring that they built broad ownership for the change.

Container Leadership in Action

So, Clark had set a new purpose for his organisation, to serve local communities not sell products, and he had reorganised structures, incentive systems and even job titles to align his organisation to this purpose.

Throughout he painstakingly ensured that his organisation did not feel overly threatened by the change, but instead that they felt excited about its possibilities, and key players in shaping its journey. This included his whole organisation from the frontline staff back to his board. A key move was to create diverse local teams who could own the change and act as support groups. Here he is empowering his local leaders.

> I gave them context; it's a big city, Newcastle, with some rural areas around it. I gave them economic data; I gave them the market share opportunity. I refused to tell them or give them any help as to how they might pull that together. I also put them into trios: so I had the community leader leading on it and in that trio I would have someone from HR or risk or operations. And then we continued to put in ongoing support around them. But the beauty of having the trio is that they weren't on their own devices, they were a threesome to get through this.

Clark even had these local trio teams present their business plans back to his board, building a greater feeling of ownership of the change. This move conveyed to his teams the confidence he placed in their capabilities and desire to do the right thing for the bank. His own role in these presentations was to stay calm and keep his nerve, and even though this had never been done before, and was high risk, he 'let the team loose' while he stood 'three to four feet back'.

Clark was not just talking, but walking the change he was asking of his organisation.

Transforming Space: Creating Movement in the Here-and-Now – We Only Ever Have the Now

Movement happens within a space, a living space. It happens as we encounter experience, not sit in a presentation of slides, or listen passively to a speech about the change journey. Change is not about thinking more clearly but *experiencing* more clearly. Transforming Space leadership is about creating change in the here-and-now of experience, and is based on the assumption that the only thing you *can* change *is* the present moment. The future is but a series of infinite presents, and the present moment contains innumerable possibilities to shift your attention, respond differently in a stuck conversation, take a risk with someone, make the decision that has been avoided. When you can alter the present moment, you irreversibly change what happens next.

There are three ways in which Transforming Space leadership can be best exercised: change the now; bring diverse groups together; and the physical design of transforming spaces.

Change the Now

Leaders who practise Transforming Space well, lead from the future in the present moment. Their attention moves from planning change to enacting change. Here, now, in this meeting or in this change process. In a sense, the present moment becomes a 'living laboratory' in which to try out new things. Changing the now requires certain moves.

First, the ability to *notice* what is present, at several levels: what is going on inside yourself, what is going on for other people and what is going on in the wider context. Then, you *read* the extent to which what is currently happening is in line with the desired change: are my feelings of sluggishness in this meeting in line with our need to speed up? Is the quality of our dialogue in this encounter in keeping with our desire to become an organisation that listens to society?

If you sense that what is happening is out of line with the desired intention, then you intervene in the present, like stepping into a flowing river, to test out your reading of the situation. 'I'm feeling a little bored by this conversation, and am wondering if this is because we haven't yet found our core purpose as a team?' 'We wish to become more innovative in our company: when was the last time we put aside our own certainty in this conversation?' And then you open the space for dialogue, 'Can we take a little time out here to see if others feel the same or notice anything different?'

These moves take systemic (not judgemental) perception and high quality intervention skill, yet when they're done, they can create extraordinary 'aha!' moments in encounters and irreversibly change the course of what happens next.

Put together Diverse Groups

One of the most impactful ways to disturb repeating patterns is to put together diverse stakeholder groups. Bring in customers, put together task forces from across different departments who all have a piece of the change to solve, upturn the hierarchy and have your CEO working with a group of frontline staff who would normally never encounter senior management. This is not about democracy, but convening representatives from the system who all have a role in solving today's issues; who, when together, can see the collective issue from multiple perspectives, and from that more systemic place build sustainable and collectively owned solutions.

Attend to the Physical Quality of Space

Finally, Transforming Space leadership is about ensuring that the places or processes within which change occurs model the desired outcome. Is the location of your next staff engagement meeting at the edge, or the centre of your organisation? Is even the physical layout of the room in keeping with the change? It's hard to enact values of 'passion', or 'trust' when people are sitting in rows of seats and looking at each other's backs. Create physical spaces that look and feel different, and that are in tune with the change you are seeking.

Transforming Space Leadership in Action

Clark took every opportunity to *live* and not just talk about the future state. In particular, he created prototypes of the new-look digital retail branches and invited diverse stakeholder groups, including customers, unions and his CEO, to come visit and help build them. He also mocked up a retail branch for a critical board meeting. Here's his underlying logic.

> Most of the people I had to go to for approval have no idea about retail banking. They come from an investment bank or they don't spend time in a branch, they have a private banker who will do all that stuff for them. So I brought it to life for them. Rather than give a PowerPoint update at the next board meeting, or just have me talking about it, we managed to convince them to create an hour and we got some meeting rooms which were turned over to various teams to showcase what they were doing, bring it to life and we took the board from zone to zone, and see real people talk about real stuff they were using in the business.

I hope by now you are getting a sense of what it took from Clark personally to be able to lead as he did.

Standing Still: The Inner Capacities – How to *Be* as a Change Leader

So we have now seen what an effective change leader *does*, the four external practices of Attractor, Edge and Tension, Container and Transforming Space. I now turn to the quality of a leader's *being*, the four inner capacities our research found were essential prerequisites to getting these external practices right: Staying Present; Curious and Intentional Responding; Tuning into the System; and Acknowledging the Whole (see Figure 3.3). These four capacities are spelt out in more depth in the next two chapters, but here is their summary now, with Clark's continuing story as illustration.

Staying Present: Notices What is Here, Now

The inner capacity of Staying Present comes closest to how Jon Kabat-Zinn – a medical doctor based at the University of Massachusetts, and a key populariser of mindfulness in recent decades – has defined the term: the awareness that arises out of paying attention, in the present moment, with intention, and non-judgementally.[2] The primary skill therefore of Staying Present is a seeing and *noticing* one. Leaders who had this capacity paid close and intentional attention to the present moment without becoming distracted, or caught up in it. They were not thrown

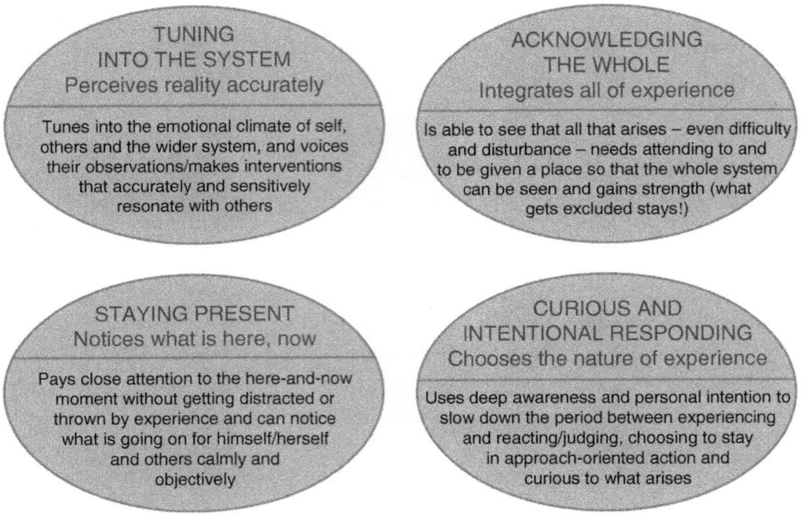

Figure 3.3 Still Moving: inner capacities – How to *be* to lead change.

by experience, simply able to observe it calmly and objectively, building a keener awareness of reality. What *is* here, right now? And can I be okay with whatever shows up?

Are, We, Here?

Paying attention to the present moment, without your mind getting distracted, sounds very easy yet studies show that for 47%[3] of the time our minds are elsewhere, reminiscing about what was or planning what is to be. And if we believe the Microsoft research that says we only have an 8-s attention span, then we can understand how our minds easily wander. We have huge habits of inattention. Yet leaders in our study who had this capacity consciously chose to be present. And they directed their attention first to the richness of their inner life.

We all regularly notice our thoughts, the pieces of information that float in our brain like the impending deadline for the next main board meeting. Who will be there, what's the agenda, the decisions I'd like to get ratified. Are we also present to our feelings and emotions? Do we feel some nervousness about the forthcoming board meeting? Or joy in the anticipation of getting our new strategy signed off? Maybe even some anger that your team has yet to get the draft board papers ready? And the impact of our emotions shows up not just in our minds, but also in our bodies.

We experience sensations such as muscle tension, stomach tightening, our hands getting hot or a raised heartbeat. All of which might lead to impulses, an urge to do something, like send off that email to your Strategy Director to get further market information, or call an emergency meeting with your staff team.

Our whole body is an extraordinary organ of perception.[4] And while we all automatically have thoughts, feelings and sensations, this capacity is about *knowing* that you are having those thoughts, feelings and sensations. Your inner experience becomes an object of your attention and you loosen your subjective identification with it. We found in our research that successful change leaders made conscious time and space during their day to notice what they were experiencing, and in particular during stressful or disturbing situations. Scheduling periods for quiet uninterrupted reflection at their desk, or taking walks outside to find a point of inner calm and perspective on an immediate challenge were simple ways to do this.

Staying Present is also about noticing what is going on in the world around you. When you arrive in the office do you give time to finding out how your team are? When you start meetings do you invest time to find out what's going on for everyone, right now? Do you have a ground rule to ensure no one checks their smartphone so that you can all be present without distraction?

Allow What is the Case, to Be the Case

The second key aspect of Staying Present is to look on what is happening in the present moment with a positive, appreciative and generous attitude of mind, using calm and objective language to describe what is going on. It is not always easy to take such a non-judgemental stance. Our minds tend to evaluate, to critique, to wish for something else to be happening, or to say that someone *should* be more like that, or that I *shouldn't* have said that. And when this natural tendency occurs, we can fret, become unhappy and dissatisfied with experience, wishing for something else. When we are wishing for something else, we cannot simply be with what *is*.

Staying Present is the capacity to look on all experience with deep respect for what is. This skill might sound counter-intuitive in a book about change, yet we found in our study that leaders who were able to simply agree to what is exuded a calmness that then allowed them and their team to find the best outcome for what had to happen next. This does not mean they were not being discerning, or were unable to judge right from wrong, but it did mean they were able to look with more kindness on current experience, in all its rich and messy texture. From this more relaxed and compassionate place they could approach the future with greater resourcefulness.

Staying Present in Action

Let's return to Clark. Recall his story of switching a retail bank from selling products through a fragmented and high-cost manual branch operation, to offering integrated services for local communities from a streamlined and efficient digital retail branch network. Throughout this change, he told us how he paid attention to being physically, emotionally and mentally fit to deal with the challenging situation. First, by taking care of himself.

> I'll slow things down and re-focus; so part of this is wellbeing, are we physically fine and I look at myself. So I make time to go to the gym, if I'm feeling tired or stressed at work and have a big decision coming up, I'll go to the gym for a while. I'll make sure I eat health-ily; I won't drink so that I'm in tune with myself. And therefore I am clear to make a decision.

Getting into the right place personally also meant staying calm and objective when inevitable wobbles occurred.

> I actually screwed up as I didn't check how many of the people who were leaving didn't have an issue working school holidays and I suddenly found myself with a shortage of people during the school holiday season, which put me under a lot of pressure. Things go wrong and I simply learn from that!

As well as not beating himself up he was also present, calm and non-judgemental towards others. He recognised that they were all on an adventure into the unknown with this digital change, and gave dedicated time and space to ensure that the local teams he had set up to build the new community-led business plans felt appreciated. He told us, 'So they worked on their plans, and some things did not go well, but I stayed with them on these calls, as I knew they were doing this for the first time'.

Curious and Intentional Responding: Chooses the Nature of Experience

Our research found that Staying Present was a baseline requirement for leading change – if you are not present you can miss vital signs – but it didn't strongly differentiate the great change leaders from the rest. What strengthens your practice is a second inner capacity: to be curious about what you are experiencing and, in the moment of noticing, *be aware of your choices and intention as to how to respond*, which might mean seeing clearly beyond our first instincts and selecting a different response. This conception of mindfulness as cognitive flexibility starts to incorporate more western-based interpretations of the capacity such as those espoused by Langer.[5]

So, the primary capacity in Curious and Intentional Responding is a *choosing* one. Leaders who had this skill used deep awareness and personal intention to slow down the period between experience and reaction, staying curious and open-minded to what arises.

Respond Not React

When our minds are not awake we impulsively react to present-moment experience, clouded by instincts formed in our early life and even our biology. If we experience disgust we are likely to reject. If we experience fear we are likely to defend. If we experience anger we stop listening to the other. Yet when we have a clear mind, an open mind, we see more choices available for how to be with experience, and with this increased cognitive flexibility and reduced emotional reactivity can respond with greater equanimity and creativity.

Leaders in our study who mastered this capacity could consciously switch their inner response to situations *within* the experience, in the heat of the action, not afterwards. It's a critical capacity to hold in change, as disturbance tends to elicit the default reaction of fear and anxiety, we seek to avoid or fight that which causes us discomfort. With greater mindfulness we have more dexterity in responding to turbulence and discontinuity.

The skill is to step above ourselves and notice our reactions to experience, and, with this wider and more detached perception, see a broader range of options on how to respond. In change contexts, this means actively *approaching* what appears new and challenging, rather than instinctively *avoiding* it. This capacity to creatively respond and not impulsively react takes a great degree of deliberate mindfulness, which I will expand on in the next chapter.

Set Clear Intention

In addition to choosing your response to experience ('I feel frustrated but will switch to accepting things'), the other main dimension of this capacity is to choose a clear intention about what you wish to *do* and how you want to *be* in experience ('So, I will now start to inquire and adopt a learner's mindset'). The successful change leaders in our study, without even requiring an interviewer's prompt, continually turned to a clear inner compass that guided how they led the change. At its heart was the acknowledgement that their leadership needed to model what it was they were asking of their organisation. For example, in one change story that required adopting a new business model in a disruptive market, a leader intentionally chose in meetings to pick the most difficult, rather than the easy route.

What Curious and Intentional Responding adds up to is *courage*. The successful change leaders relinquished the ease and comfort of habitual impulse, be that driven by their own story or the needs of the organisation's projection, and they deliberately chose a different path – one that afforded them the opportunity to change the repeating patterns in the system. The more mindful we are the more we can shape the contexts we are in.

Curious and Intentional Responding in Action

Clark was not always in his own comfort zone in the change he led. However, given its import, he had the capacity to put aside his own habitual tendencies and consciously choose a new response.

> How I prepared myself was being very clear what I wanted to do; talking a lot about context and what I wanted to see; why the change was needed; making it exciting for them and practising how I would come across on the stage. That I would come across as excited myself and that's not easy for someone who is an introvert.

And his choice of how to respond in situations was driven by a clear intention: not to provide answers but to build new leadership capabilities in the operations and create ownership for the change. This capacity is about being able to break your own patterns in order to break the patterns in the wider culture around you.

> It was involved, it was great fun. Hard going, tiring, I had to push them by saying, 'Okay, what else could you do? How are you going to think about this?' In a way, I was trying to lead them without giving them an answer.

From Mindfulness to the Systemic

The first two inner capacities, Staying Present and Curious and Intentional Responding, in a sense represent what is currently being put forward as the essence of mindfulness. *Our research found that these two inner capacities are prerequisites, but not the differentiators, of being able to lead change well.*

What *did* differentiate, and especially in change of high magnitude and complexity, were two further capacities: Tuning into the System, and Acknowledging the Whole. These two capacities moved leaders beyond the focus on observing and regulating self in relation to experience towards a wider appreciation of context and system dynamics. Senior leaders who can successfully implement large-scale change have an inner capacity to place all that happens into a deeply perceived systemic frame.

Tuning into the System: Accurately Perceives Reality

The primary capacity of Tuning into the System is a *perceiving* one, and it builds on the first two capacities. Once you are present, and have curious intention, your inner self is then a clean tuning fork with which to pick up the vibes and visible signs of what is going on around you. Unclouded by their own projections, leaders who have this capacity are able to tune into the emotional climate of self, others and the wider system and put this into an interpretation that can completely reframe for others their sense of what is being experienced.

Out of the four inner capacities, Tuning into the System was the skill most highly correlated with success in leading high magnitude change.

Visible Signs as System Intelligence

The successful change leaders constantly paid attention to situational cues that provided intelligence about the organisational system and its wider context. These signs could be as micro and as immediate as how people behaved in meetings to, at its most macro, changing customer and society's needs. And they were able to join up the dots in this reading of the system, as the primary skill of systemic perceiving is the ability to interpret what is directly present as an echo of what is happening in the wider whole.

So they connected the unrest of their operational staff unable to have a voice *to* a customer base frustrated with a cumbersome billing system; they interpreted their own team being unable to reach collective decisions *to* jealousy between different departments in the wider organisation; and they were even able to sense that what was happening in the present, for example, a team member continually causing difficulty, was in fact a systemic echo from what had happened in the past, the previous role incumbent had been disrespectfully exited from the company.

Tune into the Emotional Climate

The primary source of systemic intelligence for these leaders was the realm of emotions and feelings. In their stories, the successful leaders were continually recounting how they were picking up the mood of the organisation. They could look beyond their own emotions and feelings and pick up what was going on for others, even without needing to have a conversation. They observed expressions on faces, noticed patterns of behaviour in meetings, mapped out who was talking to whom and who was not.

Emotions enable movement. The clue is in the word, e•motion. Emotions hold a tremendous amount of energy, and especially the more dangerous ones that we tend to dishonour. As Karla McLaren says in *The Language of Emotions*, emotions are the tools of our deepest awareness. And in leading change, they are the greatest source of systemic intelligence. How your team is feeling is a rich source of data about your organisational climate; their emotions are like messages from the wider world, *not* just about immediate personalities and issues. More time will be spent on this in Chapter 5; however, a leader's empathic ability to tune into the feelings of their organisation gives them a powerful ability to interpret deeper systemic forces, enabling them to plan implementation that will move forward with greater ease.

Relate Systemic Interpretation to Others

The practical advantage of this Tuning into the System capacity is that leaders are able to describe and reframe for others the nature of reality – especially what is being experienced as difficult or disturbing. This skill holds enormous power to shift minds from judgement to openness, from defensiveness to curiosity, from complaints to open heartedness. For example, an error in a group that has led to embarrassment is reframed by the leader as an opportunity to tune into wider struggles in the organisation. An angry group of staff at a conference is spoken of by their leader as an invitation for her to take up greater leadership responsibility, and not labelled as 'awkward and meddlesome change resistors.' The positive and systemic connotation of reality is an extraordinary skill that requires much suspension of judgement and diminution of the ego. Yet, it's a masterstroke that brings systems strength.

Tuning into the System in Action

Clark spent a lot of time in inquiry, finding out about what was going on in the wider world, tuning into the changing needs of the communities his bank was serving, and reading the mood of his own people.

He was able to join up the dots and see the totality and interconnectedness of the change required.

> We did a lot of looking into the role, we did a lot of benchmarking, and talking to customers and it's very obvious that we were very manual. Lots of people doing lots of repetitive things that are cumbersome, that leaves lots of errors and not particularly a fulfilling thing to do. For example, we weren't using people for what people are good at which is using their hearts and minds to engage with others.

His sensitivity to the feeling states of his organisation enabled him to anticipate the impact of his decisions on his frontline staff, for example, the bank cashier.

> See that guy, he would be feeling, 'I am nervous about this because I'm having to talk to people without the comfort of a glass screen in front of me. But with the training I'm getting, I'm feeling really good about this and my day is much more varied, I can see a career in front of me, and I'm adding more value to the customer.'

Ultimately, Clark was a leader who modelled mindful tuning into his system, and the importance of this capacity in leading change is neatly summed up in his words.

> I think very hard about the change I'm about to do, the impact that it will have on a whole load of people. Be they a customer, be they a colleague, be it a child, be it an adult, be it someone who is much more vulnerable in society. And I test that. You've got to be really considerate as to how you ease the impact of change. Why do I do that? Well because I care, and doing things in a good way will always lead to better outcomes.

Acknowledging the Whole: Integrates All That Happens

The primary capacity of Acknowledging the Whole is an *integrating* one. Once we have noticed and selected our response to what is being experienced, and placed a systemic reading on what we see, can we then hold all experience in a wider context? Leaders who have this capacity are able to see that all that arises – even difficulty and disturbance – needs attending to and being given a place so that the whole system can be seen and gain strength.

While this capacity was the least present in the stories we analysed, it was very clear that it differentiated the leaders in the top of the sample from the rest. In fact, it only tended to show up in the most successful change leaders.

Uncover the Intention of the System

Exceptional change leaders have the capacity to step back and acknowledge all that is being experienced – including what is happening to them – to be in some way a signifier for what is needing to come forth in the wider situation. They see experience as having its own inevitable flow.

For example, far from being thrown by what could have been interpreted as a disastrous meeting with the board, one leader had the insight to tell their team that this meeting was helpful, indeed a gift, in showing up all that still needed attending to. During a major company reinvention, one leader had extraordinary back problems, and saw this not as a sign to get grumpy or take time off work, but as a signal that the structure, or backbone, of the entire company needed a radical overhaul.

It is not the norm to hold a mindset that everything that happens is in some way a signifier of a deeper whole working in our lives. We are not trained as leaders to welcome and incorporate obstacles into a change, rather, we are trained to risk manage them out. Yet this is what we saw the most successful leaders in our sample being able to do. They had the capacity to acknowledge, 'All of what is here is in some way meant to be here, let's work with it!'

Give Every Element its Place – Especially Difficulty

Senior leaders are in charge of extraordinarily complex systems comprising many dynamic intersecting elements. Some influencing elements are tangible and visible (customers' changing needs, the structure of their board), other elements less so (hidden loyalties to a former CEO, the workings of conscience in a restructuring). Being able to make this whole system visible – especially the less tangible elements – and to give each element its rightful place, requires deep systemic insight and wisdom. In a sense, it's a bit like being able to continually 'press plus or minus' on Google maps so that you can both zoom in to what is happening in one part of the system and at the same time zoom out to see how it all fits within a bigger picture.

The top change leaders in our study had this inner spacious capacity to hold and deeply respect this whole, and ensure that nothing that the system needed was excluded, even if, for a while, this included difficulty or disconfirming data. Systems are freed up when the truth is acknowledged. Take employees who have to leave the company, which is often a feature of large-scale change. If this reality, and the process to handle it, is not explicitly dealt with and respectfully acknowledged, far from eliminating difficulty, the departing employees only seem to exert an even greater gravitational pull on the system. It seems that they can't fully 'leave', and those who stay can consciously or unconsciously wish to follow them.

Yet when a change leader is able to take a wider perspective and embrace all, even the messiest parts of experience, then paradoxically the system gains strength, *because the system is then seen.* And when we feel seen and acknowledged we relax, and can move more resourcefully into the future. It really is the worst systemic crime to disrespectfully exclude someone or something from the field as it threatens our most fundamental need to belong.

In addition to holding their own capacity for non-reactivity, wider perspective taking, and the facing of difficulty, leaders who Acknowledge the Whole also consciously modelled this capacity to others so that collective systemic capacity could be built.

Acknowledging the Whole in Action

Throughout the change that he led Clark displayed his capacity to Acknowledge the Whole by putting all that happened into perspective, including the inevitable difficulty of doing such big change. He integrated many elements into his thinking – society, technology, operational people, less in touch senior colleagues, costs, emotional impacts – never imagining that this was going to be a straightforward and easy path. And he was courageous enough to test things out, build prototypes. I got the strong sense that here was a deeply reflective man who could handle complexity with insight, difficulty with courage and who could hold all of experience in deep respect. Not getting thrown. Here are some final words from this impressive change leader.

> This is the first time that we've done this as an organisation; the first time we've done it actually as leaders. So we are finding our way through it, there's not one silver bullet in isolation, its lots and lots of bits of change all coming together. So I learn as I go. The branch we've designed, the supplier to build it. We've tested it with customers, it kind of works. But we haven't tested its scale and plugged it into really complex systems and the testing environment. Things go wrong and you just learn from that!

Still Moving: Summary

Clark and his team had to learn as they go. I'm sure that this is the case for all of us in big change – particularly nowadays. But as you read this chapter I hope you have picked up some ideas on the elements of successful change leadership that can apply whatever the context and whatever the change.

Be always alert to the difference between creating genuine movement and simply getting busy in change. The first type of change requires that you go to the source of what creates today's patterns and from that place irreversibly adjust how you act. The second type of change sees you getting stuck in event level action that gets you busy and feeling you are doing something but in effect you are moving nowhere (apart from into frustration and weariness).

In order to lead from your source, and in so doing, generate system changing movement not just system maintaining action you first need to cultivate the quality of your *being*, bringing greater mindfulness and systemic skill to your inner state as a leader. Once you have cultivated these inner awareness- and perception-expanding capacities, your outer practices, the quality of your *doing*, will naturally follow. If you short change working on your inner state, when you lose your presence you are likely to lapse into a shaping style of leadership that keeps you stuck in the world of ego-led habitual reactions. The whole point is – are you aware of which state you lead in?

4

It All Starts in Mindfulness

When you lose touch with inner stillness, you lose touch with yourself. When you lose touch with yourself, you lose yourself in the world.

Eckhart Tolle, Stillness Speaks

I can recall the first time I saw Schipol Airport with a clear mind, a free mind. Until that point, my almost weekly trips to Amsterdam's busy airport only brought me heaviness, even revulsion. Over a 2-year period the leadership team of a major European company met at the Schipol Sheraton hotel to steward a major restructuring of their business. I was on that team. It was an intensely challenging, yet rewarding time. That was not the source of my disquiet. It was the airport location. Despite its convenience and superb facilities, all I ever saw at Schipol was grey concrete. Lots of it. Ugliness. And I could get caught up in that response and wish it were something else.

Then one day, a few years after this assignment, I found myself back at the Sheraton in the same meeting room overlooking the very same terminal building that had caused me such aesthetic offence. I had a few minutes' wait before a new prospective client arrived, and found myself gazing out of the window into the subtle shadow-shifts of a gathering evening dusk. And I saw beauty. I liked the grey horizontal lines in all their stark function and simplicity. For the first time I was seeing a composition, not an airport, a picture, not a place. I was alert to how the greys subtly changed colour in that hyphen point moment between dusk and darkness. And in that moment I felt still, untroubled and free.

Nothing had changed at Schipol. But the lens through which I viewed it had perceptibly changed. In that moment, I didn't want anything in my experience to be different. I was simply noticing what was in front of me for what it was – without agitation, and without judgement. Just allowing what was there, to be there. And from that place of awakened

Still Moving: How to Lead Mindful Change, First Edition. Deborah Rowland.
© 2017 John Wiley & Sons Ltd. Published 2017 by John Wiley & Sons Ltd.

sensibilities, I saw new things. A far more finely nuanced picture, the impact of light on colour and the tranquility of horizontal lines. I wasn't consciously trying to see things any differently – they just *were* different. But I noticed the change, vividly. Such moments of startling awareness are never forgotten.

Was my clearer, and more appreciative mind that evening a temporary state – for some reason my mood was a little happier – or a more enduring and underlying trait – had I become more generally able to be with life as it is? I suspect the latter. The previous few years had been intense. They had involved several major transitions, which I was able to process in a way that left me in a more aware and complete place. Along the way I encountered both lost and found. Ending a major loving relationship that sadly no longer worked. Leaving behind the wish that I would become a biological mother. With my adopted parents' blessing, tracing and being reunited over time with my biological parents, which brought resolution to the most missing element of me.

While we do not necessarily wish for all our life experiences, they offer us opportunity to grow and can cultivate a capacity for inner stillness, *if* we are prepared to look into them with courage, perspective and acceptance.

Change is All in the Mind

I often reflect on my 'Schipol moment' and the relevance that it has for leadership. One thing great leaders do is to help us make meaning from experience. The moment came after I had written *Sustaining Change* and was now leading change as an executive myself. An early hypothesis I was forming was that we live life through our minds. They both determine our response to, and outcomes from, experience. In fact our mind is the basis of everything we experience and of every contribution you make to the lives of others. I don't believe it is coincidence that the leader I met at Schipol that evening became one of my most rewarding professional partners. A still and open mind, when it is fully present and empty of need, can alter life's course. And we *are* able to regulate our minds. Consciousness is a choice.

I knew in my own leadership, however, that my inner state was not always on good form, especially in challenging conditions. Indeed, I could fly through a day during a major restructuring completely on autopilot and land at its end not quite knowing how I got there. Had I been fully present for my team? Where was my mind in that major staff engagement meeting that I led? Did any unconscious personal bias creep into my decision at the budget meeting? Was I more dismissive than curious when I had to sit with someone I did not particularly like? Sometimes, I felt even a little proud that I could operate as I did, striding through my day, tackling multiple and complex tasks and able to operate from 8:00 a.m. to 7:00 p.m. with barely a break. Yet had I showed up fully in my leadership, and what had I been modelling to others?

Mindful leadership can be a struggle. But it *is* worth it, as regulating our minds determines the quality of our thinking, our emotional state and our ability to function when we feel most insecure. In this chapter, I begin our deeper dive into *Still Moving* with where our research showed a leader had to start – in mindfulness. I outline what it means to be mindful, and set out why this is important for the leadership of change. I then describe the inner capacities of Staying Present and Curious and Intentional Responding, which we found to be the mindfulness skills most correlated with successful change outcomes. And I conclude with an illuminating story from our research that vividly illustrates this relationship.

Mindfulness in a Nutshell

One of the consequences of the mindfulness explosion is that there are multiple definitions of the concept, with subtle distinctions dependent on whether mindfulness is being situated within clinical, spiritual, psychological or workplace settings. *Mindfulness* is the English translation of the Pali word 'sati', an essential Buddhist practice that means to remember to pay attention to what is occurring in immediate experience with care and discernment. For the purposes of this book, I repeat the simple and practical definition drawn from Jon Kabat-Zinn that I find works best for leadership[1]:

> *Mindfulness is the awareness that arises out of paying attention, in the present moment, with intention and non-judgementally.*

Paying Attention

Mindfulness is a particular way of paying attention at multiple levels: you notice what is going on for yourself – thoughts, feelings, physical sensations and impulses; you tune into what is happening for others, in particular their emotional state; you notice what is occurring in the wider situation; and you notice the interrelationship between all of this. You cultivate situational awareness with deeper and more connected sensibilities.[2]

This special way of paying attention lifts you outside of yourself so that you view your experience as it were from a balcony, and with this greater detachment see wider points of reference than just your own projection. You *notice* that you are constructing a story about the situation. You *notice* that you are having feelings in response to experience. This skill of *meta cognition* enables you to de-centre yourself in experience and avoid ego-led reactive impulses.[3]

So when you are paying attention you start to *observe*, and not just *be*, your experience. Experience becomes an *object* of our attention; you are no longer *subjectively* identified with it. Rather than thinking to yourself, 'I am angry', you notice, 'I am feeling anger right now' (you know this state will pass). You become less enmeshed in your own narrative, or drama, about what is going on.

Many studies have shown that people who pay attention in this way have improved cognitive and emotional regulation and have more balanced interpretations of reality. Our problems, fears and anxieties are magnified when we are locked within them.

In the Present Moment

When you are being mindful the focus of your attention is on the present moment – what is here, now? Not what is happening elsewhere, or what was experienced yesterday, or what might happen tomorrow. Your focus is on what is being sensed, thought, felt inside yourself right here right now, in this meeting, in this conversation, in this encounter. This is easier said than done if you recall the research that shows we are only available in the present moment for just over 50% of the time,[4] and have an attention span of a mere 8 s.

Our minds naturally wander. In a conversation with a colleague we might be thinking about what remains to be done before we leave the office. It is very rare to be with someone who is giving you the sustained gift of their attention. But when you are being mindful you stay present, you are totally available for the now, welcoming all current experience, receptive to the other. This is a real gift. People feel seen, heard and valued when you are truly present. You divest yourself of any feeling of superiority. You acknowledge the mutual interdependence of you and another's presence in that moment.

This availability for the now has a further advantage in leadership. It ensures that you don't miss something vital: a tiny defect that could escalate; a whiff of change in your customers' needs; an opportunity to shift a troubling relationship that would otherwise remain exactly as it is. By the conscious direction of our attention to the present we can make better choices in the moment as we see things that would normally pass us by. If we are not present, we miss the chance to bring in the new.

With Intention

When you are mindful you know you are being mindful. You set an intention to pay attention in the present moment. It's a deliberate, conscious act. Your mind is fired up and alert to experience. The classic way to intentionally practise and cultivate your capacity for being mindful is to meditate, and focus your attention on your breathing: the act of your in breath, and your out breath, and the pause in between. The power of holding an intention is that you then recognise when you forget that intention, you notice your mind wandering away from present-moment awareness and into the whirl of troubling thoughts, you observe you are no longer noticing your breathing, and you consciously bring your attention back.

The good news is that this is perfectly okay. The act of remembering and forgetting your intention, time and time again, lays down tiny neural deposits in your brain that studies show lead to increased working memory capacity, enhanced creativity, greater empathy and improved mood regulation. It's not bad that your mind wanders. That's what minds do. The trick is to be conscious of what it's up to and get into a different relationship with what you find there. Your attention is like a muscle that can be exercised just as you do your quads at the gym. Repetition. Practice. Tiny switches teach the brain and your body that you are in charge.

When you are mindful you come away from living your life on autopilot and you consciously choose, or set an intention, for how you wish to be with experience: with this person, in this situation, in this precious tiny moment on earth that is called life.

We only have the now; let's make best use of it.

Non-Judgementally

Mindfulness encompasses a set of attitudes such as patience, non-striving, openness, curiosity, kindness, non-reactivity and non-judging. There is little moaning and groaning or huffing and puffing. Instead, you encounter all of life with calmness and equanimity, even good humour. Mindfulness is not antithetical to evaluation or judgement. It means you are not overly critical and avoid being excessively judgemental – especially on encountering something new, different or disturbing.

In particular, you allow what is the case to be the case. History has delivered this moment and we can't do anything about that, so, how do I want to be with it? You also avoid the tendency to self-critique and beat yourself up. You catch yourself saying, 'I should have done it like that', or, 'I shouldn't have gone to that meeting' (indeed, I am always on the alert now for the 'should' word, either in myself or others), and you start saying 'Hmm, I wonder why it was meant to be that way? How was this helpful to me?' When you are in a place of judgement, be that of your own self or others, it bars you from being able to hold a systemic interpretation because when we hold something as negative we stop exploring (something beneath the surface could be at work here).

When we are being mindful, we don't block things or wish for something else.

Just imagine, now, the quality of awareness that could result from these four mindfulness principles. What might you be missing from your perception?

Mindfulness and the Leadership of Change

In *Sustaining Change* I signalled the importance of self-awareness. When you know your ego's reactive tendencies you can avoid shaping, a leader-centric style that tips the four leadership practices into their shadow. When Attractor leadership is led purely by your own needs you slide into *seduction*. When Edge and Tension leadership is fired by personal prejudice you veer into *intimidation*. When Container leadership is caught up in personal anxiety, you swing into *protectionism* (both of yourself and also of others). And when Transforming Space leadership is guided by your unconscious needs, your intervention to change the present moment is felt as *manipulation*.

It's a fine line in your mind that distinguishes between serving egotistical and situational needs. But sharpening your awareness to this distinction is vital. The shaping behaviour outlined above leads to change failure.

My research and personal leadership experience, combined with the gift of having worked alongside a deep mindfulness teacher and practitioner in a major change assignment (see Chapter 9), points towards mindfulness as being the foundation for doing the four change leadership practices well. I have already alluded to the advantages of mindfulness for change: by becoming fully present you increase attention to novelty, and can expand the space to create something new; when you are non-judgemental you sit in experience with an open mind, able to explore new possibilities; and acting intentionally takes you away from your habitual routine and creates choices about how to take action in the world.[5]

Now let's step up to your role as a leader taking a large complex system through change. Here are my concluding thoughts on how becoming more mindful enables you to accomplish this challenging task well.

Mindful Leaders Approach, Not Avoid Difficulty

Change, especially big change requiring internal psychological adjustment and transition, is stressful. When we are anxious our amygdala, the brain's threat detectors, send out warning signals and flood the body with hormones such as adrenaline and cortisol. Our nervous system is activated. This neurochemical stress response (which happens in a nanosecond) raises our blood pressure and increases the flow of blood to our main muscle groups so that we are ready for fight or flight. Such a response was highly appropriate for our ancestors foraging for food in the forest, on constant look out for bears and other predators.

Yet such a physiological and behavioural response is no longer appropriate when the board asks us to restructure the company and its top team; external regulation requires us to radically change our business model; other departments aren't pulling their weight in implementing a key new process; or we find ourselves facing awkward questions about the change in our staff meeting. In these circumstances, if we are not mindful, it is likely that the right-hand prefrontal cortex in our brain will get activated, which leads us to get anxious and avoid or defend against difficulty.

How do you function when you face disruption and difficulty, but don't (yet) know the answers, or feel insecure? In situations such as these, my natural tendency is to become anxious, maybe a little angry. I might be tempted to defend my position, or provide overly long explanations for why it will all be fine (as my adoption story to please kicks in again). In these challenging situations, I'm sure we can all react to apparent threats as if our life depended on it.

When we are mindful we catch our emotional response in a difficult and disturbing situation, and as soon as we notice we have choice and can more flexibly respond. We train our minds to switch from anxiety to curiosity, firing up the left-hand prefrontal cortex in our brain, which leads us to approach and not avoid challenging contexts. What's going on here? What does this difficulty teach us? And as we stay calm and more able to approach and not avoid difficulty, we can approach turbulence with greater ease.

Mindful Leaders Create Psychological Safety

It is very important to be relaxed as a leader because if we become anxious in a challenging situation, so will our organisation.[6] A leader's mental states and emotions are contagious and can spread like wildfire, especially in times of change when people are most on the alert. If the leader feels insecure (even if their language is that of conviction), the whole organisation feels insecure. Just as ever-watchful monkeys in a forest are alert to danger and take their cue from the alpha male (or female...), human beings also automatically tune into the inner mind state of their leader. If the leader feels safe, we feel safe.

It is a central task of a change leader to help their organisations to feel secure in transition. This does not mean the elimination of difficulty – far from it in fact. It's about creating a feeling that tough things can be talked about, that people can take interpersonal risks and innovate even if that will mean a failure along the way, that the leaders at the top are open to being challenged. While jobs or roles might feel insecure, people nonetheless feel that their leaders are communicating with openness and transparency. While the future direction might feel unknown and uncertain, people see that their leaders support a process to find new solutions.

When leaders are mindful they become calm, centred and more connected to the task at hand and resonant with their people. They can hold a space that feels safe and secure enough for others to speak up, take risks and walk into new places. A relaxed leader is an inspiring leader.

Mindful Leaders Don't Shirk the Big Calls

So, getting on top of yourself and your responses to experience enables you to regulate your emotions, be at ease in difficulty and create a more secure and hence resourceful climate around you. Becoming more mindful has a further advantage for change leaders. You can feel fearless when you have decoupled yourself from negative and troubling thoughts, especially excessive worrying about personal security, image or reputation. In such an ego-free state you don't shirk the choices, you take courageous decisions, and you make bold moves.

Without the help of my personal coach in processing my adoption story and its troubling legacy in the present, I would not have been able to pluck up the courage to trace and meet my biological parents. Once I had accomplished that task, taking major restructuring decisions, handling tricky big leadership meetings or facilitating volatile leadership group dynamics didn't seem to phase me as much. Basically, mindfulness can make you more resilient.

And change requires leaders to make and implement tough decisions, often with a human cost attached. When your personal baggage doesn't weigh you down, you see the situation free from your needs and insecurities and unflinchingly do what's needed.

Change, by definition, entails a betrayal of loyalty to what has gone before – including your own conscience and 'safe prison'. I had to unhook myself from a story of not being wanted. This can be a very seductive story in adult and leadership life, which means you excuse yourself from fully committing to a relationship, an assignment or to a team. Yet it holds back your life and it holds back your leadership.

People who are better at working with their minds and their mental states do not allow their own story to get in the way of what has to be done. They see disturbance not as dysfunctional, but as a necessary companion in change. In a sense, they are ready to forfeit their innocence and can endure the guilt they feel from making and implementing tough calls.

Mindfulness and Still Moving

Let's now turn to the two mindfulness-related inner capacities I introduced in the previous chapter: Staying Present and Curious and Intentional Responding. In the following section I share the specific elements of these two capacities that our research showed mattered most when leading change, illustrated by a short quote from a leader in one of our research stories that brings the element to life. In the full story that concludes the chapter, I show how these two inner capacities combine to enable a leader to put into action the full range of the external practices so essential in change.

Staying Present (see Table 4.1)

Uses Language to Describe Experience and Doesn't Get Caught Up in the Response to the Experience Itself

The following quote illustrates how a leader avoided an amygdala hijack. He tuned into his emotional response in the heat of a challenge without allowing his feeling to colour his interpretation of experience or lead him

Table 4.1 Staying Present.

Pays close attention to the present moment without getting caught up in it, so is not thrown by experience but can observe it calmly and objectively (intimate detachment)

Uses language to describe experience and doesn't get caught up in the response to the experience itself

Focuses upon what is happening in the present moment and consciously avoids distraction for a sustained period of time

Pays attention to what is happening in the present moment with a positive, appreciative and generous attitude of mind

Consciously makes time and space during disturbing situations to process what is going on

Remains calmly curious and objective in novel and/or disturbing and difficult situations into impulsive reactivity. When you are Staying Present you view moment-to-moment experiences with clarity and objectivity, and can use language that gets to the heart of what is being called for (not an outpouring of your unchecked feelings).

> So it was very hard to ensure that that emotion didn't just spill out. And so trying to speak slowly and trying to come back to that rallying cry and actually talk through what we've accomplished and what we want to do next.

Focuses on What is Happening in the Present Moment and Consciously Avoids Distraction for a Sustained Period of Time

The next quote illustrates how a leader places value on taking time out in the hurly burly of a major change to simply rest and relax the mind, creating spaces for inner stillness.

> I needed to find some space for myself; so lunch times I decided not to go down to the canteen but to have down time in my office. And every time that I did that I would sit down and I would eat my sandwich but I wouldn't actually work. I would sit there quietly, often with my eyes closed, just breathing deeply, trying to centre myself. Not planning or thinking really just trying to let the, kind of, adrenalin soak out of me and get myself into a calm sense of mind.

Pays Attention to What is Happening in the Present Moment with a Positive, Appreciative and Generous Attitude of Mind

When you are Staying Present you do so with an attitude of warm kindly curiosity, allowing what is the case to be the case, being wholehearted in your approach to work. This mindful leader avoided getting grumpy with her team and instead chose to draw out and amplify their qualities.

> I'm a non-exec on a small digital business, they move on decisions a lot faster, and I think what I'm trying to do here is move to clarity fast, even though that can be a little awkward. But what I would say is I think you have to do that with a spirit of generosity. They know that what I'm doing is never personal.

Consciously Makes Time and Space During Disturbing Situations to Process What is Going On

Another key feature of Staying Present is the capacity to process distressing thoughts or feelings. This capacity to find words for emotions *as you experience them* promotes both intimacy with and detachment from the source of the distress. Physiologically the act of labelling emotions activates the higher prefrontal cortex enabling the mind to become more resourceful. Here is how one leader sought not to eliminate difficulty, but by processing it live in a team meeting brought instead perspective and equanimity.

> I think you have to be very wary of conversations that are going around the meeting, so you might see or sense a couple of people that are a little unhappy about one element, or they're threatened by the restructure. We've got it now and we're looking at another cost saving drive, and I had an incident recently where I had to say, 'Look, I sense that a couple of us feel too threatened by this so let's actually have this out as a team', and I'm building huge levels of trust and openness among my top 12.

Remains Calmly Curious and Objective in Novel, Disturbing and Difficult Situations

Finally, a key aspect of being able to Stay Present in difficulty is to put the presenting challenge into a wider context of awareness. Negative experience is just a mental event. This leader had to deal with an extreme period of difficulty in his organisation but managed to stay balanced and calm in the eye of the (very public) storm.

> I spent 5 months running the whole organisation in a time of enormous crisis. It was front-page news – it was huge – and I think people were shocked that I would just disappear for an hour and say, 'Right, I'm just going for a cup of coffee'... I care desperately about the business, but it's not the meaning of my life. I think the best executives have balance. They really can understand that quietly sitting, thinking, actually taking a day off is one of the best things you can do for the business because you begin to really think things through. That quiet period is really important.

Staying Present is a necessary foundation for the four external leadership practices. Without this capacity to sustain present-moment awareness you are unable to tune into the day-to-day stories that guide the inspiration for Attractor leadership. The capacity to be calm in the face of difficulty ensures that the straight talking of Edge and Tension lands on receptive, and not closed ears. By being non-anxiously present and available for people in times of challenge you provide secure and affirming Container leadership. And with this deep capacity to process difficulty as it is happening, and not leave it to gossip or corridor talk after a meeting, leaders provide the moment for a Transforming Space intervention.

When we notice, we can exercise choice. Let's now move to Curious and Intentional Responding, the capacity that uses present-moment awareness as a springboard for a new and creative leadership response.

Curious and Intentional Responding (see Table 4.2)

Notices and Processes One's Feelings and Emotions as Observable Data and Does Not Impulsively React with Them

This capacity moves beyond calmly noticing your thoughts and feelings to actively using them as helpful signals. You process the content of your mind as a rich resource, a window into what is going on for the culture at large. Our minds are extraordinary organs of perception – and not just for self-awareness. Here is a leader who consciously used his mind state and his feelings about his team as cultural data, rather than impulsive judgement. He turned his noticing into a hypothesis about the leadership inefficiency in his organisation.

> Yes, I certainly felt a bit surprised, maybe even somewhat guilty as well, because I obviously had underestimated the mental imprints that were there. I thought if I say what I'm going to do, why are they not then immediately acting on that? Why am I not then getting the information on this? So I felt a bit ... I wouldn't want to say, confused, but at least disappointed, I think that was the feeling, and to a certain extent also frustrated because I then

Table 4.2 Curious and Intentional Responding.

Uses deep awareness and personal intention to slow down the period between experiencing and reacting or judging, staying curious to what arises

Notices and processes one's feelings and emotions as observable data and does not impulsively react with them
At any moment is conscious of both one's options on how to respond to what is being experienced and also the choices that one takes in response
Approaches what arises in any situation with curiosity rather than judgement, including interactions with others where you seek to understand before you evaluate
Uses personal intention as an inner compass to guide how one is, and what one does, in any situation
Is not afraid of uncertainty and trying out new things in order to bring about positive change and move beyond autopilot

got called in, in such a late stage that it was for me a considerable extra effort to get things back on the rails.

At Any Moment is Conscious of Both One's Options on How to Respond to What is Being Experienced and also the Choices that One Takes in Response

This is the point at which you now actively pivot your mind from one state to another. And here's the rub for why mindfulness is so key to leading change. Because what shows up in your mind is not just a result of your own personal impulses, but also a window into the wider system, when you start to regulate your mind you are also able to shift the source from which the wider system operates. Below is a leader who overcame his cognitive defensiveness to feedback. If he had not switched his mind from an ego-impulse to a systemically required state, this leader would have missed the trick to get buy-in to a big restructuring necessary to save his company.

> Emotionally, I was not enthused, but something inside me, there was some voice saying, well, he might have a point. And he was an external coach, there was clearly no hidden agenda on his side. So I somehow forced myself to swallow my pride, and my anger, and discuss with him how he would go about achieving the goal I had so that my Finance Directors would be more likely to build and own the solution.

Approaches What Arises in Any Situation with Curiosity Rather than Judgement, Including Interactions with Others Where You Seek to Understand Before You Evaluate

A further dimension of this capacity is to see others free from your own insecurities and desires. Far from experiencing difficult interactions as threatening or disappointing, a mindful leader uses such encounters to provide vital clues about the system they are seeking to change. Notice how this leader was able to free herself from a judgemental stance, and from this more consciously curious state was then able to tune into the source of the difficulty that was keeping her organisation stuck.

> I was noticing that people had been on a journey themselves because we'd done lots of conversations, which I had found a little bit frustrating because I thought, well, I know where this is going but I then realised that people have to go on their own journey and I was noticing that we'd, everyone had moved on to, wow, we really want to do this now and we just need to nail it!

Uses Personal Intention as an Inner Compass to Guide How One is, and What One Does, in Any Situation

Great change leaders command through intent, not personal control. The successful leaders in our study continually reflected on the overall goals of the change and then made sure that their own personal leadership reflected that intent. Here is a leader fully conscious of how his leadership had to break, and not maintain the repeating patterns in his company's culture. In strong cultures people will (unconsciously) project onto you a need to keep the system exactly in its current state. Beware!

> People say, 'you are the CEO; tell this joint where to go.' And it's tempting to step into that and say, 'I've given it some thought, here we go.' But you need to be very careful with that because people are asking for solutions in a direct control environment that they're used to work in. So very often I'm consciously not doing that in order to create the vacuum that people then are forced to start making their own ideas.

Is Not Afraid of Uncertainty and Trying Out New Things in Order to Bring About Positive Change and Move Beyond Autopilot

Finally, successful change leaders in our study fearlessly and deliberately chose a different path to the norm, even if that came with risk (of looking silly or incompetent) and resistance (to trying out new things). Here is a leader who had managed to fire up the left-, and not right-hand prefrontal cortex area in her brain, so that she could approach novelty with poise, knowing that no one ever falls off the universe.

> But I guess the first bit of the journey was actually committing 100% to an unknown thing, with unknown measures of success, and unknown idea about what that would mean to my career path, etc. There were easier parts to do other than jump in there!

While Staying Present was a foundation for leading change well, our research data told us that *Curious and Intentional Responding was more distinguishing* – it began to visibly set apart the great change leaders from the rest. Here's how it enhanced their practice.

The intentional modelling of what was required in the change, leading from the future and not from today, enabled strong Attractor leadership to flourish. By viewing difficulty as an objectively systemic clue not a subjective source of frustration, Edge and Tension leadership was never hijacked by personal needs and its challenge became directed to the wider good. Container leadership was strengthened because leaders approached all of experience with genuine curiosity and so their people felt safe and able to talk about difficulty. All put together, Curious and Intentional Responding gave leaders the systemic command and personal courage to make present moment experience a Transforming Space. It's impossible to change the now unless you can think and act from the future.

Mindfulness in Action: Bold Transformation of a Global Human Resources (HR) Function

In order to illustrate the two mindfulness inner capacities in action and how they enhance great change leadership, I'd like to introduce you to Steve. I first started working with Steve 20 years ago and had always been impressed by his ability to be generously present with whomever he was with at the time, able to put aside distractions and focus on your needs and the matter at hand. I also remembered him for his capacity to openly process what was going on for him – he made his thoughts and feelings and responses to experience transparent and visible – in a way that felt reflective and open-minded. I never felt he had a controlling personal agenda but he worked with a clear leadership intention that guided how he was and what he did.

His story over the past 4 years is highly illustrative of a leader who remained calm and purposeful during the trials and tribulations of a very large transformation. Within the continually changing environment of the financial services industry, he boldly transformed his global HR function to be fit for the dramatically new requirements of the post global recession world. It was bold in that he secured $100 m as an upfront investment to fund the implementation of a new HR system that was ahead of its time, anticipating future service demands, cost requirements and industry regulation. Not always an easy sell to your boss the Chief Executive, and your colleague the Chief Financial Officer, let alone to your 800 staff, 25% of whom were going to have to pay the price for this change with their jobs.

What he did fell into four phases: starting with customer feedback, i.e., his company's business leaders, combined with external benchmarking, he built a model of HR in the future; next, he put together the business case for this new look HR function, which included selecting an external vendor as partner for the services delivery platform; the rubber hit the road when he secured his HR Leadership Team's (HRLT) commitment to the new model, and created the conditions for them to visibly own the implementation of the radically new structure; finally, he led an implementation and sustainment phase that incorporated feedback and adjustment to the new model.

I'm sure this sequence of steps sounds familiar. It is *how* he led the change that made the difference to its successful outcome. Let's step into his process.

Building the Future HR Model

First, listen to how he embarked on the change with *Curious and Intentional Responding*. He tuned into his feelings at the start of this adventure, and was fiercely intentional in deciding that, while he wanted to do something transformational, he wanted to introduce the change in a way that stretched yet didn't alienate his people at the first hurdle.

> I think my job as a leader is to look down the field as far as I can see and make sure that my team is actually headed in the right direction. So the vision I had is we have got to get way ahead of this thing, make a big change while things are pretty good, and set ourselves up for what might be several more years of better than expected cost performance. Now, I didn't talk a lot about that because I think at that stage of the game you're going to turn this into a cost project and you're going to scare the heck out of everybody. But that's what's going on in my head at the time. I don't want to make an incremental change. I wanted to make a transformational change.

Given the boldness of his vision, he knew he had to pay special attention to building ownership, especially in the initial stages with his direct reports, the HRLT, who could have felt very threatened. He intentionally took months at the outset to secure their ownership, but, as you will see later, the price of building ownership was well worth paying. It's a good example of how the inner capacity of Curious and Intentional Responding enhanced his strong affirming Container leadership practice.

An early example of this is when he chartered a team of junior HR leaders to assess current reality and make radical proposals for the new organisation. Instead of leap frogging his direct reports to make his own appointments (something I have often seen leaders tempted to do) he spent an inordinate amount of time working with his HRLT to build their ownership for the team's selection.

> I really felt for something this big everybody had to own this. I'm not going to just say, 'do this for me'; I wanted them to own it and really feel it and believe in it. So I spent a lot of time with my direct reports picking these leaders who they felt would carry their vote.

A critical early encounter, which could have thrown him off his intention to be both bold and inclusive, came at the very first meeting when this delegated task force gave their feedback to the HRLT. Listen here to how he combined Curious and Intentional Responding, the inner capacity to be able to creatively deal with what arises in the moment – especially when under pressure – with the capacity of Staying Present, being able to calmly and objectively observe what is going on. Indeed he was so present in that meeting his recall now 4 years on takes us right back to being in the meeting with him.

> It was really hot and it was in the afternoon, and the conference room was kind of sticky, and the pressure was high and things were on. And I just remember the (delegated) group really being embarrassed to say, 'we have a long way to go. We might think we're pretty good, but we have a long way to go.' And I think they were nervous to say that to the senior team because it's our function and they might think they're throwing rocks at a glass house. But I think what they were looking to me for was that this was my first big test as to whether I was going to say, 'I think you're right and I really want to do this', or, 'I think you've gone too far'. So I remember that moment pretty vividly and it was really clear, to the team's credit, we had to change. So at that moment I started to think not about whether we needed to but how would we, as opposed to should we or should we not.
>
> So I said, 'I am convinced that we should move to the next step. I think there's enough here, that we ought to try to turn this into an actual undertaking and a project.' And I said, 'I'm looking for enough of your support that you'll give me your teams, their time, and that you will give it your own time and your own commitment that we're going to try to lead this together. Now, I'll still give you an exit, that if at the end of this chapter two, the business case doesn't work, we learn that we can't build the technology for it, we'll all look at that again. So you don't have to vote that we're going to go all the way, you just have to vote that we're going to go to the end of the next chapter.'

Notice how his calm detachment in the moment, Staying Present, and his ever alert inner intentional compass to make the stakes manageable for people as he went, Curious and Intentional Responding, enabled him to exercise straight talking Edge and Tension leadership, and inclusive contracting of expectations, Container leadership. He skilfully got them moving down a transformational path – yet reasonably so. The offer of a credible exit ramp in the event that things did not go as planned showed that his intention was to serve the system, and not his own ego gratification.

Securing the Business Case and the Vendor

Politics flared as Steve then had to secure the backing of his Chief Executive to do two things: ask the Chief Financial Officer to loan him the €100 m necessary to fund the HR restructure and installation of a new IT platform; and agree to sever the relationship with the existing services provider, whose own Chief Executive was on the main board of his company. Note how he paid special attention to the time and place for this critical encounter with his Chief Executive, and how he was processing his feelings at the time, likening them to an encounter with a parent.

In this respect, he was well able to step above his feelings and observe and describe them with curious detachment. And this distancing ensured he could regulate his emotions and be totally available to have the tough conversation – to clearly spell it out to his boss that he needed to make a bold (expensive) move now in order to be able to service the business further down the track.

> Over dinner and a bottle of wine I said, 'I've delivered everything I've ever promised you and then some. I've looked at this, and you have my word that this is a good deal. Tell me that you support this and I'll make sure that the rest of the organisation understands it's a good deal.' And he said yes. I likened it to asking your dad if he would loan you a hundred million dollars, and while you might have felt great about the yes, you also felt 'I really have to deliver now'. A hundred million dollars in an HR organisation is a lot of money!
>
> So I prepared a lot for that. I picked the spot that I had the conversation with him. It was part of a year-end discussion we normally have. There's generally plenty of goodwill at a dinner like that, just the two of us. And I wanted to give him some space. I said, 'I'm worried about that 2 years from now you're going to ask for more and I'm not going to be able to deliver it'.
>
> I believed it needed to happen, and I felt like I wasn't hysterical or overly dramatic. I framed it in really solid business terms. I felt like I left him some room to consider it in a way that didn't feel like I took advantage of a personal relationship or a bottle of wine or doing this at dinner. I felt like it was a really clean pitch. And I remember walking out of that conversation feeling really good.

Steve's inner capacity to remain calm, objective and intentional during testing experiences not only built the trust of his Chief Executive, it also carried through into the sticky moment when he had to sever the relationship with the existing vendor (whose Chief Executive, if you recall, sat on their main board). Here is an excerpt from his story when all

Staying Present elements were out in full force. He used language that was clear of his own impulsive response. He stayed focused on the present moment without getting distracted. He maintained a generous and appreciative stance. And he could consciously process what was going on in a sticky encounter. All the while remaining calm and objective!

> It was one of the more difficult conversations because I think this person expected the business and had made some inferences that they didn't think the process was fair. I was ready for it. I was sitting in a taxi stuck in heavy traffic on my way to a business dinner; he called at 5:45 p.m. It's not the kind of conversation you'd prefer to have on the phone in a car, but that's when he wanted to talk about it, and there was some looming perceived urgency on his part. So I would say I met his escalation, when he got a little more animated, I tried to match that a little bit, but not to make it any worse.
>
> I said, 'Well, here's the process. Here's how you scored in the process. You came in dead last of the others. It wasn't even close. You want me to keep going? I will tell you as much as you want to hear, but don't say that this wasn't fair. You've been with us for several years, that should give you an advantage in this, not a disadvantage. Lots of your plans for the future were all sort of vision stuff, and I can't put my future on that cloud smoke as a project.'

Notice how Steve's inner game, which was so attuned that he mood matched the other person during a testing exchange, enabled him to stay free of anxiety and calmly deliver a difficult message while playing a straight bat: the hallmark of a leader who can combine Edge and Tension with Container leadership.

Empowering Others to Own Big Change with You

In the meantime, Steve had followed through with the key members of his HRLT to secure their visible ownership to lead this change. A key masterstroke in this regard was how he secured the leader who could have been the most resistant to be the one in charge of the change. Here he is in a key encounter with her where again his intentional inner compass of being bold yet inclusive guided how he was and what he said. Erring on the side of including people who disagree with you can be a counterintuitive yet effective tactic in leading change.

> I said, 'I'm worried that this outsourcing work that we're thinking about doing isn't going to work as well as if we did it ourselves and your generalists are going to be withering in their criticism and you're going to be the chief critic of that on their behalf'.

I said, 'So I'm going to ask you to lead this entire transformation.' That was, I think, the boldest political move that I made in this entire project because I actually gave her enough gunpowder that if she wanted to kill this thing, she could have. On the other hand – I was betting that her ownership – and her leadership – of this project would greatly improve the odds of the project's success. I was betting she would rise to that challenge, and she over delivered on that bet.

After Steve had worked with his HRLT to design the new organisation, he realised the moment had come for him to come clean with all his people about the new structure and the people impact. With his HRLT's backing, he drew deeply on his inner capacities to stand up in front of his people to deliver the difficult message. You can just feel from his account of the occasion how present and empathically connected he was to his people, and, as always, staying intentional to make this change one which was felt to be done *with*, and not *to*, people. His skill enabled him to hold his nerve, do the difficult stuff and still be available for others. You can hear in this excerpt all four of the change leadership practices in action.

I am generally known for my transparency. So what comes along with my brand is, even as uncomfortable as it might be, I am more likely to tell you what is exactly going on. So I prepared for the town hall meeting. I always try to picture one person in the audience that I'm really talking to and imagine what they are thinking, what they are worried about, what they want to hear, what they need to hear, and I tried to tailor my pitch to that.

And I just remember I came out from the podium and away from my notes, and I said, 'I want to talk about the hardest part of this. And that is the impact on some of our colleagues around the world. Because, at the end of the day, we're going to be able to deliver a better quality product with less of us in the organisation.' And I put a slide up, I said, 'We're going to have to go down by a couple of hundred positions', and there was a gasp in the auditorium. I said, 'We have a long time to do this. That's good and bad. It means that we can make some really great decisions in who stays and who goes. And although this is never fun news to deliver, we have total control over this and this team can make this work. We have a chance to do this right. I know you don't love it and I don't love it either and it's the hardest part of leadership to deliver bad news, but you deserve to hear it, we're in this together, we're going to be as respectful as we can and I'll take whatever questions that you now have.'

Implementing with Poise

Steve got a lot of credit for this moment of leadership. After the meeting he processed long and hard his inner conflict in implementing big, tough change, noticing his ambivalence in holding both excitement for the new and regret at having to let so many people go. And this acute ability to get in touch with his inner response enabled him to see that he now had to talk more about the future, and in a heartfelt, rather than cognitive way. He consciously switched his mind from focusing on those who were not going to make it to those who were. And this capacity to notice and switch mental states, to set an intention for how he wished to be as a leader, and then use language to describe the change experience in words that people can relate to, enabled him to raise his Attractor leadership game.

> I actually took this as Hannibal crossing the Alps. When I was in high school I studied how this African Carthagean general moved his entire troop of African soldiers across the Alps in Spain and into Italy to attack from the north – which no one expected. And he took elephants with him and people and animals that had never been in snow or never even seen snow. It was one of the greatest military campaigns ever. They still study that campaign. And to me I thought this was a great change management exercise in what I was trying to do. And so I went back and I read Hannibal as I thought about this and I thought, he had to create a picture of Italy for his people. He paints this picture of what it's going to be like when they get into the fields of Italy. By legend it was a signal to me that I needed to talk more about the future and the promise of the future and get those excited who wanted to go on that journey, and to probably start worrying more about them and less about the ones who were not going to make it. You know I had to be compassionate, I had to be understanding about that, but there was a crowd of people who wanted to turn back and they were not going to want to go on to Italy and I just needed to kind of pour it on.

The launch of the new organisation was a bit anti-climactic in that it worked so well. There were some restructuring business challenges that affected the timelines but Steve saw these merely as 'another little speed bump we had to get over'. Throughout the whole process he had been inspired by an early email he had received from someone complaining that HR only ever delivered US, and not truly global solutions. Far from rejecting this email, or reacting to it impulsively and personally, he called on all of his Curious and Intentional Responding capacity and used it as his guiding light.

I used that email as my note in the locker room that we *were* going to deliver a truly global solution. A lot of people said when we delivered it, 'Well that's what you said you were going to do so you're not going to get any medals for this'. But I know how hard it was. We did the entire world in two waves. You're talking about seven languages in service centres in different parts of the world and doing several countries at once. That's pretty awesome.

Summary – When You Lose Touch With Inner Stillness You Lose Touch With Yourself

Being mindful of self and others, not rejecting things, or people, you don't like, staying on top of your emotional responses to experience, setting a clear intention and using that to drive all of your game, were all hallmarks of Steve's leadership. And it enabled him to achieve a very successful change outcome. Perhaps, not surprisingly, we also learned that his capacity to be mindful as a leader was something he actively cultivated. He meditated daily, and also took regular physical exercise, in his case, weight lifting.

I can't think of a more fitting way to close this chapter on the power of mindfulness – where you learn to build your ability to pay attention like a muscle – than this final excerpt of Steve in his (mind) gym.

> I do a lot of weight lifting and it's a great way to measure the power of your mind in terms of what focus can really do and how your performance changes as a result of that. So let's say I can lift 200 pounds, and I know that. And every day you go in there and you can lift 200 pounds. There are some days you can't lift 200 pounds, isn't that weird? Like on Tuesday you can and on Thursday you can't. And the variables to that, there aren't many of them. I eat about the same thing every day, I sleep about the same amount every day, but what has a lot to do with it is what's going on upstairs. What's on my mind, am I distracted by something, is something bothering me? And when I have my best lifts and my best sessions is when I feel like I can really channel my mind into that. You've just gotten rid of all the monkey brain stuff that goes on and you are just a little bit sharper.

If increased mindfulness clears you of all the monkey brain stuff, what can it release the *Homo sapiens* leader inside of you to do? The next chapter takes your inner capacities one step further.

5

The Power of the Systemic

The greatest thing a human soul ever does in this world is to see something, and tell what it saw in a plain way. Hundreds of people can talk for one who can think, but thousands can think for one who can see.

John Ruskin, Modern Painters

My journey towards seeing the world from a deeper level of reality was accelerated dramatically one evening on a Tuscan hilltop. I had travelled there to participate in a workshop on how to lead emergent change, an approach that I knew worked best in contexts characterised by uncertainty and creative disruption, conditions that my clients were increasingly facing. Chris, the moderator, had become a trusted partner in my consultancy practice, where he regularly held supervision sessions to quality assure our skills in effective client system diagnosis and intervention.

On this particular evening he helped me see a troubling situation through a completely new lens, a systemic lens, and the basis for this different way of perceiving experience irreversibly changed how I made sense of and showed up in the world. This later enhanced my capacity to lead accelerated large system change in contexts of uncertainty. But let's return to the story.

In hindsight, it was such a tiny matter that had made me so distraught that evening, a state not even a balmy Tuscan May evening could dispel. I had just taken up a new coaching contract to support the leader of a global manufacturing operation in transforming her business into top quartile industry performance. It was a high profile assignment, and I was very keen to make a difference. It included working with her top team to examine their leadership dynamics and impact on the performance of the organisation. A top quartile organisation needs a top quartile leadership team. Based on my conversations with her team, and the reputation that went before her, I had deduced that this leader,

Still Moving: How to Lead Mindful Change, First Edition. Deborah Rowland.
© 2017 John Wiley & Sons Ltd. Published 2017 by John Wiley & Sons Ltd.

let's call her Jody, was pretty fierce. Her team were in fear of her intellect and seeming inability to tolerate mistakes and underperformance. And that night I had made what I thought was a major error.

I had missed the time that I was to call her, due to my confusion over the time difference between Italy and Houston.

The call had been scheduled to give her feedback on how her team experienced her leadership style, and had been set up through several confirming messages with her personal assistant. I had prepared carefully and was more than a little nervous about how I was going to share messages with someone who was reported to be resistant to hearing any feedback. When I realised my error over the missed time I left the Tuscan workshop participants to their dinner, and, with heart thumping, stumbled out of the restaurant to get some air. These were the days before smartphones, and given there was no phone signal either in that moment I had no idea how I was going to contact Jody to confess my mistake and reschedule our call. And, as you may imagine, my old adoption story of being on the brink of being discarded was playing out in full-blown Technicolor in my mind.

Sensing my distress Chris had followed me out of the restaurant, and, prompted by his gentle inquiry, I explained what had happened. I noticed how he wanted to find out about the context to the call and what was going on in the dynamics of my client's situation. While I was still stewing in the immediate drama, he spent a moment looking up into the night sky and then turned to me and simply said, 'Well, isn't this a fortunate situation for you, as you now have the chance as Jody's coach to explore how she does respond to error. This seeming wobble must be the work that you and she need to do together on behalf of her team and on behalf of her organisation. Use this disturbance to notice and change things!'

In a flash my mind switched from labelling this experience a mistake, to seeing it as an opportunity. Far from me issuing an apology, I could now offer an invitation, and his systemic reframing enabled me to see myself not at the centre of my own drama but rather enmeshed in a wider organisational dynamic of fear of failure. It was as if I had pressed the '–' button on Google maps and zoomed up above my location to see a much wider and interconnected landscape. And I felt calm, resourceful and surer of the potency of my place in the complex contours of my client's system.

Systemic Thinking is Not the Same as Systemic Perceiving

With further processing, I realised that up until that moment I had thought that *systemic thinking* was undertaking root cause analysis of events and conducting largely rational analyses of how the elements of a system were interconnected. I had not yet understood the notion that whatever shows up in present-moment experience – including your inner state of thoughts, feelings, sensations and impulses – is in some way a part of a wider whole. And that the task of *systemic perceiving* is to therefore tune into what is being experienced *right here* as some kind of signal as to what is being experienced *out there*. Inner experience is not just the drama of your own story, or what other people are doing to you. We dance within the dynamics of a wider field that has its own tugs, invisible contours and intentionality.

In this chapter I will explore the dance in more detail. And its moves are important to master, as I have now found that *a leader's skill to tune into system dynamics and perceive all of experience within this wider integrated field is the inner capacity that makes the biggest difference to how well they can lead big complex change.*

When I eventually got to call Jody the following day, I shared my systemic insight about the missed call incident (it was very challenging for me to stop myself saying, 'sorry'). And she responded with great empathy and curiosity. I instantly relaxed and thought this kind of systemic expertise works! We noted how her response to how I had been feeling ('Well, I had way underestimated the perfectionist shadow of my leadership!') helped her get in better tune with the emotional climate of her organisation, which was still stuck in lower quartile performance. We closed by agreeing that she would do something very risky at the start of her forthcoming leadership team meeting.

I can recall now the faces of her team as she warmly opened with an invitation for them to give her frank and open feedback (no need any more for me to be the messenger). Gingerly, they all stepped up to the plate, and her invite led to a cathartic conversation in which the whole team processed their felt fear and anxiety of not being good enough, and how this story was disabling them from taking up their full leadership responsibility in this team and the wider organisation. Far from weakening the team, this full frank acknowledgement strengthened it. This was clearly not just about Jody (though, for sure, she owned her part in the dance too).

I then changed tack, and asked them, 'So, if you all are feeling like this how do you imagine your organisation must be?' With slightly shameful faces, this top leadership team decided to change how they were approaching the manufacturing plants' underperformance. While not relinquishing the tough performance goal, they now framed it as an opportunity and subsequently put in a lateral network process to join up and engage the plant teams across the world in finding solutions. The organisational atmosphere began to change, as did their results – for the better.

What a result from a missed phone call. It led to a top team openly processing their fear of their leader's 'scary' leadership style, which resulted in them relaxing and leading at their best, which in turn freed up their own teams' ingenuity and felt responsibility. But without Chris's ability to *see* the system behind my little perturbation it could have ended so differently. The Tuscan sky had a business outcome.

In the rest of this chapter I continue to set out the case for why becoming more systemic as a leader is an indispensable skill when you are implementing big change. I continue by illustrating the two inner capacities of Tuning into the System, and Acknowledging the Whole, which our research clearly demonstrated differentiated successful change leaders from the rest. And I finish with another story from our research that shows superb systemic change leadership in action. You might find the content of this chapter new and more complex than the others – and hence more challenging to read. However, stay with me as this edge might hold the most important insights for your leadership.

The Potency of Systemic Leadership

The two mindfulness capacities in the previous chapter, Staying Present and Curious and Intentional Responding, allow you to stabilise your attention in the present moment, regulate your cognitive and emotional response to experience and in that less reactive and impulse-led state afford a clearer and more open-minded comprehension of what shows up. This is what's here, let's work with it!

The question is, *how* do you work with what shows up? That evening in Tuscany Chris could have stopped at calming my mind and helping me see that my drama was just a projected personal narrative. But he did more than that. He helped me see that my place in the system – of my client's organisation, Jody's leadership team, her personal leadership and the wider goals of the change – had its own energy charge. Consequently, my behaviour and effectiveness as a coach was subject to wider system dynamics (not just my own skill), the influence of which I could both better see, and more wisely act upon.

Completely strange, unknown currents can shape our leadership. I am sure in your own leadership role that you sometimes feel you are being pulled into a collusive dance with the system. It might be invisible, but it is still felt. You may wonder where emotional experiences such as envy, shame, rivalry, joy, fear, anger, sadness, pride, guilt, boredom, disgust, scepticism or attraction come from. *Leaders in our research who were the most successful at leading change were alert to their inner emotional experience as a signal about the outer system that they led.* They didn't just put it down to a bad night's sleep or a personality clash with a colleague. They recognised their inner experience as a property of the system.

Systemic perceiving is a vital skill for change leaders. Cultivating an inner systemic ear enables you to do four things: discern that what is here is also there; monitor and regulate your response to organisational projection; approach difficulty and disturbance as a resource; and create strong and flourishing whole systems.

Discern that What is Here, Is also There

When you view the world through a systemic lens you interpret what shows up in directly observable, present-moment experience as in some way a symptom of a deeper and wider field. Just as a Geiger counter detects radioactivity, what you are experiencing can detect systemic dynamics.

Let me provide an example. At the start of one leadership development programme designed to build the skills to lead a major change, I invited my fellow faculty team to stand and introduce themselves to the participants as their guides for what was to be a 6-month journey. For the very first time at a programme opening, and we had run seven previous waves over the 2 years, a participant stood up to introduce herself during the round of faculty introductions. I felt at that moment all eyes were on me, was Deborah going to point out the participant's mistake, or just kindly ignore it?

I am now always alert to a systemic signal – which usually appears as a wobble, or process deviance. In that very moment I did not see the participant standing up as a mistake. Instead, I read it as a signal that the leaders in this organisation (i.e., beyond just those in the room on this programme) were now ready to do their own guiding. The time for us as a faculty team was coming to an end – the job was almost done.

I invited the (now somewhat embarrassed looking) participant to be seated and offered this systemic interpretation to the group. Despite some puzzled looks I felt them become relaxed and resourceful – an energetic quality that remained through their programme. What had occurred on that first evening (systemic perceivers always pay special attention to how things start) was not simply a participant standing up in error: it was a vital signal that the wider organisation had progressed well along its transition.

This is not the normal way to view experience – we tend to make sense of what happens at face value. Systemic perceiving halts habitual and conventional interpretations. And when leaders can instantly and non-judgementally read what shows up in experience with a deeper lens, they achieve two things.

First, they create richer meaning of what is being experienced, which completely reframes how others make sense of what is occurring. This is particularly helpful when people are going through the inevitable rocky times in change. It relaxes and strengthens people when they can see that what they are experiencing is part of a wider dynamic.

Second, their systemic interpretation of experience gets into a deeper and more accurate contact with reality – far more quickly, I would argue, than running laborious cultural diagnostics. There is so much systemic data in front of us that, if we are not present and attuned, can easily pass us by.

This offers high leverage potential when leading change. *If what is experienced here is also a microcosm of the wider field, by changing what is here, we de facto change the wider field.* When you see the world as interconnected, a bit like a delicate children's mobile all of which trembles at the slightest touch, you realise your own power to make change happen from your place in the system, however small and insignificant an act that may seem.

This dynamic is particularly applicable to top teams who carry such systemic charge (remember Jody's team). They are the only group that holds a fragment of each part of the wider system. So what shows up in top teams is a Geiger counter for wider cultural dynamics. Poor listening skills in a top team, for example, might signal that the organisation at large is out of touch with a changing customer base. The corollary is, that when top teams can improve what might feel like a tiny element of how they interact, it has an amplifying effect on the wider culture. Before top teams roll out (expensive) values programmes to change their organisation's culture, how about shifting the way they as a team operate first?

Monitor and Regulate Your Response to Organisational Projection

Let's continue with this a little more. As a senior leader your role carries a systemic charge like a field of energy particles in the world of physics. While it might sound humbling and challenging to the ego, your behaviour and effectiveness in role can have less to do with your own skills, and more to do with these wider so-called systemic dynamics.[1]

These dynamics can come from your role's place in the hierarchy; for example, the more senior the position the more likely you are in this place to feel the organisation's need for you to provide the answers. The dynamics might come from the relative weight your role has in the balance of organisational exchange. If your role contributes more wealth to the overall enterprise than others, you might feel a little more 'owed' and superior to those in support functions. How you perform in role might even flow from skeletons in its history. If a previous incumbent in your role experienced some upset, for example, and this has not been acknowledged, you might now find they are a spectre on your shoulder and you now feel scapegoated by others, even though you are giving your very best.

When leaders tune into the system, they are able to differentiate what is *their stuff*, the residue of impulses and habits that show up in their leadership based on their story, from the *system's stuff*, what is being (often unconsciously) projected onto them in their role. And, most importantly, they can see the interplay between these dynamics and notice how they might be getting hooked, pulled and mobilised into unhelpful collusion with the system's need.

Let me share one pattern I have frequently seen in a change context, a pattern that can keep the leader trapped and the organisation stuck. When the future looks uncertain, what to do is still unknown and past approaches are clearly outmoded, a confused and anxious system will search for the heroic leader who can provide the answers. And, if your personal story contains any tiny grain of the responsible-solver-of-all-problems pattern, you can easily slip into providing those answers (even though you know that seeking their ideas is a better option). This is a rescuing pattern that keeps your organisation stuck in learned helpless-ness and funnily enough defensive resistance to your new ideas (even though they are asking you for direction). Strangely, you never seem able to satisfy their need for more strategic direction. So, you give more answers, which makes them more passively resistant, and, and...

When a system is not able to operate systemically, and see how each role is locked in some kind of unconscious contract, then these collusive patterns, while strongly felt, go undiagnosed. While each person has responsibility for getting out of stuck patterns, as a senior leader, you, systemically, have the greater weight. It is your task to be able to spot systemic dynamics and do something about them. This requires that you become awake to your own story and alert to the organisation's projec-tion. While there might be a wish of the system for you to be, or to act, in a certain way, it does not mean that you have to!

As a personal example, a collusive contract I often find myself in as a leader is when my adoption story of wanting to please, to belong, gets hooked by the organisation's need to have their leaders carry the load. So off I go and take it all on! Sorting out how you get entangled in organisa-tional projection is not always an easy task to accomplish, but when unrav-elled things appear much more conscious and straightforward. When I *am* able to appropriately take up my leadership role in a system I require more of others, and in so doing end up recruiting my team to have more respect and unprojected confidence in me. I have appropriate command, and they want to do their best. And that's when change can start to flow.

Approach Difficulty and Disturbance as a Resource

One leader described leading change to me as like white water rafting. Just when you think everything is going smoothly you will suddenly hit an unexpected rapid and have to adapt in the moment, staying in balance, but also going with the flow, as any move to control the raft could flip you over. You need to work with, and not against, the energy of the rapids, putting the oar in lightly just when and where it is needed.

In the next chapter I expand on the importance of being able to work with, not negate disturbance in change. Our research showed that bringing appropriate Edge and Tension to a system was the foremost leadership practice to get successful change outcomes. However, it's not the felt natural thing to do (we tend to work round, not through, disturbance) and is generally done very poorly. Our research showed that this is because Edge and Tension needs to be backed up by strong internal systemic skill. Here's what that takes – from the inside.

First, *have the wisdom to recognise that disturbance is not wrong but a systemic clue into the organisation's story.* Just as emotional triggers can set off your own personal story, so whole systems have their sources of entanglement and difficulty. It is more natural to respond to difficulty by finding a place of comfort. Yet, until you have uncovered troubling dynamics, acknowledged them and cleaned them up a bit, a system will be unable to move forward. Change flows when difficulty is seen.

As an example of this I have worked with an organisation one of whose business units was facing terminal decline. At the same time, they had set up a new innovation team to find revenue streams to take the company into a different future. The leaders felt unable to cleanly face the fact that the part of their organisation that had contributed much wealth and benefit to society in the past, was fast approaching its sell by date. Until the source of the difficulty was seen, in this instance the strongly felt feeling of betrayal among their staff that society was now putting them to one side, the whole system remained stuck and the innovation team seemed strangely unable to find its place. When interventions were made to bring out the feeling of betrayal, and true acknowledgement of this business unit's past contribution was expressed, the whole of the organisation relaxed and the leadership energy flowed, even though that meant closing down parts of their business. Systems gain strength when difficult truths are acknowledged.

The second essential and related inner capacity is *to be comfortable with not being comfortable.* As one leader once said to me during a very challenging moment, 'more movement happens in the non-comfortable!' It can be heart thumping and nail biting, but approaching difficulty is a potent force for a change leader because it enables you to create movement in the here-and-now. Seeing disturbance is like having a target marker in front of you, go towards it! If you are having a difficult team meeting where you feel that it is almost impossible to reach agreement, do you keep pushing for compliant decision-making, or do you take a time out to name the difficulty and uncover its source, however awkward and dangerous that might feel?

Moments of disturbance offer powerful opportunities for revelation and development. So, anticipate and welcome wobbles, they are sources of intelligence as to what is still holding your organisation back, opportunities to build key change skills such as self awareness and straight talking, and opportunities to intervene and change repeating patterns – thereby accelerating change.

Create Strong and Flourishing Whole Systems

Given the contextual challenges set out in Chapter 2, I believe that the core task of a change leader today is to create the right conditions within which a system can do its own changing. Clearly, you also need to make sure that your strategic choices are sound. It's no good being great at leading change if the direction of travel is flawed. But I have seen more change efforts fail not because of faulty strategy, or lack of vision, but due to poor change implementation. And the task of senior leadership is to create a flourishing organisation that can deliver the desired outcomes.

Successful change leaders therefore invest special attention not just on setting vision and strategy, managing tasks and numbers, or attending to key external stakeholders, but also on cultivating the health and vitality of the complex social system that they lead. Mindfulness expands to become a collective capacity as Weick et al. have comprehensively researched.[2] Challenges from without an organisation put the internal system under psychological stress. And when these challenges concern the system's very viability to survive in its current state, the anxiety and ambiguity are all the greater.

When you work as a systemic leader you increase your capacity to be able to hold all of this troubling nature in your vision, and you address the need for the system *as a whole* to be attended to.

Practically speaking, what does this mean? I am indebted here to the sagacious and compassionate guidance of Judith Hemming, a leading systemic thinker and intervener, who has done much to further my ability to attend to the health and hence transforming power of whole systems. She has helped me see that all human systems gain strength, and can therefore move towards difficulty and change, when four basic universal laws governing collective life are attended to.

First, *belonging*. We all have a basic need to belong to a system: a place where we can matter and feel secure – be that one's team, company, profession, family or nation. We do, of course, have multiple allegiances, which brings a sense of disloyalty when we spend too much time in one conscience group at the expense of another – for example, too much time in head office at the expense of being present for our local team. In times of change these loyalties can radically change – such as when a country-based organisation is required to restructure into a regional product-based structure. In major restructurings we can even find that we no longer belong.

Systemic leaders have an acute radar for this most fundamental of human laws. They pay attention to whether their systems support or threaten belonging. This means ensuring that everybody has the same right to a place, that all voices are heard and recognised, and that nothing or no one is excluded. If dismissals are necessary, then the departure is handled with great care and an acknowledgement of all past contribution is given so that people leaving can truly leave, and those who stay are free to move ahead.

Second, *time*. From our early ancestors to today all collective life is governed by time. When I stood in that Neolithic trench during my archaeological studies the impact of the past was noticeably present. But time also exerts a gravitational pull on the present moment in subtler and less visible ways. If spectres such as an organisation's founder who has not been suitably honoured, or past upsets such as unfair treatment of people or aggressive takeovers remain unprocessed, then there will be unease and drag in the present moment. It's a bit like driving your car with the handbrake on.

You can only look forward with confidence when you know the truth about your past. Systems are therefore unable to move into a different future until all important past elements have been seen and acknowledged. It is why good change leaders spend time exploring an organisation's history before they attend to its future. Furthermore, the future is as capable of causing the present as is the past, and can have great impact on the system's present dynamics. The felt future can exert both positive anticipation and fear. Good change leaders tune into these emergent dynamics as important signals of transition, of a need to relinquish the old and give place to the new. By attending to both past and future dynamics change leaders can stand strong as a bead in this necklace called time.

Third, *exchange*. This systemic law seeks to maintain a dynamic and proper balance between what is given and what is received, as no one in the system should be allowed to have a felt advantage over someone else. When there is imbalance, when one group feels they are owed more than they owe, or they are carrying a disproportionate burden in a change effort, then they will not give their best. It sounds simple, but clear and heartfelt acknowledgement, saying 'thank you' to your team, who are putting in an inordinate amount of effort in a big change, can work wonders.

Conversely, when a group is felt that they owe more than they are owed, they have been given too much, then they can carry a conscience of guilt and a burden of over gratitude, as giving someone too much can make them feel small and forever indebted. In which case they have to leave in order to feel stronger elsewhere (a dynamic often seen in personal relationships). When there is a good balance of giving and receiving, then there are no unhealthy ties that bind and people are free to give of their best.

Finally, *place*. An organisation is an interconnected system of role relationships and when flourishing there is a clear structure in which each person, team, department and even abstract elements such as financial resources, or the organisation's vision, has a right, safe and legitimate place. When structures are made visible, every person and team has a sense of purpose, their competence is assured and they can function well. Systemically speaking, the role, or function, and its relationship to the organisation's purpose are more important than the individual. This explains why when leaders try to build new structures for special individuals, and there is ambiguity about how this role fits into the overall picture, the leader in that structure will always have a struggle even if they have great gifts and skills.

Systems also hold important natural hierarchies, such as age and length of service or affiliation (note here how *place* and *time* intersect), as who comes first has more systemic weight. It's sometimes surprising how, by making these natural hierarchies visible (just get your team standing in line according to length of service, or how long they have each known you), the group is immediately settled and strengthened and able to get on with their task. In restructurings people are often brought together into awkward new groupings that override these innate hierarchies, such as younger people joining from the outside into more senior roles. As long as this is acknowledged, there will be no difficulty, if it is not, then it somehow takes more effort to get work done and there is not a good flow of leadership energy.

When these four systemic ordering forces of belonging, time, exchange and place are well attended to, an organisation has the best chance to flourish and people give of their best.[4,5] If they are not attended to, there remains an unhelpful undercurrent in a system. You might get busy, but you won't get movement. And, the greater the actual or anticipated disruption to a system, the greater the life of this invisible undercurrent. So in big change, ignore these forces at your peril. In my experience attending to them skilfully only requires a subtle move here and there (get people standing up in their loyalty groups – simple!), and makes you realise how moving an organisation is sometimes more about the art of the nudge rather than making bold dramatic moves.

In summary, systemic change leadership is about discerning where a few choice interventions will most enable movement in the deeper field – the source from which your organisation operates. And clues to finding such interventions can be found within these four areas: spotting and changing systemic patterns in the here-and-now; staying alert to organisational projection and not getting caught up in its unhelpful, stuck patterns; using difficulty and disturbance as a resource for diagnosis and movement; and finally, attending to the four forces governing human systems that can either strengthen – or threaten – organisational vitality.

Let's now get a little more specific as to the inner skills you will need to be able to do this. Our research revealed two: Tuning into the System and Acknowledging the Whole.

Tuning into the System (see Table 5.1)

This capacity was the inner skill that most differentiated between successful and less successful change leaders. It was omnipresent in the stories of the leaders who can lead change well, in particular change of high scope and complexity. And here's how it breaks down.

Pays Attention in any Given Situation to the Visible Signs that Give the Leader Intelligence About the Organisational System

We found that successful change leaders operate with a systemic radar, spotting signs in front of them as indicators of the wider context. Nothing passes them by – even the micro cues in their environment. Listen to the

Table 5.1 Tuning into the System.

Tunes into the emotional climate of self, others and the wider system and voices their observations/makes interventions that accurately and sensitively resonate with others

Pays attention in any given situation to the visible signs that give the leader intelligence about the organisational system

Puts into words current experience in ways that other people can relate to

Even when feeling upset, finds a way to put their experience into words

Notices and tunes into (changes in) the emotions and feelings of those around them and in the wider system, so can bring awkward facts to light

Consciously anticipates and empathises with the impact of actions and events on others and the wider system forensic anthropological insight of this leader, which he used to be able to successfully launch a bold new initiative for his company.

> There were no people on laptops. There were no people checking their phones. I noticed a very diverse spectrum of opinions in the room. Some people were declaring the opinions, some of the people were just not declaring, but you could tell with body language, with facial expressions, with who they were looking at, that some people either didn't understand the topic, or were in the no camp but were waiting for somebody else in the room to declare. But it was definitely very emotional. There are some companies where when everything goes to the room, all of the conversations have already been had. Here is never that sort of culture.

Puts into Words Current Experience in Ways that Other People can Relate to

Leaders who tuned into the system well were also able to tell what they saw to others in simple, plain language. See how this leader came back from the field and confronted his sales team with language that he knew would resonate (note also how he had picked up an imbalance in the systemic law of *exchange* with his frontline staff).

> I went out into the field and I saw a frontline organisation that was not being leveraged, and I thought, we could do better. I found that the technical guys had to pay for their own work boots, and I'd assumed we already did, as they have to have a steel toe. I said to my team, 'Guys, we need to stop thinking of our frontline as a cost centre, they are in some ways our most important strategic asset. They are the voice and the ears with the customer.'

Even When Feeling Upset, Finds a Way to Put their Experience into Words

Successful change leaders were able to tune into troubling inner states and convey what they were feeling in language that could describe their emotions, without being overemotional. This is because they knew that their emotions were not just personal, but a carrier for wider forces. Here's one leader who overcame her fear and did this very well. Her sharing of her emotions led to a key moment in her company's history that was going through its own difficulty. Her wobble – and the fact she survived it – systemically enabled her team to pull together to face their collective crisis (and note, again, the systemic law of *exchange* showing up in how she expressed her needs).

I still had this beat-up point in my brain that leaders had to have a strong front, I was still afraid to share on that level of personal information of, 'Hey, I'm going through a really difficult time, and I've never crossed this bridge before and I'm scared. I'm going to need your help.' I want them to know that I'm strong and capable, but I also want them to know my emotional state, because it's important that they know that it's a little wobbly right now, and that doesn't mean I'm going to steer the car off the cliff.

Notices and Tunes into (Changes In) the Emotions and Feelings of those Around them and in the Wider System, So can Bring Awkward Facts to Light

Successful change leaders therefore also paid close attention to the emotional experiences of others. Emotions, while deeply felt, can often remain unspoken and unaddressed. Yet they are vital in change as emotions fulfil unmet needs and hence are the basis for movement. I find *grief* a common emotion in change – mourning for what was. Its task is to enable you to move from having something to no longer having something. Yet our grief often goes unacknowledged (by ourselves, not just by others), and when unprocessed easily becomes *anger*. Unprocessed primary emotions therefore easily move into stuck secondary ones. Here is a leader who tuned in superbly to the primary mood state of one of his team members before it escalated into an unhelpful emotion, and in so doing made a transforming intervention.

I sat down with them and Pam took me through it all and I said, 'Pam, can I check, do you really believe in what you're saying?' It was very, sort of, task-focussed and toneless, it wasn't with excitement and passion. And she said, 'Well, not really'. And I said, 'Well, what would you believe in?' And so she said, 'Well, we've just been to a company and they do it a completely different way'. And I said, 'Well, what do we think would really help the business?' And the team went away and what they actually came up with was amazing. But it all arose out of that first conversation when I just had this sense that they didn't believe in what they were saying.

Consciously Anticipates and Empathises with the Impact of Actions and Events on Others and the Wider System

Every action we take has a cost and a consequence. When you are leading big change this can be magnified across a whole human system. The most successful leaders in our research spent considerable time anticipating the systemic impact and side effects of the intended change and their behaviour. Here is a good example of a leader who consciously anticipated the impact of his every move on the system in order to change its repeating patterns (note also how, by building felt security, he addressed the systemic law of *belonging*).

> I think it helps if you arrive in a new situation that isn't great because you don't own it as much. But what wouldn't have worked is the typical local approach of being downbeat and pessimistic, to the point of finding the person to blame, because that would have reinforced existing instincts. *And so I actually did the opposite.* I said, 'Well, this is something we can eminently fix. What we need to first agree on is that we have a healthy future. And I'm sure we'll get there.' Which caused a lot of surprise. And, at first, a reaction of, 'Here's another typical westerner, completely naïve.' But if you stay with that story, then, at some point, they actually start believing you. And that's when, quite quickly, things turned around.

This inner capacity of Tuning into the System ran like rivers through how leaders in their stories deployed the four external leadership practices. By noticing day-to-day visible signs, they could weave together a compelling narrative for their change that connected to reality – strong Attractor leadership. With the ability to empathise with people's emotional states, their Edge and Tension could be heard, not rejected, and it built the necessary trust of Container for others to talk about risky subjects. And with the interpretative capacity to see all of experience as a sign of wider forces, it enabled them to perform pivoting Transforming Space interventions in the here-and-now.

Acknowledging the Whole (see Table 5.2)

This inner capacity of Acknowledging the Whole is a rare, but important breed. It is rare in that it did not show up very much in our study. It is important because of where we found it. And this was among the very top leaders who could successfully navigate change of high magnitude across large complex systems. This role requires you to move beyond empathic tuning in, and to lead from a larger more integrative place, which includes *the radical allowing of all experience.* With this capacity leaders saw no pathology in their system, only intelligence. They had come to the realisation that the ultimate task of the leader is to sense and embody the system's intention and then step out of the way, seeing leadership through to its ultimate non-existence as a distinct entity.

Here's what it takes.

Table 5.2 Acknowledging the Whole.

Is able to see that all that arises – even difficulty and disturbance – needs attending to and integrating so that the whole system can be seen and gains strength (what gets excluded stays!)

Notices and uses data about one's own feelings, impulses and physical sensations as visible signs as to what is being felt and experienced in their team, organisation or wider society

Views all experience as what, in some way, is meant to happen – giving everything that arises a place, and a purpose (senses the *system's* intentionality)

Has an open-minded, expansive and inclusive mindset that is able to use multiple interpretations of what is being experienced in order to build up an accurate picture of reality

Views difficulty and disturbance not as obstacles or barriers but rather as important resources to learn from and be acknowledged so that the whole system gains strength

Is conscious of how their systemic leadership can model to others non-reactivity, wider perspective taking and the facing of difficulty so that they build the capacity for greater mindfulness in others

Notices and Uses Data About One's Own Feelings, Impulses and Physical Sensations as Visible Signs as to What is Being Felt and Experienced in their Team, Organisation or Wider Society

Deeply systemic leaders have the ability to interpret their inner experience as an indicator as to what is needed to happen in their team and the wider system. Redolent of what the Massachusetts Institute of Technology's (MIT) Otto Scharmer would term *presencing*, they have the capacity to tune into their own deep source as a signal for the emerging future. Here is a leader who had been experiencing severe back pain, which he diagnosed as a symptom of what he was having to carry for his company's restructuring – even if this was contrary to his peers' position. He took action on his pain – but not just with an osteopath, and it led to a necessary restructuring of his company.

> For me it was clear because it was a long process for myself, not feeling well, and I would have gone further on in this not well feeling because I had the impression for months that I'm against a lot of things which my colleagues will do and I tried to bring it more to the operational ground. And then for me it became clear where we should go, and when we go this way together – we will have success.

Views All Experience as What, In Some Way, Is Meant to Happen – Giving Everything that Arises a Place, and a Purpose (Senses the System's Intentionality)

The second key element of this capacity is to see all of experience as having some kind of purpose that is building towards where the system needs to go. Successful change leaders hold a sixth sense about the future already emerging in the present moment. You can hear in the excerpt below how this capacity is about sensing the direction and then stepping aside. This leader did not control what was happening. Instead, he gives space to others and everything flowed in the right direction (notice the systemic law of *place* operating here). Successful change leaders can gently guide their system towards its destiny.

> I was quite able to let the team, let the process flow, you know? I didn't feel, after I'd introduced it I didn't feel I needed to direct it that much. I just sensed that this was the right way to go for the whole company. When we went on plant tours I would make sure people presented it, so it was a hearts and minds campaign upwards to get people to recognise how it forms.

Has an Open-Minded, Expansive and Inclusive Mindset that is Able to Use Multiple Interpretations of What is Being Experienced in Order to Build Up an Accurate Picture of Reality

Acknowledging the Whole challenges our natural craving for alignment: it requires that we are able to see any situation from several perspectives. It's not about making everything the same, but like creating a rich tapestry, or bringing together different notes into a harmony. This is the only way to orchestrate large change across a complex system that needs to retain its requisite variety. At its most basic, but essential level, it involves the capacity to ensure that all views are equally included and respected in any interaction, *and* that people are encouraged to give up something of their own strong views in order to be able to create a whole. Here's a leader who did this very well.

> I think emotionally I had the team with me to finally talk about the real issues. I had people ready to be constructive. I also brought data, so rather than having people say 'Oh, blah, blah, blah' – they brought real examples. So I think unlocking emotionally, and also data driven factual, talking about concrete things as opposed to dumping problems. And being part of the solution was also important for the team. So we built bridges between people who are very easy to entrench themselves in their own problems.

Views Difficulty and Disturbance Not as Obstacles or Barriers but Rather as Important Resources to Learn from and be Acknowledged so that the Whole System Gains Strength

I have already written about how systemic leaders are willing to embrace the shadow of experience as a glimpse of what is needed to heal. They are able to differentiate between difficulty as unnecessary partisan protest and difficulty as vital systemic message. If we view all difficulty as negative we stop exploring it, and this is dangerous. Reframing difficulty as inherently meaningful is *not* about sugar coating difficulty and simply spinning a positive interpretation. This is a denial of reality. Instead, it is the capacity to see the systemic role that difficulty plays in experience; it can be a signifier of what is held to be precious and what still needs attention.

Notice how this leader embraced a disturbing meeting as a source of systemic intelligence – not pathology. He didn't dismiss the meeting as a disaster, or blame the organiser, or beat himself up, but instead used it as a signal that the change effort needed to change tack – in this instance from an emphasis on today's problems to one that anticipated the future solution (note here a leader addressing the systemic law of *time*).

> The meeting was really awkward. So it was – for me – enlightening as to why this company was stagnant. While we spent a lot of time talking about what's called the burning platform I think we spent too much time there and not enough time trying to create a picture of what the future could look like. We got people very energised, but not pointed in one direction. So there was a little bit of chaos in that meeting. It was dramatic, and people got worked up about it. People had lots of ideas about what this should be, but more than anything they were confused and they were worried.

Is Conscious of How their Systemic Leadership can Model to Others Non-Reactivity, Wider Perspective Taking and the Facing of Difficulty so that they Build the Capacity for Greater Mindfulness in Others

Finally, leaders who could Acknowledge the Whole consciously turned themselves into a vehicle for the future. This capacity needs to be distinguished from shaping and controlling others, expecting others to agree with you or be exactly like you. That's cookie cutter leadership. Listen to how this leader consciously set the overall tone for expected behaviour in her organisation, a commercial subsidiary of a public service parent organisation. She encouraged her team to be present in a conscious and adult state, not caught up in unhelpful projections or colluding with the chorus of organisational dysfunction.

> So I'm not going to do the eye rolling. I'm not going to say 'Ugh, public service'. I used three words – positive, partnerships and collective problem solving. And hopefully, that will set the new leadership tone for how we're going to work in this new world. And I feel good about that.

This inner capacity, Acknowledging the Whole, was a vital enabler to all four of the external leadership practices. When you can sense a system's intentionality you can naturally practise purpose-led Attractor leadership. Viewing disturbance as a systemic clue not pathological problem helps to contextualise Edge and Tension so that it can be heard. The fierce allowing of multiple voices creates a secure Container for people to bring the whole of themselves. And the deep capacity to tune into one's own experience as a source of systemic intelligence is the necessary first step in Transforming Space leadership.

Now here's a story of all of this in action.

Systemic Leadership in Action – Building a Global Networked Enterprise

This is a story of how a leader courageously and patiently built a $2bn global charity organisation out of what had previously been a $1.2bn loose confederation of 30 separate country-based entities. It's a story of high magnitude change, to build a single vision, strategy, governance structure and modus operandi for an organisation of 25,000 staff members who had all been used to running their own programmes. And, to take an organisation on a journey from self-interest to collective alignment, across so many different cultures, required an acute ability to Tune into the System and Acknowledge the Whole. And this lady, lets call her Angie, had both of these capacities in spades.

Letting the Opportunity Emerge

In the early days after Angie had been appointed to run the UK branch, she sensed that the disparate nature of the whole charity was no longer fit for the twenty-first century. Yet her instinct was not to declare this to the rest of the organisation (shaping), or to set up a project team to study new organisational options (directing). Instead, she tuned into the proudly localised culture and used that systemic awareness to gently steward her peers along a pathway to sense for themselves what had to emerge. So, she began by building a deep foundation of trust and alignment among the various country Chief Executives.

This was done by meeting up informally in each other's homes around the world, travelling together and even doing job swaps. In doing this she modelled to her peers how to tune into a whole system, build strong emotional connection and take a broader perspective on what could be achieved. And she did this all with no set agenda – she had the capacity to sense the intentionality of the whole system and simply nudge it on its way. Here's an early excerpt from her story when her colleagues met for the first time at her home. Notice her ability to simply hold a Transforming Space for whatever work needed to happen (and attend to the systemic law of *belonging* and *time*).

> I invited everybody to my home. I made sure they had nice places to stay at night and that there were some nice walks that we could go on. We didn't have an agenda. I just welcomed people as they arrived. We didn't start early, we started whenever everybody could get there. We just sat and talked. I asked people to sketch out – I had flip charts available and pens – to draw a little picture, what it looks like where they're sitting. I got people to talk about what their realities were. And then we just had some lunch, and then we went for a walk. Came home – it was wintertime – so we then had a fire and then we went out for dinner. We were just really talking, getting to know each other, talking about what our hopes and aspirations for our organisation were.

Angie had a deep capacity to not shape the change, but instead intuit what the organisation needed. She shared with us this reflection about those early days, 'I had no real expectations. Now, with hindsight, you can look back on it and say, "Oh, that's where it all began". I didn't realise I was beginning anything then. *It just felt like a really good idea to do something like this.*'

Stepping Up to the Leadership Plate

The next critical event in her change story came at a large meeting of the 60 country directors. She was on a panel with her peer group of seven regional Chief Executives, who by now had spent a lot of time getting to know each other, tuning into the reality on the ground and imagining their future organisation. What transpired at this event sounded like a stand off between the Country Directors and the top team – the systemic law of *place* was out of balance as more junior staff members felt that their senior leaders were not taking up their appropriate role in the system. Here's her recall of this dramatic flexion point.

> We were on the stage, and those country directors could ask us questions. I do recall the audience really pointing up to us and asking – virtually demanding – to know when we were going to get our act together as Chief Execs because we were all running separate organisations and, on the ground, they were feeling the brunt of that. That was, at least, how I interpreted it. *It was good actually* because it was starting to be not just a good idea to make a change, the pressure was starting to build from the grassroots to think about organising ourselves in a more efficient and effective way.

Notice Angie's capacity to be present in difficulty, to tune into the emotional experience of others and to see this disturbance as a helpful force for change – not an unruly audience. She didn't react personally, or defensively. She wasn't worried about her own ego and not looking good in front of others. Her response *in the moment* was to see this as helpful intelligence, which she then picked up in order to exert gentle peer pressure with the other Chief Executives. She said to them immediately after the meeting (notice good Attractor and Edge and Tension leadership), 'Guys, this is a leadership challenge. We have to live up to what our people are asking of us. I feel a sense of responsibility here, don't you?'

Nudging the Organisation to its Destiny

After this Country Directors' meeting, Angie patiently did the heavy lifting work of securing multi-stakeholder alignment to the vision. And she not only had to align her fellow Chief Executives but also the separate Boards and Chairs that they were accountable to. At all times, she was demonstrating her capacity to hold a wide space for everyone's views, focusing on how to build the strength of the whole. After one key encounter with a Country Chair, where she had managed to secure a 'yes' vote to creating a global organisation, her team were pressing her to have convinced him to agree to a faster time frame. Here is her response, an example of her holding the whole and not getting distracted from the bigger picture. 'The moment passed. I didn't want to turn it into a big confrontation. It was a victory that he said that he agreed – little by little.'

Along the way there were big leaps forward, glimpses of getting agreement to a proposed single management structure, rows with external advisors, and yet despite moments where it felt like she was 'wading in treacle', Angie simply kept moving, seeing the humour in confrontation, and frankly holding it all both seriously, and lightly, at the same time.

She said to us, 'These all were just little moments along the way. It wasn't a logical process. It wasn't, "Oh, then A, then B, then C". It was much more of a meandering kind of progress with two steps forward, one step back, and a step to the side.'

Angie was a leader well able to dance at the still point of the turning world.

Breaking through the Dark Days

Eventually, at an annual general meeting (AGM) the motion was passed to move the organisation into a single global management structure, and Angie was selected as International CEO. Now the 'dark days' kicked in. Moving to a global organisation takes more than a new organisation chart. Coming down from 30,000 feet to the ground Angie encountered all the restructuring ins and outs of changing ways of working, dismantling and rebuilding new legal entities, and losing key talent. You can hear below what the change required of her (and pick up the systemic laws of *belonging* and *place* under threat).

> I was engaging the different members and negotiations were going right around the clock for weeks on end, with Australia who would pop up with an objection at one time. Then just as the UK was going to sleep, the US would come in, and the issues ranged from the sublime to the ridiculous. They were genuine debates about fundraising rights, but people were even arguing over where a comma was placed in the agreements. I had never attempted anything like this before, so there were some real dark days for me here.

Good change leadership can be seriously threatened when it gets down to the heavy lifting of implementation, where Container leadership – the channelling of anxiety – is particularly called for. The organisation will transition through a state of insecurity and emotional turmoil, naysayers will point to all the things that are wobbling as justification for their doubt and old loyalties will impede movement. It can be tempting in this sea of insecurity for leaders to get hijacked by their own anxiety, and avoid visibly engaging with their organisation, just at the time it is needed most. Angie though could hold all of this – but she needed to resource herself.

Through these dark days she used two tactics to enable her to stay the course: daily journalling, which kept her 'sane', and frequent one-on-ones with her Chair to cope with the 'ups and downs'. This demonstrates her inner capacity of Staying Present, regulating her emotional response to experience, and this capacity in turn enabled her to keep Tuning into the System so that she could regulate the emotional response of her whole organisation – superb Attractor and Container leadership. She confessed to us, 'I don't think anybody knew I had doubts because I was just always saying, "This is the right thing to do for children. Remember we've all agreed how fantastic it is. We are going to be the leading NGO."' And indeed, the change that she led exceeded everyone's wildest imaginations.

Systemic Change Leadership Can Be Done, Yet It Starts in Emotional Contact

Despite the organisational and inner personal turmoil, Angie throughout kept the whole system on track. She didn't hide behind the scenes during turbulent times. She even dragged her team huffing and puffing on one occasion out to Nepal (a notoriously difficult place to access) in order to help them see the positive change that was happening on the ground, as local teams joined up their effort around the world. Towards the end of her interview with us she shared her biggest reflection, that 'the feelings side of things is incredibly important. Getting people trusting each other. If you don't have that, everything else is hopeless. It can be built. But it's a mistake to just focus on what's logically right.'

As I conclude this chapter I want to pose the question – if getting in contact with feelings is so important, indeed primary in change (and is what makes the biggest difference between systemic thinking and systemic perceiving), *why do we tend to avoid emotional contact in business, and in our leadership?* Maybe you don't. Maybe I've just spent too much time in rational and logical cultures. But I've been around a fair bit in my almost 30 years in the field, so I do feel I speak from a generalisable place.

Do we operate our defence mechanisms – avoiding tricky meetings with unsettled staff, or attending them but overly focusing on the business case and not people's innermost fears and desires – because they keep us safe from uncomfortable feelings? Emotions will arise in these kinds of situations, especially primary ones such as fear, grief, anger and dare I say it, joy and love. If these primary feelings were not there, then we wouldn't be human and we wouldn't be leading change. What do we risk when we show our deepest emotions? That others will not feel as we do and therefore we end up looking exposed and feeling hurt? Maybe we feel we don't have the right language for such feelings in a business context. Or we do have the words, but we fear that others will take advantage of us if we share emotions (a sad hypothesis that one leader recently expressed to me).

If we as leaders cannot face up to our own emotions we cannot be in emotional contact with others. We will then miss a sense of relationship. And, as I showed at the start of this chapter, without feeling ourselves in relationship to others, we cannot operate systemically. If we cannot operate systemically we cannot move our communities. And leaders such as Jody will be unable to transform her organisation to better the world.

I have no simple answer. But let's keep Still Moving…

6

Make Disturbance Your Friend

But that shadow has been serving you!
What hurts you, blesses you.
Darkness is your candle
Your boundaries are your quest.

Rumi, Enough Words?

I have always struggled with the practice of Edge and Tension. And while it has been a lifelong journey to embrace it, I persisted. There was a wobble or two during my adolescence, and thank goodness I did learn about boundaries then (thank you Mum and Dad). But, for the most part, I grew up in my adopted family wanting to please everyone and be the perfect child. They say that adopted children can go one of two ways. You self-destructively rebel, waiting for that double rejection just to prove that you are indeed unlovable. Or, you make it your quest to prove that your adopted parents made absolutely the right choice when they selected you as their child, and that your biological mother got it wrong. I chose the latter path.

And so I trod gently and carefully through my life. I applied myself diligently at a middle-of-the-road school to earn a place at a special university, where I focused on my studies and left with a first class degree. Never wishing to put a foot wrong, I strove in my professional life to be the most needed consultant, the most responsible leader, the friendliest colleague. Needing to feel I belonged and could be loved, in my personal life I tried to be the kindest friend, the most dutiful of daughters, the best possible life partner. And yet try as I might, I was always on this tightrope, in an oscillating balancing act between being as nice and as perfect as I could possibly be, and at the same time acting out and testing people's boundaries, sometimes to the extreme. I felt protected in politeness and scared in confrontation. And neither felt a very safe place to be.

Still Moving: How to Lead Mindful Change, First Edition. Deborah Rowland.
© 2017 John Wiley & Sons Ltd. Published 2017 by John Wiley & Sons Ltd.

So a major part of my journey has been to learn how to confront the truth about a situation without fearing rejection, to be able to approach difficulty without worrying about causing upset, to be able to disagree with someone clearly and cleanly without obsessing about causing irreparable offence. To be in community and in relationship with others – be that professional or personal – requires you to connect with niggles, awkwardness and tensions, not just joy, harmony and ease. To be in discomfort, knowing that you won't fall. To encounter danger, trusting in your safety. To risk opening up, knowing that you won't be hurt. It's a far less rewarding world without these capacities. Love removes us from our centre and asks that we find our edge.

And this learning became vital as I started to take up leadership roles, where I discovered that most movement happens in the non-comfortable space. I have already discussed how difficulty is a source of systemic intelligence and your target marker for creating change in the here-and-now. If as leaders we ignore disconfirming data, brand those who disagree as 'resistors', or exclude anyone from our leadership team whose views rest uncomfortably with our own, we can become dangerously out of touch with reality. Worse, we risk taking our organisation down the wrong path. And if we fail to uncover the sources of current difficulty, which often requires a delving into the murky world of strongly felt emotion, we not only risk staying in fantasyland, we miss the chance to dislodge what might be most holding us back.

Moreover, the leadership of big change ups the ante even further. By definition it requires you to go to the edge of your system where most innovation occurs, taking others and yourself out of comfort. Not only that, you have to keep holding the tension there because our natural tendency is to retreat to the safety and security of what is known. Going towards the new will also require some form of betrayal of former loyalties, as strong allegiance to past products or ways of working makes new futures very difficult. Organisational change can be like a surgical intervention and you might need to muster a degree of ruthlessness in your leadership. For the reasons described above I have found this very hard to do. However, it has been vicariously reassuring to experience the reality that not many leaders *can* do this practice well. It's one of a top leader's most difficult challenges – critically needed, yet chronically hard to do.

But as hard as it is, it's a challenge that needs to be overcome. *Our research showed that the skilful exercise of Edge and Tension leadership was the external practice most related to the ability to lead high magnitude change well.*

In the rest of this chapter I describe what Edge and Tension is – and, just as importantly, what it is not. Since I wrote *Sustaining Change* I have come to see more clearly how it can be mistaken for a range of practices that are pure shaping behaviour. And when Edge and Tension is done clumsily it can be more damaging to an organisation than not doing it at all.

The answer to doing it well came through loud and clear from our research. There are some crucial inner capacities that you need to get right first. Recall the need to be able to stand well before you are able to move. I will build on the last two chapters and describe further how these inner capacities help you practise Edge and Tension effectively. I conclude with a story of a change leader who had mastered superlative Edge and Tension leadership, enabling her to bravely break her organisation out of a very stuck place.

What is Edge and Tension Leadership? (See Table 6.1)

Tells It As It Is; Describes Reality with Respect Yet Without Compromise

The number one skill in Edge and Tension leadership is to speak plainly, not to be overly polite, pussyfoot around issues or avoid them. Nor to offload issues or to blame others. But to tell the truth (as you see it), without compromise, and with compassion.[1] People respect the truth, however hard it may be to hear. Straight talking can enrich relationships. It builds trust. And it enables clear choice. Like it or not, people know what's what. It's then down to them to decide what to do with this reality. And then you know where you stand too. You do a far greater service to yourself and others by talking straight; it's profoundly disempowering not to do so.

Table 6.1 Edge and Tension leadership – *truth is a turn on.*

Amplifies disturbance in order to shift the organisation's capacity to perform to its potential

Tells it as it is; describes reality with respect yet without compromise
Stays constant when the going gets tough; does not withdraw from difficulty, holds people's hands 'in the fire'
Spots and challenges assumptions; creates discomfort by challenging existing paradigms and disrupts habitual ways of doing things
Sets and holds high standards for others using differentiating consequence management; stretches the goals and limits of what's possible
Does not compromise on talent; pays attention to getting and keeping 'A players'
Focuses on a few big priorities, not lots of small distractions

Here is a cracking example of how a leader was well able to speak plainly. And I know that he was in a context that had been previously bereft of clear, unambiguous, straight talking leadership. Due to his fresh leadership style, he was able to drive through a significant restructure.

> I remember having some of the toughest conversations around the restructure. For instance, we'd be on a videoconference and some of the countries would say, 'Look, we want to form a different brand'. Or 'We want to do our own logo', things like that, and I was having to be quite brutal, 'Just so you're clear, this is non-negotiable and this is not your call'. I know it sounds horrid, and I did it with a smile on my face, but I did it hard. One of the tensions and problems of the restructure was people understanding what they do control and what they don't control in the new system, so I had some awkward moments where I would say, 'No, sorry, you are not calling it that. The model here is licensing and we're not going to do it.' And they say, 'Well, we looked at this, and we think it can work'. Then you get to what I call the point of awkwardness. The point of awkwardness is when you have to say, 'No, we've got all the team here and unless anyone's got a strong different point of view, this is a no, we're not going to do this, look for alternatives'.

Stays Constant When the Going Gets Tough; Does Not Withdraw From Difficulty, Holds People's Hands 'In the Fire'

While the first step in Edge and Tension is to go towards a 'point of awkwardness', the second key step is to make sure you can hold it there and move even further. The brain can take a while to update its operating system and adjust to a new reality. A leader's task in change, a bit like how my osteopath works on my back when it's gone awry, is to keep nudging the organisation towards its edge, rocking it gently in that new, more uncomfortable position, until it becomes bearable, the minds adjust, and then taking it one step further (crack!).

Listen to how this determined leader made sure that others did not become complacent with just one move forward to address a major systemic issue. She kept moving her colleagues away from self-congratulatory relief and continued taking them towards the necessary edge.

> Everybody thought it was great. It was their success. Now we seemed to be where we wanted to be. But I forced them to go deeper, to recognise that because of the past there are still big gaps. We are still far away from consistent quotas between male

and female candidates on every single management layer. I forced them to see that it is not enough to have 1-year cohort consistent promotions to really be successful on diversity.

Spots and Challenges Assumptions; Creates Discomfort by Challenging Existing Paradigms and Disrupts Habitual Ways of Doing Things

All of the external leadership practices are about enabling sustainable big change, addressing the source from which the system operates. They are not about fixing surface-level minor problems. What Edge and Tension leadership does beautifully in this regard is to hold up the mirror to reveal the assumptions that are governing how the system behaves. It exposes old scripts to a reality check. So, a further key aspect of Edge and Tension is a leader's ability to work *on* and not *in* the system – by noticing and challenging its deep assumptions.

Here are two good examples of leaders who could see beneath the surface of how their teams were operating, name the assumptions and repeating patterns, and then require – indeed model – a different way of operating. In the first instance, a leader of one European region needed to highlight the 'not invented here' dynamic in his team as he required them to adopt a best practice from the UK. The second example highlights the challenge of breaking open the prevailing control mindset in a finance function.

Notice that they don't tell their people what *not* to do; they only state what they would like them *to* do. Very skilful, as we know again from brain science that behavioural change best occurs when we are invited to approach an opportunity, not be criticised for doing something 'wrong' (as hotels found out when they switched from telling us *not* to put our towels on the bathroom floor if we wanted to keep using them, to inviting us to help the environment if we put our towels back onto the rail – the latter strategy achieved much more success!).

> 'Be curious', I said, 'I'm expecting every employee here to be curious. You are coming with an opinion that this programme is dead, but only because in the UK they have issues in terms of customer dissatisfaction. This doesn't necessarily come from the programme. It comes from totally different areas, like IT.' So I was trying to have good arguments at hand to say, 'Be open and curious. Once, we have to try it out and then we see whether it works or it does not work.'
>
> I thought he was completely right in saying that we should empower and expect leaders in the organisation to be changing

and driving things. But we need to show up and give real clarity on what our expectations are; and that was definitely not being done. So we started to really experiment with being the voice of discomfort where it wasn't happening naturally.

Sets and Holds High Standards for Others Using Differentiating Consequence Management; Stretches the Goals and Limits of What's Possible

Edge and Tension leadership is also about ambition. Closing that performance-to-potential gap. And, I'd say, creating a *burning ambition* in your organisation is far more likely to bring you change success than building a *burning platform*.

When I worked at PepsiCo I had the great fortune to work with Daryl Conner, a change guru who was helping us through a major international restructuring. The term *burning platform*, which he derived from the tragic Occidental North Sea oil platform disaster, in which the sole survivor realised that the only possible way to get out alive was to jump off the platform into the burning sea, was coined by him as being an essential prerequisite for achieving change. There has to be 'felt pain' in a system, created by pointing out all the things that will go wrong if you don't change. Only then will people be prepared to risk stepping into uncertainty.[2]

I have worked with that notion, and found it very helpful to invite leaders to reflect on the *cost* of bringing in change (as no change comes for free) versus the *price* that will be paid if you maintain the status quo. Putting those two expenses alongside each other can create a stark readiness for change equation: will it be less expensive to change than not to change? However, in my own leadership practice I came to learn that people respond more creatively to desire and enterprise than they do to threat and fear. And this was backed up by my research, where I found that a further aspect to Edge and Tension leadership is to continually raise the bar for others, clearly specifying performance requirements and putting in measurement and planning processes that liberate ambition. Here are two good examples of how this was done.

I said, 'I think you're being spread too thin. I want you to be as close to the customer as we can get, and therefore we might try and flatten your structure a little bit so that you're closer to the complaint numbers and that you're doing more coaching personally. And some of these additional reports of yours that are more technical reports, more change people, I want to take those away from you and have them report to the centre so you can focus on two things – delivering customer and colleague outcomes. Customer outcomes measured by quantity and quality of complaints; colleague outcomes by your ability to attract people to work for you. They're the only things I want you to talk about.'

It was literally, 'Look, you know, we're 17th in the market, why aren't we third? What would you do to get to third, what's growing, what's not growing, where are there partnerships, let's be ambitious and take some risks here!'

Does Not Compromise on Talent; Pays Attention to Getting and Keeping 'A Players'

Jim Collins in *Good to Great* uses the term, 'first who, then what', to describe one of the hallmarks of companies who can continue to excel. Essentially, it means getting the right people on board before you finalise what has to be done, as great talent will naturally determine the right thing to do. Moreover, your selection of leaders to key positions in a change effort sends out strong signals to your organisation about what you (really) value. This does not always mean having to hire new people from the outside to bring about change, but it does mean paying careful attention to not just competence but also character when appointing people into key roles. Remember, cultural change is about *how* things get done, not just what gets delivered. Here are good examples of leaders who held the line and were uncompromising in their insistence on getting selection calls right, including the choice of their consulting partners.

> I needed to shake up the organisation, change responsibilities, and get people on board for that. So one of the strong 'I' people in Canada, who I thought was by the way a very bright person, who had great skill, was very strategic, was an action-oriented person that could make things happen, but was not going to allow anybody within Canada to really change. I mean, he might say it superficially, but it was still going to be whatever he wanted. So I needed to move him out.

> We had a discussion about the Lean programme and we had two consultants in there doing the beauty contest. One had already demonstrated a good track record with us; the other one was cheaper. The people wanted to go for the cheaper solution. I said, 'Wait a second – we've just seen the people that were involved in the first project saying, it depends very much on the quality of the consultant, and do we want to experiment without being sure that the cheapest option not only whether it is as good but whether it will fulfil all the criteria?' That's a kind of wake up call. People say, 'Oh, yes. We're drifting down a path that is going in the wrong direction.'

Focuses on a Few Big Priorities, Not Lots of Small Distractions

I always recall at PepsiCo what Roger Enrico would say to us, 'Which side of the decimal point are you working on?' If you find that your 'to do list' is mainly on the right hand side of the point, you could be filling your day with interesting yet irrelevant distraction. Conversely, if you find that your list is mainly on the left hand side, you are focusing your effort on the fewest items of highest leverage. In change it's very easy to swamp the system by launching programmes and layering on initiatives that might be nice yet irrelevant distractions, while in the meantime, the underlying operations have to keep running. Where do we focus?!

Good change leaders can differentiate between push back from the organisation – 'There are too many programmes and priorities!' – as a change avoiding defensive routine, to the voice of a system that is genuinely overburdened. However, I see two things that leaders continually underestimate in leading change: one is attending to the human dynamics of transition; the other is regulating the demand that major change places on the organisation. As it's not just the literal volume of work that might go up, it's also the demand on attention spans. In big change people get distracted, a lot of energy is consumed in speculation and coping with uncertainty. And in times such as this, successful leaders ruthlessly focus on the few things that matter most.

Here are two good examples of leaders who courageously pushed back on their hierarchy in order to get focus and hence greater productivity in their change. Notice also their clear straight talking.

> We had in the people strategy 27 things to deliver, big projects. And it was probably 20 too many. So I decided to prioritise; so I met with the people in HR who were driving the people strategy. And went through with them what seemed to be the business priorities. I remember a guy who said the HR director is not going to accept that. She's already agreed it with the board. It all has to be delivered.
>
> And I said, 'Well, it all has to be delivered but it doesn't all have to be delivered at once'. So I went back to her and I just said, 'Look, there are 27 different initiatives here, I haven't got a proper team in place, people are working 60-, 70-h weeks; we just can't do this. We need to prioritise and we need to prioritise in time and what's really important to the business. Particularly as we've got a huge restructure going on at the same time'.
>
> I had a conversation with him that went like this, 'You could roll out the strategy maps, or you could continue to roll out some of these other things, but we can't do it all at the same time.

People are overwhelmed. I'm getting complaints day in and day out. People are feeling like they don't have time to do one thing before you've started something else. They're feeling like you've gotten scattered, and you're doing too many different new initiatives at one time, and I think we need to sit down and really map this out. You're going to lose your credibility. You don't want your good people leaving. You've got to slow down.'

The Challenge of Edge and Tension

All of the above examples sound so straightforward to do. But I also know from having read each one of the 88 change stories in our research that moments of skilful Edge and Tension leadership ask a great deal of the leader. This is a practice that is so easy to get wrong. In fact, it's naturally easier to do Edge and Tension badly than well! Here's why.

It's Easy to Lose It

I have already talked about how my personal story led me to feel protected by politeness and scared by confrontation. So I would tread carefully through life, anxious to please and say the 'right' things, fearing causing any upset. Whenever I was taken to the edge and needed to put things on the line, my goodness would I stew about it. And even if I prepared well for a risky encounter I could still lose it in the heat of the moment and switch from the calm naming of reality to a sudden impulse to attack, defend, justify, blame, apologise (how many times do you catch yourself saying 'sorry' when you have to say something difficult?). Or, at times, simply bail out from the difficulty. Things that we care about arouse emotions. And while losing it in this way is natural and seductive, I always let others and myself down.

I am not arguing here for leaders to be nice, friendly and harmonious, or cold and clinical and unfeeling – far from it. I hope you detect much passionate taking-the-bull-by-the-horns in the excerpts from the leaders' stories above. What I *am* inviting here is that leaders pay special attention to the *quality of how* they acknowledge difficulty. In none of the above examples do you hear: intellectual debate, disagreement and point scoring; overly criticising someone or the situation; excessive complaining or annoyance; false threats, frustration, anger or hyperbole. And yet very often I hear leaders say of someone when they see this kind of behaviour, 'He is being very edgy!' or, 'She's bringing some edge and tension to this meeting!' This is a complete misunderstanding of what Edge and Tension truly is.

I have seen organisations get results with this poorly done, or what I call pseudo, Edge and Tension leadership, as so-called 'movers and shakers' turn around their organisations. Sometimes they get lucky with a technological or market breakthrough that can mask poor leadership. But the question is, for how long does the impact of this kind of Edge and Tension survive, what operational and cultural legacy is left for their successor, and what is the (human) price of the collateral damage?

So, why is it so natural in our lives and in our leadership to either avoid Edge and Tension, or do it poorly? I believe it's primarily because we have not sufficiently attended to our own anxiety and inner needs, and how the projection of these impulses might sabotage what is actually called for in the situation. Here's a story of a time when I *was* able to go against my natural grain, do good Edge and Tension leadership, confront reality in the face of extreme denial, and deliver an outcome that was important for my business and for the sanity of all parties concerned.

Overcoming My Story

It was an extraordinarily difficult situation to confront – yet the experience was an indicator to me that I was becoming more able to exercise good Edge and Tension. And on reflection, I can see now how the time consciously invested in my personal and professional development was paying off. I had become more able to not get unconsciously thrown by experience but to recognise my response to it as a product of both my story and the system's story, as Chris had helped me do that evening on the Tuscan hilltop. I was learning to stay calm and connected rather than fearful and anxious in troubling situations, which allowed me to act in service of the whole and not just act out of my own projected needs (needs which at times, meant that I not very helpfully did nothing).

I had to close down a division within my consulting company. Twelve months earlier we had set up as a subsidiary of the main consultancy business, a new product-led division, and had brought in a Commercial Director. In that 12-month period much goodwill and effort had been expended in market sensing, creating a product range, sourcing and training a distribution network, and conducting a high profile sales and marketing campaign. Each month I would receive sales updates with red, amber and green new business opportunities, and I was told we were always on the brink of converting an amber prospect into a green fee-paying client. Yet, at the end of 12 months, a sale had still not been made.

I felt torn. My Commercial Director was still saying that success was just around the corner, that it was far too early to pull the plug, but all the indicators were telling me that this was an illusion. Twelve months in and we had sunk 20% of our annual profit into the division's launch and yet still no income. The Chairman and Chief Financial Officer were getting jittery, and I needed to make the call. Personally, I didn't want to hurt the Commercial Director, and I feared the reputational risk of owning up to failure, but this time I was able to put my fear of confrontation and loss of relationship or impending rejection to one side, and squarely face the difficulty to say, 'This can't go on'.

At a specially convened board meeting we took a vote on this fledgling division. I had all the data, and I described the situation simply as it was. There was nothing pejorative, I just laid out how much had been invested, with minimal return, and quite ruthlessly went through each future client prospect to reveal how far we were from securing a sale. I went beyond the facts to describe how I was feeling about the situation – torn between my loyalty to having this division and my colleagues succeed, and my prime responsibility for ensuring the viability of the whole business. The board took a vote, and it was to close the division down.

It was, of course, a difficult message to take on for the Commercial Director (who had to leave) yet I was now able to not take on the anxiety-led projection of others. I was sad at the decision and the impact it had had on people, yet at the same time it brought me a newfound confidence to tackle difficulty in a more detached yet still empathetic way. And in subsequent years, as I increasingly found myself in front of large groups, either as a business leader or as group moderator, I have found this inner capacity to not *introject or mirror* other people's anxiety to be essential in holding my nerve and doing good Edge and Tension. I'm sure as a leader in your own organisation you too might recognise the dynamic of anxious groups (unconsciously) placing the sole responsibility for their difficulty at your door. Don't take it on.

Not Having a Systemic Interpretation of the Difficulty

So the first challenge in doing Edge and Tension well is the difficult task of managing your own and others' anxiety. The other main trap is to fail to recognise that any difficulty that is being experienced, be that in yourself and/or others, is also a property of the wider system. It is very easy to get wrapped up in the discomfort yet familiarity of personal neurosis and be blind to the systemic signal of your feelings and emotions.

When leaders are unable to read difficulty systemically, their Edge and Tension will be targeted only at the surface level of events. It will be about people and their performance – what they have done or not done, or about dissatisfaction with an incident – what we did do or failed to do. This is all very well, and might address immediate problems, but it is not Edge and Tension leadership that gets to the source of the presenting issue, it will only be tending to the symptoms that this issue has created.

You might confront the fact that your team always seem to speak over each other, yet fail to dig down to the murky depths of inter-departmental rivalry.

And when Edge and Tension is only applied to event level and not underlying systemic difficulty, people are more likely to feel a little blamed, or judged and get defensive. Edge and Tension will feel like being told off by a teacher or critical parent – you did something wrong, you should have done something differently. The immediate mishap is not interpreted from a wider and deeper perception. People will end up feeling corrected, but not enlightened, and likely to repeat the unhelpful pattern again.

Another risk of failing to see difficulty or disturbance as systemic data is that you might not exercise Edge and Tension at all. It all feels so inter-personal and awkward that you end up, in your own anxiety, giving others a comfort blanket of security. Strangely, such unwillingness to approach difficulty can only make people around you feel even more anxious. I once worked with a leader who was so unable to contain his own fear of uncertainty in a turnaround – where the solution to get out of today's problem was far from obvious – that he put even tighter control over his people, at the same time telling them 'Not to worry, I will figure things out'. The consequence of this avoidance was his whole organisation ended up in an even greater panic than if he had been able to face the difficulty alongside them.

In short, I'm not surprised that Edge and Tension leadership – the skilful confronting of reality, and in particular underlying assumptions – is so misunderstood and hard to do well. I have shared why I find it personally difficult to do, even though I think (intellectually) I understand it better than most. The biggest trick seems to me to be the capacity to view reality as always friendly. However disquieting, unpleasant, heart breaking or gut wrenching, reality always allows something new to appear. Look on it wisely, both through the lens of your own story and the lens of the wider system that in difficulty more than ever requires your leadership.

Edge and Tension – How to Do This Well

We found in our research that the critical skill of Edge and Tension is strongly related to change success only when it is accompanied by particular inner capacities. If the inner capacities were not present in the leader's story, Edge and Tension tipped into shaping and intimidatory behaviour, or, was simply not present at all (the leader bailed out). Both of these scenarios lead to unsuccessful change. So here's where and how by using the inner capacities set out in the previous two chapters, you can learn to excel at this much-needed change leadership skill.

Edge and Tension with Staying Present and Curious and Intentional Responding

We found through our research that these two inner capacities were the starting point in enabling leaders to confront difficulty while staying personally non-anxious. And it was the following elements of Staying Present and Curious and Intentional Responding in particular that made the biggest difference to successful Edge and Tension leadership: uses language to describe their experience and doesn't get caught up in their responses to the experience itself (speak plainly and clear of personal projection); focuses upon what is happening in the present moment and consciously avoids distraction for a sustained period of time (stay with the problem); notices and processes one's feelings and emotions as observable data and does not impulsively react with them (stay cool); and at any moment is conscious of both one's options on how to respond to what is being experienced and also the choices that one takes in response (if it gets rocky, stay flexible).

Edge and Tension with Tuning into the System

Staying calm, connected, conscious and curious is therefore the starting point for effective Edge and Tension leadership. It allows you to confront difficulty without causing excess fear and anxiety in those around you, so your messages can be heard. Our research showed that what raises the quality of your Edge and Tension game a significantly greater notch is a leader's ability to tune into the emotions and feelings of the whole system around them, and having the capacity to anticipate how difficult decisions and actions will land. This helped the leaders avoid another Edge and Tension pitfall – defensiveness in others – as they place the naming of difficulty into an empathic, not judgemental place. However it goes even beyond the tuning into others and the empathic naming of difficulty.

Edge and Tension with Acknowledging the Whole

We found that Acknowledging the Whole was the inner capacity most closely associated with skilful Edge and Tension leadership, especially among the leaders who could pull off major change across large complex systems. How come? We burrowed a bit deeper into the stories, reflected on our own experience and came to this conclusion.

As a senior leader you do not always know what the difficulty is, as it can be hard from this more operationally distant place in the hierarchy to put your finger on the source of what is holding your organisation back. And this gets amplified in high power-distance cultures where people tend to only pass good news up the hierarchy. The ultimate skill of great Edge and Tension leadership is therefore your inner capacity to hold a big enough space for your people to take risk and to name and face their own difficult reality. These leaders could uncover difficulty and amplify disturbance *with* their organisation. And simply by being the bearer of an edgy *process*, and not the teller of an edgy *message*, they could build the organisation's own ability to navigate through difficulty.

In a sense, it is like being able to help people walk across a dangerous threshold, while holding your own nerve. It starts with a stated intention to *systemically* find out what is going on – not to discover more symptomatic issues such as interpersonal conflict, areas of operational deficiency or resisting groups in the organisation. The leader then uses simple inquiry to help others find their way through the jungle, *at all times not allowing people to run away from the difficulty, blame others or bail out.* You don't have to be the describer of the difficulty, but you do have to be a strong convener of the safe space that enables underlying difficulty to be revealed.

I recently helped convene such a space with the executive board of a company I have been coaching through a multi-year change effort. It's a good example of how the inner capacities were called upon in order for them to bring skilful Edge and Tension leadership to a critical event in this change. It was a great team effort, and they stepped up to the plate and provided me with one of the best examples of Edge and Tension I have witnessed.

Edge and Tension Leadership in a Transforming Space

The board were hosting their annual 2-day senior leadership event, with 360 people gathered. The four board colleagues had had a tricky first day to the conference. The external and financial pressure on their company had become immense, and anxiety and uncertainty were dripping off the walls of the conference venue. In times such as this people need to see an inspiring and aligned top leadership team, and this is not what they had experienced on the first day.

The four leaders had appeared overly scripted, not relaxed and unaligned. Moderators were running the show, which made it difficult for the top leaders to engage, as a team, in any intimate way with their people. Moreover, I also noticed that it had felt hard for participants to be able to voice difficulty or doubt in the room. When this was done their very well intended board leaders were, far from acknowledging difficulty, instead encouraging everyone to be positive and upbeat. I was sitting in the audience wincing each time this occurred – and I could feel the bristling of others around me. Who was going to be brave enough to say anything hard to hear now! But I knew I needed to choose carefully the timing of my intervention.

Fortunately, the board were now used to the importance of tuning into the system, and during the first afternoon were coming up to me to share what they were feeling inside about how the conference was going. They couldn't quite put their finger on it but they knew that there was a not good feeling in the room. At the end of the day, they courageously invited volunteers who had been observing the dynamics of the group to come onto the stage and share their feedback. It was while this group was struggling to name the difficulty that I took the microphone. I had been sitting attentively appreciating the bravery of the observers to get on the stage in front of their 360 colleagues and share what could be heard as a negative message. But I felt that the message needed to land a little more provocatively.

I offered a systemic hypothesis that one of the reasons it was hard for this observer group to describe what was difficult was because whenever an awkward subject had been raised in the large group during the day, its reality was being denied and excluded. The observers were themselves part of this pattern. And I linked this pattern in the room to the wider difficulty that this organisation was experiencing in society, where issues such as climate change, and the cost of moving to a carbon-free world were not being squarely faced (by multiple parties). I closed by inviting the group to learn a little more about how to steer towards their edge in this meeting.

The intervention opened up a space. And it gave permission for brave leaders to take the microphone and in front of a large group talk about their deepest fears and anxieties about survival, and their feeling of impotence. No matter what the company did to ensure its future viability, market, political and regulatory circumstances kept taking them back down again. It was a special and emotional end to the conference day, and overnight the four board members and I knew that they had to capture the moment and come out in a radically different way the next morning.

Over breakfast the four calmly and openly shared with each other how they were feeling personally, what they thought about each other's leadership on the first day, and what they had heard in the informal conversations over dinner. They had read the mood music perfectly. They were not blaming the conference designers or moderators, they were not angry and projecting their anxiety onto anyone. In situations such as these the top leaders I work with can often say, 'Our leaders just don't get it', or, 'They need to take more accountability!' Not this top team, who were masterfully exercising their capacity to process difficulty without getting personally caught up in it, or projecting it onto others. I only had to moderate this conversation with a light touch.

And with minutes to go before the whole group got back into their seats for day two they agreed their game plan for the opening session – for the four of them to get onto the stage, without a moderator, and basically name and process the difficulty in the room, starting with themselves. And so they did, they spoke clearly and plainly, 'Yesterday we failed you, we were not inspiring enough'. You could have heard a pin drop. Nothing apologetic, no attempt to ask for forgiveness, they just named reality. And they continued, 'There are extreme difficulties in our business, which we must face. And we need to be able to do that together. Let's all raise our game in the room today. If we can't do it here we can't do it outside this room either'. They also invited the group to break up into smaller peer groups and identify the big dangerous questions and concerns that were still causing trouble, and there was space created to voice these to the board in front of all their colleagues.

This was Edge and Tension in action par excellence. The four leaders opened up the space to allow their 356 colleagues to walk gingerly together across a challenging threshold. Not walking around, but going through difficulty. And they did this with great sensitivity, poise and systemic insight. Even making light of the experience from time to time (well-placed humour here and there can always make Edge and Tension more bearable).

I hope by now you might be realising how challenging, yet how vital it is for leaders of change to be able to exercise superlative Edge and Tension leadership. I guess if Edge and Tension were in itself without edge and tension then you might not be doing it! I conclude this chapter with a final story of a business reinvention, featuring a leader who could combine the inner capacities and external practice of Edge and Tension leadership to dramatic and transforming effect.

Edge and Tension in Action – A Leader Who Could Face Her Fear

What follows is a remarkable story of a leader, let's call her Andrea, who landed in a foreign country (a Latino in a North American context) to become the new CEO of a $4bn business that had not made any money in years. Head office had just fired the business's previous CEO, Commercial Director and Production Director. And the whole organisation was in the long-term grip of a bad contract with a major customer who had forced down prices to the bone. It was a stuck and frightened organisation that she described as having, 'Tried to do change by doing the same things, nobody wanted to face the customer, or to say bad things. They had been a happy family that had never made any money. Everything started the moment we realised we were "busy fools".'

When Andrea left the business 3 years later, this fearless leader had almost doubled the annual operating profit from $120 m to $225 m. She had not only diversified the business's customer base, she had also confronted the organisation's worse fear and taken on its biggest customer, securing a new longer-term contract – all despite doing the previously unthinkable and implementing a 20% margin rise; and, she left behind a far happier, empowered and inspired organisation now believing it had a long-term future.

What had this leader done to pull off this turnaround, which all of her predecessors had failed to do?

As ever, *what* Andrea did is relatively easy to get your head around: she traded volume for margin by raising prices, taking the consequent hit of lower volume and increased capacity to create the space to upgrade the production and distribution system, and develop more innovative products; this attracted new customers, and she used the additional earnings from the higher price position to plough back further investment into the business; she upgraded the leadership team by promoting great talent from the lower ranks into more senior positions; and she fundamentally created a more open culture by removing power distance between her and the operational staff and moving all of the administration unit to open plan offices.

This set of actions might sound obvious, but the strategy was radically counter to how the organisation had been run for decades, and Andrea had to overcome significant resistance, scepticism and even personal threat to get it implemented. And here's *how* she overcame all the hurdles, using, primarily, world class Edge and Tension leadership. She confronted the organisation without being confrontational – a good summary, in a sense, of this practice when it is done well.

Edge with Empathy

Let's start with how she convinced her own organisation to be up for this radical new strategy, as this is where her special skill started to kick in. Imagine now you are a production manager in one of her factories: you know that you haven't been making money for a while; you have just seen your boss, and his boss the CEO being fired; and you jump at every demand of your major customer, who is calling all the shots. You would be more than a little nervous for your job and a touch defensive when you saw a new CEO arriving. Is she going to take a hatchet to the organisation? Will she point out how bad my performance is?

Andrea was extremely sensitive to the history and current mood of the organisation. Her leadership began with *tuning into the system*. Far from leaping to premature judgement and haranguing her organisation about their poor performance, she personally spent weeks in the manufacturing plants and out with the sales teams getting to know the operations and their story. When it came to the moment to create the new strategy, she knew that she had to hold up the mirror to her organisation in a way that her team could see their unhelpful repeating patterns. Listen to how she calmly took them to their edge and held the tension there, despite their pushback and projection onto Andrea as being some kind of madwoman.

> I remember exactly when I presented the work. I prepared just the logic. I did not prepare a huge presentation. And everybody agreed, 'You're going to be punishing our customer. You are going to lose capacity.' And I said, 'Yes, that's exactly what I want. Because I believe based on what I see at the marketplace, there will be other players who will buy this capacity at a fair price.' And everybody was extremely afraid about this punishment, because they were kind of slaves to our customer. They were vocal about that. They said, 'Are you crazy?'

Andrea was firmly holding the line, but while she did that she had the inner capacity to sense that her team didn't really want to be in this current state of affairs either, she was acting from the intention of serving others, not her own personal glory. And it was through this deep empathy with her people that she was able to eventually secure their agreement to the 'crazy' plan.

> Nobody wants to face slavery, nobody wants to be submitted to another company, so what I presented to them was hope. Hope and better profitability. Hope and a better future. By now I knew them all by name, and they wanted to do it although they didn't know how. So my question for them was, 'Guys, do you have any other idea about how? Because if you don't, what I'm presenting to you is something that may succeed. I'm not saying will succeed, but may succeed. We have a chance. The only thing that I know is that doing nothing we will not succeed.'
>
> They asked me if I'm ever going to change my mind, and I remember saying these words. 'Guys, every time I change my mind I feel smarter. If you have a different option, please share it. If you don't, please support.' And they did.

It can be disarming – and incredibly effective – to initiate what people are expecting to be a testy exchange, with a gesture of empathy.

Staying Present While Under Fire

The next hurdle was convincing her board that the seemingly crazy plan to push up prices would work. Again, she faced resistance and initial scepticism, but she bravely held her nerve and got their approval. This was no quick victory as after the board decision their major customer came calling and she had to calm the nerves of her anxious Chairman. Notice again how she could approach difficulty and challenge assumptions while at all times remaining calm and collected, not taking on the anxious projection of others.

> My board were more than sceptical, they were cynical. They said, 'Ha ha ha.' They believed it was a kind of joke. And when I finished I said, 'Okay. Maybe it won't work. So tell me, if we don't do it, what's going to happen?' And there was a huge silence, and I said, 'I think we're going to die if we don't do it.'
>
> The board approved the strategy. Although they approved it, I remember when I raised the prices and my customer's leadership started to call the company and say, 'Look, this is absurd. You guys are destroying the relationship.' I remember I received some phone calls asking me if I knew what I was doing and I said, 'Yes, I did.' And I remember I asked my Chairman, 'Unless you know how to do it different than me, I will keep going.'

Now comes the heat of the fierce pushback from their major customer. And again, as cool as a cucumber, Andrea didn't waver, or take things personally, but kept the tension and held the course.

> I remember there was one event that happened, and the main guy from my customer went to my CEO and complained about me saying that I was not being supportive and, what's worse, I was being disrespectful.
>
> What I said is, 'Look, first of all I believe that there are no boundaries among the companies. Naturally, I understand that you have to make decisions and you have to do what is better for you but you got to understand from the same logic that we are going to do what is good for my company.' He was distant, but he could not go against this logic. So he said, 'Yes, we understand, but let's see what's going to happen.' And so he left the table with a threat. The threat was if you don't behave, you're going to lose your job.

With No Fear You are Just Stupid

In the face of such personal attack, Andrea's inner capacity to notice, process and regulate her own emotion and that of her customer helped her stick with this extremely difficult path. She was able to be so good at Edge and Tension not because she was an insensitive and uncaring character, but because she had the inner capacity to understand where her own and her customer's discomfort was coming from – and to see this difficulty as an important resource, not something to be feared or attacked back in return.

> You can't fight emotion with emotion. You got to understand and put yourself in his shoes, you got to understand his feeling. It was the first time he was being challenged. So that was to be expected. My position was to be polite, respectful, good, yet assertive.
>
> I felt fear for sure, because I was being threatened personally. This guy could smash my head any time. Yet when I have fear, I try to rationalise the fear, and understand that fear is part of progress. With no fear, you are just being stupid. So you need some fear in order to balance your decision and question yourself. Fear is good and necessary.

Andrea's empathy went even as far as going up to the CEO of her customer at a major industry awards ceremony to congratulate him, showing there was no rancour on her part. This lady can do Edge and Tension from a deeply respectful place. I could continue with further stories of how Andrea did not buckle under fire, and also of how she engaged her frontline organisation to support the change, but I do not have the space to do so here, and wish to focus this story to illustrate how Edge and Tension can be done so well when you have mastered your inner capacities, as I believe this is such a missing skill in leadership today. Here is a final excerpt that for me sums up Andrea's character to put the good of the system around her as her number one priority, the source from which she draws the courage and sensitivity to do the difficult work of Edge and Tension.

> One thing that is very clear, I feel fear, especially when working in a new position in a different country, and it was my highest position that I had in my life in that moment. Naturally I felt a lot of fear. But the same time, I knew I was doing what I should do and that's what we needed to survive. When I know I'm doing my job in my best way, and I'm doing this in a very honest way in order to provide the best result to my company, that's what I need.

And the consequences will come. The fact that I will be squeezed or damaged by the organisation and by the decisions that I take is one factor. The other factor is that it will not stop me doing what I have to do.

Edge and Tension Summary: It Must Come from a Still Place

So my research found that Edge and Tension leadership is the number one external practice needed to do big change well. Most movement happens in the non-comfortable space. It is the top practice because the skilful confronting of difficult reality is needed in order to go to a system's source and confront its repeating patterns. Yet, while critically needed, it is also the leadership practice most poorly used or avoided. This is largely due to our inability to attend to our own anxiety in discomfort, and also because we do not interpret difficulty systemically and end up confronting only surface-level action. This is just getting bolshie, not true Edge and Tension leadership.

What enables you to do good Edge and Tension leadership is to be able to deeply hold the belief that reality is always friendly, however painful and dangerous and awkward it might feel to confront. For this, we found that the inner capacity to Acknowledge the Whole became Edge and Tension's requisite companion. When you have the inner capacity to graciously and wisely give all of experience its place and its purpose, Edge and Tension feels like a helpful illuminating laser, not a misguided missile.

In the closing story I have already mentioned the stunning results that Andrea delivered from implementing her brave, countercultural strategy. You may be wondering how she developed her inner capacity to be so calm in fear, empathetic when under attack and systemically wise during personal fisticuffs. Well, she meditated throughout the 3 years of the business turnaround to build greater self and system awareness, yet has discovered since that time that she did not have the discipline to continue for the long run.

So, she searched for another practice that could have the same effect, and has now taken to the daily reading and rereading of poetry. There are many paths that lead to a skilful inner state. I invite you to discover one of your own.

7

Holding the Fire

We can make our minds so like still water
That beings gather about us that they may see,
It may be, their own images,
And so live for a moment with a clearer,
Perhaps even with a fiercer life
Because of our quiet.

W.B. Yeats, Earth, Fire and Water

Mum and Dad were very quiet the moment I told them I wished to trace my biological mother and father. They took my tumbling words and faltering sentences with calmness and grace. My emotions were raging inside. I desperately wanted to take this step to grow and feel complete, yet deeply feared the difficulty in doing so, anticipating a second disintegration in my life – the rejection of the two people who had picked me up and taught me love. Let alone facing the very likely pain of re-identification, and the unleashing of unfathomable emotions in tracing those who had given me life. I don't think it is a coincidence that in one conversation with my mum and dad I suffered an anaphylactic shock, which subsequently could not be traced to any physical source.

Yet I got through it. I stayed on course. And my mum and dad were a significant part of the *containing structure* that took my tumultuous anxiety and channelled it into purposeful discovery and ultimately joy. I continued with my primary task, to complete the missing element in my story, and was eventually reunited with both of my biological parents. My mum and dad took this in their stride, supporting me non-anxiously with 'minds so like still water' all the way.

The containing presence of Mum and Dad had begun very early in my life. They were secure enough in themselves to have told me from the outset that I was adopted – one of my elder brothers had been too.

Still Moving: How to Lead Mindful Change, First Edition. Deborah Rowland.
© 2017 John Wiley & Sons Ltd. Published 2017 by John Wiley & Sons Ltd.

And I was always encouraged to ask questions about the circumstances of my birth and talk as much about it as I wanted to with them. Such an emotionally risky subject made their invitation a difficult one to take up. But growing up I felt secure and deeply reassured that I could always speak with them if I felt I needed to. My adoption was never a non-discussable subject. Their love for me was uncontaminated by their own needs for reassurance of their own worth as parents.

Yet while I rationally knew that I had their full backing, if ever I wanted to do the trace, my anxiety was still palpable when it came to the fiercest of moments in my life – the physical reunions with my biological parents. In my anticipated fear I tested the security of my mum and dad's love – I'm sure my anaphylactic shock that day was an unconscious hurdle I put in front of them to see if they could stay with their ungrateful daughter, who had collapsed very publicly in a heap in a pub outside Marlborough. They did.

And while staying compassionately present with me in that moment, they also had the humility and strength of character to stay out of the way further down the track when it was only I who could take responsibility. With great patience and generosity they did not interfere and demand any communication with me when it came to the two separate reunions. They let me walk my own path across the precipice.

Going to the Edge Requires Container Leadership

All of these features of my mum and dad's parenting are characteristics of what I call Container leadership: being secure enough in themselves to be non-anxious and available for me when approaching difficulty (not letting their own story, or needs, get in the way); making it completely okay to talk about difficult and disturbing topics; providing a reassuring and affirming presence to enable me to move more comfortably through challenging emotions; and ensuring that I, ultimately, took full responsibility for my own transition. Turbulence does not always bring out the best in us. But Mum and Dad's containing parenting brought out the best in me.

In the previous chapter I talked about the necessary and transforming power of Edge and Tension leadership to effect change – the ability to talk straight, name reality, challenge assumptions and ruthlessly focus on what counts. However difficult, facing the truth is a transforming act as it allows something new to occur. Yet if this facing of the truth is not combined with the channelling, holding energy of Container leadership, the turbulence that Edge and Tension generates becomes so overwhelming it can lead to behaviour more related to the playground than to the boardroom.

Disturbance is only developmental and not dysfunctional when it is accompanied by the alchemical power of containment. In this chapter I set out how this can be done. Like Edge and Tension, Container leadership can be misunderstood and poorly executed. And yet I have found that it is a vital skill for top leaders to deploy when successfully stewarding their organisations through big change. Here's a chapter to burrow deeply into the subject and dispel its myths.

What is 'Containment'?

Psychological containment is an aspect of resilience, and refers to the capacity to internally manage the troubling thoughts, feelings and behaviour that arise as a consequence of anxiety. Having this capacity allows you to approach and not avoid difficulty. Containment is *not* sweeping things under the carpet.

Through her pioneering psychoanalytic work in stress-inducing workplaces, such as studying nurses in hospitals, Menzies Lyth[1] (and the Tavistock Institute she was associated with[2]) has contributed greatly to my understanding of the importance of containment in leadership. She maintains that all social structures are a form of a defence, ways to avoid the experience of anxiety, guilt, doubt and uncertainty. In that respect, all workplace systems are partly designed to protect people from anxiety. Via their rules, processes, role allocation and task delegation mechanisms people can feel secure enough to go about their work. Any change that disrupts these systems will lead people to feel insecure.

As a result, great change leaders need to understand and work with troubling emotions and the process of containment. The success and viability of a social system are intimately connected with the techniques it uses to contain anxiety.

For leadership, it's partly about managing your own inner state – more of that later. But containment is also about regulating the emotional state of your organisation. Containment is the energetic space between you and your people. It is the atmosphere you create that conveys a sense of safety, allowing your organisation to manage *its* troubling inner thoughts and feelings when approaching challenging times. Change is not just a rational but also a psychological task. An organisation needs to feel 'held' to feel strong, which means you as a leader openly acknowledging and managing difficult feelings so that people's minds can be freed to engage constructively with their work.

The Consequences of No Containment

When containment is underplayed in change, the stress that change generates gets dissipated into unhelpful defensive routines. These are the mechanisms we use to alleviate anxiety. Common ones I encounter in a change context are denial and avoidance of the difficulty, dissipative and opaque accountability and decision structures, grandiose ideas about pie-in-the-sky solutions and convenient upward delegation – often manifesting as blaming the CEO for all the organisation's problems. All are ways to take the heat *out* of a difficult situation.

I find the metaphor of a crucible helpful when describing containment. A crucible is a vessel that can hold hot and transforming processes. When dealing with molten metals, for example, a crucible can be subjected to extremely high temperatures. The word crucible also means a severe trial, or any situation in which different elements must interact in order to create something new. Highly relevant, I would say, for organisational or societal transition. When molten metals and difficult experiences have no adequate holding container, all energy dissipates and the change task becomes impossible.

Here are two scenarios I have seen when an organisation's leaders were stoking up the fire with Edge and Tension – talking straight about reality and naming what needed changing, yet providing very little Container – securely holding and channelling the ensuing disturbance into resourceful movement. Both scenarios – Edge and Tension with no Containment – led to stuck systems.

One organisation had openly acknowledged a threat to its very survival, and as a consequence its leaders knew they had to radically change its operating system. But senior leaders did little face-to-face engagement with impacted people and in the absence of safe places to talk about hot topics – such as the difficult decisions and people's troubling feelings about those decisions – uncontained Edge and Tension spread wildfire panic through the system. It bred politics, self-interest and rivalry, and led to very biased and partisan narratives about the truth. It became a very unsafe place.

The other organisation, conversely, was feeling proud and complacent and not aware it had to truly change. In these conditions, its natural immune system fought against the exposing Edge and Tension leadership brought in by the new CEO. In the absence of any clear guidance on how to hold people responsible for change, the system extinguished any transforming energy at source. Uncontained Edge and Tension created an irrationally felt-safe place.

Going through change requires 'lighting many fires' – how often have you heard that expression? How often have you heard leaders also say that they need to create the psychological safety for people to channel the anxiety that those fires will create? I suspect, not so often. I'm not talking here about leaders issuing reassuring communications or offering daily counselling sessions to make people feel better. No, those are only, and justifiably termed, 'touchy-feely' attempts to take the pain away, not channel the latent energy in anxiety towards creating something new. We need adrenalin. Yet it also requires a secure navigable passage. This is good Container leadership – providing just the right amount of structure and felt safety to endure the at-times painful process of transition.

Containment Does Require Managing Your Own Inner State First

Yet in practice, when life inevitably heats up and gets risky in a change, leaders gravitate towards two very natural responses. Neither represents good Container leadership, and they are consequences of the leader in all the hurly burly being unable to manage their *own* needs and anxieties first. This is where the inner capacities need to come in. It's very hard to do Container leadership when you are not in charge of your own needs and feelings, as then your own story will get in the way. Your people will feel *your* issues filling the space (even if you try to hide them). They will not feel in safe hands.

I exaggerate the two typical responses to make a point, but I hope you might see even a tiny fragment of your own leadership in them.

Too Much Containment Constricts

When we take on the sole responsibility for the anxiety of others we tend to try to protect and rescue. In our own unprocessed anxiety ('Gosh, I'm the leader here, I better try to solve all this!'), and at times deep affection ('Your pain is my pain and I wish to take it away'), we try to make ourselves feel less anxious by stepping in to take charge. We offer to take on the burden, we tell others not to worry or we even apologise (my tendency) for any difficulty and cut people slack at the first expression of discomfort. Yet these strategies only keep the other party festooned in cotton wool and dependent on you. This doesn't create new capacities; it evokes learned helplessness in the system, and, at times, outright rebellion if people feel too smothered.

In these circumstances are you leading or substituting for your people? We short-circuit other's growth and development when we do not require that they take their own steps to work through difficulty. I am very glad that my mum and dad did not get on that plane to Dublin and accompany me even part of the way for my reunion with my biological mother, even though (at age 43) I was quaking in my shoes. Their knowledge that as parents they were responsible *to* me not *for* me enabled me to find out just what I was capable of. Great change leaders powerfully build accountability and ownership for tackling difficulty throughout their organisation in order for the system to grow.

It takes a strong leader to be able to let go of complete responsibility, especially when you see others in difficulty.

Too Little Containment Creates Unsafe Places

Here's the other extreme. We shut ourselves down from our feelings and become out of touch with the anxiety of others. Or maybe we are in tune with others' and our feelings yet in our insecurity of not knowing how to respond we stay out of the fray. In both circumstances we end up letting people struggle on their own. The outward explanation I most often hear for this, in response to my suggestion to engage with staff going through a testing time, is, 'Deborah, they are all grown ups here, we've communicated the change timetable and what's what. I know it's tough, but the best thing we can do now is simply let them get on with the business.'

I sense that at times the subtext might be, 'And, by the way, I never got any support in that last restructuring, and I'm still standing!' or, perhaps at its deepest place, I can both feel in my body and hear, 'To be honest, I just don't feel equipped to go and have these squirmy kind of conversations, especially as I think they are angry with me at the decision I have just had to take. I simply don't know how to handle this kind of awkwardness, and I'm frightened I might lose it, and do more damage than good.'

And so leaders stay in their offices and resort to sending in the human resources (HR) team to find out what's going on. Or, they ask their communications team to set up nicely impersonal and orchestrated webcasts during which they broadcast a set of messages, maybe having time for a question and answers session at the end to allow a few brave souls to pose a question, usually through an anonymous and mediated digital channel. This is far too little containment in times of anxiety and big transition. In these times people need to be able to feel the personal presence of their leader, checking at all times if their leaders are non-anxious and secure, as then they too can relax and confidently approach the tough stuff.

Great change leaders don't avoid duck out of containment; they are calmly available to channel the anxiety of their people. At times all it takes is simply guiding people with clear lines of responsibility and a few firm rules which then allow people to get on with what they have to do. I still chuckle at one memory of my mum. I was about to take one of my earliest oil paintings to Dublin to nervously show to my biological mother (who, we discovered, is an accomplished artist). Sitting still in her arm-chair she very gently, yet firmly said to me, 'Darling, you can take that oil painting to show her (it was hanging on my mum and dad's wall), but, you need to bring it back, as it belongs to me'. Perhaps that oil painting was an unconscious metaphor for her daughter, yet, I do know that the clear rule removed any ambiguity from me as to how to relate to having two mothers. While she didn't accompany me to Dublin, I nonetheless went with her firm guiding hand.

Organisational Containment, Big Change and Top Leadership

One of my objectives in this latest round of research was to revalidate the four change leadership practices set out in *Sustaining Change*. In the previous chapter I have shared how important we found the practice of Edge and Tension leadership to be. I was still convinced of the need for Container leadership in challenging times. What surprised the research team and I this time round was that Container leadership did *not* differentiate between the successful and less successful change leaders. Good research is spacious enough to hold disconfirming data, so in a sense this was reassuring. It also led us to a more powerfully nuanced understanding of this practice.

We interrogated the data further by doing several things: we looked more specifically at the impact of Container leadership in change of the highest magnitude, i.e., the most complex change impacting many people; we separated out the different levels of leadership seniority to see if organisational hierarchy was an influencing variable; and we ran separate correlations for the different elements of Container leadership. Specifically, separating out what I call the more *intra- and inter-personal elements* of Container, such as providing a strong affirming and non-anxious personal presence, from the more *structural elements* of Container, such as setting up performance contracts for what work needs to happen and how. Finally, as the clear second objective to the research was to look at a leader's inner capacity to lead big change well, we investigated which of the four inner capacities set out in Chapters 4 and 5 was related to any of the above.

Latest Research Findings on Container Leadership

And here's what we found. In contexts of high magnitude change, which is complex and affecting many people:

- Container leadership is vital for the very top leaders in an organisation, where it strongly differentiated between success and failure at this level.

- The intra- and inter-personal elements of Container significantly differentiated between success and failure. Structural elements were present in success but they did not differentiate.
- Acknowledging the Whole was the inner capacity most strongly present alongside Container in the most successful top leaders.

The message is loud and clear: the emotional health, strength and security of top leaders to channel anxiety and difficulty across a whole system in transition are critical variables in ensuring successful change outcomes.

The most successful leaders in our study did not act out their own insecurities, needs and issues. Nor did they project judgements onto difficulty – in particular, misinterpreting apparent resistance as something negative to be eradicated. Instead, they modelled courageous stewardship of their organisation. They remained calm and secure when the going got tough, even when under personal attack; they authorised others to take responsibility for resolving difficulty, focusing on building the strength of the whole system; they provided as much structure and consistency as possible during periods of change, such as articulating its scope, and communicating a clear timetable; and they paid extraordinary attention to fostering a supportive culture that contained safe and secure spaces for the processing of difficult emotions.

Far from overly protecting people, or letting their organisations drift in a sea of choppy anxiety, they powerfully took up the role that has to be the prime responsibility of senior leaders in a changing system – to provide strong enough organisational containment to deal with the anxiety generated by uncertainty and the insecurity of not knowing.

The Power of Container to Channel Edge and Tension Towards Big Change

While in the previous chapter I shared my lifelong struggle with the practice of Edge and Tension, I do feel I am pretty effective at Container. This is no doubt partly due to the role models of my mum and dad – and, in particular, learning leadership at the feet of my dad when I grew up in the 1970s. During this decade, as head of personnel for a large UK Government department, he skilfully navigated his organisation through some of the toughest industrial relations unrest of the century. This early impressionable modelling, combined with my natural affinity for tuning into human systems and fiercely empathising with the deep emotional insecurities of transition, had given me a bit of a head start.

Containment and Restructuring

Having said that, the challenge is constant. I discovered this when I found myself as the People Director responsible for delivering a major global restructuring. It was an instructional leadership experience for me in how to set up a change process secure enough to take anxieties – and their defences – and move people through difficult transition (Container) into a radically different future (Edge and Tension). In this instance, it meant moving a company that had been organised in a centralised, product-led structure, to a devolved country-based structure. This entire shift had to be accompanied while still retaining product and brand consistency across the globe. No small task.

This required the careful setting up of an organisational design (OD) process that was: contracted with and owned by the organisation; visibly open and transparent to the business; able to hold a space for the difficult contracting of differences between multiple stakeholders – in particular, the relationship between my organisation and its parent; and, finally, secure enough to allow leaders to come up with radical new solutions, even if that came with a human cost. Here are the main elements to the change, the OD process and my leadership that illustrate the alchemical power of Container leadership alongside Edge and Tension.

Overall, I advocated that the OD process be run in a professional and holistic way – not by dreaming up a new organisational structure on the back of an envelope, or designing an organisation around special favours to certain individuals (I have seen both of these approaches used in restructuring and they breed difficulty). To that end, I brought in a very talented OD leader who quickly gained the trust of my boss, the CEO and my executive team colleagues. When a professional OD process was laid out, incorporating several work streams of business processes, people and culture, as well as the structural elements of organisational design, it created confidence in the organisation that this process would be objective and well run, even if there was natural anxiety as to what the solution and outcomes might be.

Building Networks to Reduce Anxiety and Liberate Creativity

I set an essential 'hard rule' for this OD process, and that was that the entire design be leader-led, i.e., run and owned by our business leaders, not outside consultants, nor subcontracting the task internally to the HR function. This rule took a lot of fierce holding, as I was asking for the commitment of 10 internal business leaders for almost half of their time over a 6-month period, all of whom were key senior talent running significant parts of the commercial operation. I needed to gain the trust of my executive team colleagues to release their key players. But I remained non-anxious and firm in asking for this, at one point saying, if it were not done this way then we should forget about doing it at all.

With my CEO and colleagues bought into the containing structure of the OD process, and signed up to commissioning this 10-strong working team to drive the effort, I also asked for a sub-group of the executive team to work with me. The primary task of this group was to steer the efforts of the working team and, ultimately, determine and recommend the new organisational model to our executive colleagues and the CEO. This reduced anxiety and feelings of loss of control at the top – a frequent (and uncontained) occurrence in many restructuring efforts that are delegated away from the top team.

The establishment of the working group of 10 business leaders became a major success factor in the OD process and the change as a whole. It brought strong cross-business ownership (across contentious and even competing product organisations) and intimate knowledge of the drain-pipes of the organisation. Their task was to do the necessary leg work of analysing the current work processes, roles and organisational structure, interrogate the future business needs and come up with organisational design options that could take the business into this future. This team met, unfailingly, every 2 weeks on a Monday morning. While this sched-ule and the various work streams provided a good structural container, it was the atmosphere we created at these team meetings that made all the difference.

I aimed to be at every one of these meetings, providing a consistent, affirming and encouraging presence. In addition, my executive sub-team colleagues joined. We had many crunchy conversations – which had been well prepared and were well moderated in the meeting itself (another good containing element). An important advantage of the con-taining structure of the OD process was that it directed and channelled energy to the real issues – not the political fluff – and moved all conver-sations away from assertion to fact-based dialogue. One of the hard rules was, 'no sacred cows' for the organisational design, so you can imagine that we encouraged this working team to be radical and take risks, at times requiring them to come up with a solution that might threaten the security of their 'home' organisation. Having the executive members alongside them, as well as a newfound holistic knowledge of the whole company, gave them the encouragement and air cover to be bold.

Never underestimate the containing anxiety-settling power of setting up networks across your organisation's boundaries, which allows leaders from different parts of your system to be able to see and appreciate the whole.

Containment that Transforms Conflicting Relationships and the Insecurity of Not Knowing

While this OD network team was working away, building extraordinary ownership for the process and its outcomes, another major task for me was to manage the sometimes-awkward relationship between my organisation and our parent organisation. In the face of some cynicism and scepticism, I insisted that our parent organisation not be seen as an obstructing difficulty, but rather as an important resource that required a place and a voice within the design process.

I therefore set up an interface group at this boundary, comprising senior members of both my organisation and our parent, whose primary task was to take the emerging outputs of the OD team and propose any necessary adjustments – based on the mission and strategic direction of the parent. Again, this took some tough conversations, and much eye rolling on both sides, but I persisted in keeping the two parties in contact, and, for the first time in a long while, some real breakthrough ideas emerged for one of the key commercial processes that sat across the two entities.

Finally, another key feature in the change was how to keep the wider organisation informed and up to date. Very often restructurings are done 'in the dark' for fear of creating even greater insecurity in the organisation, but I knew that if this fear were to be left unexpressed then it would only make matters worse. To that end, I implemented a series of 'Just Talk' sessions in all major staff locations. These were monthly engagement sessions open to any staff who wanted to show up for a 2-h conversation, including lunch, when they could interact with executive team members and raise any subjects that were on their mind. I recall even now the anxious faces of my colleagues when I made the proposal, 'But, what will we talk about Deborah, if we don't have anything to say, and what if people raise dangerous subjects, or, have questions that we don't have answers to?'

I stuck to my guns, coached my colleagues on how to simply hold a safe and open conversational space, without getting defensive or overbearing, and we went ahead. I confess I also felt a little nervous when I stood up to introduce the first Just Talk session in front of around 50 staff, not knowing at all what was going to happen. However, by framing it openly as an opportunity to raise difficult subjects, during which *everyone* could support each other – this was not just about staff members putting their top leaders on the spot – it somehow made the process a lot more open and human. Of course, the sessions did have difficulties and some conflict, but I had said that the more edgy they were, the greater I would see their success. The sessions provided some means to build trust and receptivity to the organisational design process. And, by the time we got to implementation, our staff members already knew what was coming – even if they didn't agree with the solution.

Containment Allows Tough Transitions

Container leadership is not just about providing safe spaces for processing difficult emotions, it is also about doing the necessary things to keep your organisation safe and viable – but done in a mindful way. Facing up to tough decisions, holding consequences and sticking with unpopular decisions are all part of this. While people might not like what you choose to do, the essential thing is that you are transparent, robust and consistent, and that they feel they are in safe hands.

In this story, the OD solution was certainly different. It entailed a complete tilt of the organisation away from central control to an enabling central organisation and an empowered local organisation. A completely new role was created at the executive team level, which necessitated a major change to several roles and positions in the top team. New, more agile product development and business planning processes were installed. All of this came with a price, including human impact. While I'm not saying it was the perfect OD process, and my leadership had as many wobbles as good qualities, we nonetheless made and implemented some tough decisions that helped take the business to a different level.

When I was at my best in this restructuring I knew I was consciously attending to the quality of my *being*, and not just my *doing*, as a leader.

Container Leadership – Combining the Internal (Being) and the External (Doing)

Table 7.1 summarises the essential practices for doing effective Container leadership. To remind, it is the first three practices that are the crucial differentiators: robustly and non-anxiously standing up for your beliefs; providing affirming and encouraging signals to others; and creating safe spaces to have the difficult conversations. While the other two practices – setting and contracting boundaries, and creating aligning networks – are important, they do not make the difference between successful and unsuccessful change. I hypothesise that is because they also require the least emotional risk.

As I mentioned earlier, our study showed that the senior leaders who were the most successful in pulling off large complex change combined the externally exhibited practice of Container leadership with the internal *being* capacity of Acknowledging the Whole. In Table 7.2 I repeat its

Table 7.1 Container – *safety strengthens.*

Holds and channels disturbance into purposeful energy

Is self-assured, confident and takes a stand for one's belief – is non-anxious in challenging conditions – works to create the space to be 'off the stage'

Provides affirming and encouraging signals: builds ownership, trust and confidence

Makes it safe to speak out and say risky things and have the hard-to-have conversations through empathy and high quality dialogue skills

Sets and contracts boundaries, clear outcomes, expectations and hard rules so that people know what to operate on and have the trust and freedom to make it happen

Creates alignment at the top and builds networks of relationships to ensure consistency and constancy of approach

Table 7.2 Acknowledging the Whole – *integrates all that happens.*

Is able to see that all that arises – even difficulty and disturbance – needs attending to and given a place so that the whole system can be seen and gains strength (what gets excluded stays!)

Notices and uses data about one's own feelings, impulses and physical sensations as visible signs as to what is being felt and experienced in their team, organisation or wider society

Views all experience as what, in some way, is meant to happen – giving everything that arises a place, and a purpose (senses the *system's* intentionality)

Has an open-minded, expansive and inclusive mindset that is able to use multiple interpretations of what is being experienced in order to build up an accurate picture of reality

Views difficulty and disturbance not as obstacles or barriers but rather an important resource to learn from and be acknowledged so that the whole system gains strength

Is conscious of how their systemic leadership can model to others non-reactivity, wider perspective taking and the facing of difficulty so that they build the capacity for greater mindfulness in others

description as a guide to understanding the superlative Container leadership shown in my final story in this chapter. A leader's capacity to hold and work with difficulty, using their inner experience as a guide to creating movement in their surrounding system, is the *sine qua non* of successful top flight Container leadership. Read and absorb both these tables, and start to note the connections you see between them. For example, it is nigh on impossible to encourage others to have the risky conversations (Container) if you don't first possess an open and inclusive mindset (Acknowledging the Whole).

Top Level Container Leadership in Action – Successfully Moving an Entire Organisation Through Extreme Difficulty and Transition

I knew I could be secure around this leader – let's call him Harry – when we were both on stage together in front of an audience of 2,000 leaders. It was a nerve-wracking situation. I was responsible for interviewing, or let's say, grilling, the top executive team of my client's organisation that was going through unprecedented change. As I stepped up onto the podium, and moved into position alongside Harry, he accidentally knocked over the glass of water on the table between us and it soaked my dress.

In front of the 2,000 leaders, and with the remaining 60,000 employees in the company joining the event online, Harry gave me a small yet reassuring smile. He took out his handkerchief, very calmly offered it to me to help pat my dress dry, and then asked for it back so that he could mop up the water sluicing between us on the table. We continued with the interview. A small vignette, yet for me highly illustrative of Harry's firm-and-empathetic-under-fire leadership style.

Harry's organisation was in a major disruptive transition. After almost a century of supplying society with essential energy supplies, the market had, within the space of a few years, radically altered. As consumers were moving towards cleaner sourced forms of energy, the wholesale price for his organisation's main product had dramatically collapsed. What's more, changes in the political regime had brought in a structural supply decision that was to wipe out a large chunk of his operating profit. Society, which had benefited greatly from this organisation in the past, was now shunning it for polluting the planet. His division, 23,000 staff members based throughout Europe, were feeling under siege as activist groups physically attacked plants and endangered employees' well-being. To add to the humiliation, an organisation that had been used to providing two thirds of the generated wealth back to its parent was now a major drag on all current and future earnings. Understandably, the internal climate was an emotional melting pot veering between pride and shame, anger and resignation, acceptance and denial.

Yet, despite this extremely challenging situation, whose inherent Edge and Tension could have been paralysing, Harry's leadership achieved extraordinary outcomes: his organisation delivered €1bn of cost savings 1 year ahead of schedule, through a process that was *internally* owned and led; through extensive dialogue with both central and local politicians his team created a market model solution that can now be bought into by the various, conflicting, interest parties; and he has done all of this while retaining the motivation and dedicated commitment of his board and direct reports. In fact, this is a very good story to illustrate that when a whole system is going through the turmoil of major disruption, Container leadership is not just an individual property – it has to be a collective capacity held by the entire senior leadership team. And here is how he did it.

Trust as the Foundation for Container

Without trust there can be no psychological safety. And the resulting anxiety will distract people from their primary task, impacting negatively on productivity. I was very struck when I read Harry's Behavioural Event Interview (BEI) transcript by something he said to the interviewer right at the beginning. He gave her complete permission to be in charge of the interview. Now, I read all 88 of the BEI transcripts, and it was standard interviewer protocol to say early on that the format would be rigorous and structured, necessitating that they probe and intervene in the interviewee's story. Normally, everyone would say in response a simple 'Yes, that's fine'. However here's what Harry said.

> Yes, for me it's fair if you interrupt me; if you say, okay, yes, I don't want to hear this or that, I want to know about that, I think it should be something that contributes to our call here, to your research. If I'm on the wrong track to what your expectations are, please feel free to guide me so that I can come to that.

What a container statement back to the interviewer. For both interviewer and interviewee, the BEI can be an anxious process. Two complete strangers, usually by phone, conducting an in-depth interview that is being recorded, and which will be assessed both for the interviewee's leadership and for the interviewer's BEI competence. Notwithstanding this stress-inducing circumstance, Harry had an inner capacity to instinctively give trust to the interviewer to own and run the interview. Not only that, he gave voice to this trust, which led to the interviewer saying in response, 'I promise I will do that'. Already, just 5.44 min into the interview, a trustful, secure and energetic relational contract had been created.

I next noticed the title that Harry gave to his story, a task that, again, was standard BEI protocol. He chose to title his story of leading change, 'Taking people along and motivating them for ambitious targets'. If *taking people along* is not a container-redolent title, I don't know what is. He could, just as easily, have chosen words such as, 'Rescuing an organisation on the brink of bankruptcy'. Before I even started the quantitative coding of the story's behavioural data, it was becoming clear to me that Harry trusted his organisation to do this change with him. Here he is recounting how his team took that early fateful decision, a bold decision that became the key ingredient as to why this change was so successful.

> So the external frame is that we are in a tremendous change of our market environment, so we had to work on improvements of the organisation, reduction of costs and change of business model. Before the organisation formally started, from the very beginning, my board colleagues and I took the risk that we trusted our team, that they will deliver the ambitious contributions needed to meet the market changes.

Harry made a conscious and explicit choice to empower his organisation to deliver the change – *I took the risk that we trusted our team.* And this was not because he and his team had no ideas themselves, as they did, rather, he knew that the only way to get through this tough situation, and get through it quickly, was to build his entire organisation as a trusted and capable team that could deliver. This is precisely what is meant by the second Container practice, 'Provides affirming and encouraging signals: builds ownership, trust and confidence'. Harry was secure enough in himself to adopt this strategy even though he acknowledged it as a risk. In that respect, he also demonstrated the third inner capacity in Acknowledging the Whole, 'Has an open minded, expansive and inclusive mindset'.

Authorisation Around Real Work Builds Energetic Action

Upon Container's bedrock of trust, Harry and his team then set about giving clear, unambiguous performance guidance to the organisation. Here he is describing how he kicked off the change at a leadership meeting. Notice how he not only contracts with his people *what* they have to deliver – solutions to address the performance problems, he also makes very clear his expectations for *how* this it to be delivered.

> At the kick off we taught them about the market conditions and our environment, and said, 'How would you solve the problems? You, our direct reports, are to make proposals to us and we will discuss together.' There was a certain surprise that we from the very beginning said that you are the guys. They felt this was a very authentic first step, coming from their former organisation where it was more top-down. The team then understood, 'Okay, we have to solve our own problems and not wait for the board to give us targets.'

Impersonal command and control leadership can be a defence against anxiety. It's a style that makes you feel in charge even when not in control of the situation. However Harry knew that this style of leadership would only create helpless dependency on the organisation's leaders – a dangerous approach in such a fast-moving market. It would short circuit the building of adaptive capacity deep in the organisation to be alert to finding new solutions for the ambitious cost reduction targets.

It was, however, a completely countercultural move to the preceding leadership style. So Harry had to keep fiercely modelling and reinforcing this radically empowering approach, holding his own role authority, while at the same time requiring his whole organisation to be independent and resourceful.

> Some of our direct reports said, 'Yes, who on the board will take care of this?' And, I said, 'No, the next step is with you and you amongst yourselves. Most of the things you know better than we do. Organise yourselves and come up with a proposal.' It was a very important signal that we weren't asking for feedback all the time. It's about personal commitment and personal demonstration that we trust them.

In the end, his organisation delivered a €1bn performance improvement ahead of schedule that far exceeded what was thought possible.

> The crucial point for our executives and our employees is that it was very motivating and they are proud of the targets that they set themselves, and which they delivered on. So they have been both committed and successful, and in fact, have accelerated delivery. And the self-organisation of them was really the first step; this was the accelerator to come to a really fast solution.

So, across this change story Harry demonstrated the fourth Container practice, 'Sets and contracts boundaries, clear outcomes, expectations and hard rules so that people know what to operate on and have the trust and freedom to make it happen'. This, combined with the early-established bedrock of trust, brought his whole organisation to life, even though they knew that they were creating solutions with painful human impact. When Container leadership is strong, and you have created the right psychological environment, it challenges the truism that says you can never use a change approach comparable to turkeys voting for Christmas.

And notice how Harry's clear authorisation for the organisation to find its own way through the change demonstrated another crucial element of

Acknowledging the Whole, 'Is conscious of how their systemic leadership can model to others non-reactivity, wider perspective taking and the facing of difficulty so that they build the capacity for greater mindfulness in others'. At all times, Harry intentionally used his personal leadership to convey strong signals to the organisation. This took a lot of skill, and it began with him being able to tune into his own inner state and regulate his emotional response in stressful situations.

The Fierceness of Authenticity

When people show up in all their humanity it enables others to do the same. This is strong Container leadership as, whatever the feelings or insecurities or difficulty, people feel secure in the presence of truth. This is how strong containment enables Edge and Tension to be bearable. Whenever there is disturbance, leaders need to create spaces for people to be able to discharge their feelings. Here is Harry describing how he likes his leadership to be.

> It is a personal principle for me – but I also know it from the feedback I get – it is really being authentic, no story telling but really telling the truth, explaining how the situation is and nothing else. Saying, okay, what do I know and what do I not know? And really showing that I am present, and recognising what is going on, in a small conference, or in a meeting. I try to find out what are the worries, and what are the insecurities not only with regards to the business but also the personal.

Here is an example of when he put this self-assured truth-telling authenticity into practice. Container leadership requires that you also stick to your guns.

> I still have an issue with my executives, some of them remain a little bit black and white and I'm still feeling that we are in a certain comfort zone, and that they feel we have time to change our business model. So on the one hand I want to keep the people motivated, but on the other hand I had to tell them, 'Okay, you should also feel uncomfortable. This situation will not change, we will not come back to a stable situation that we have had over years and years, and if we do not contribute to this, then at the end the company will not survive.' In the long run these kinds of people cannot stay in the company. It demonstrates to the organisation that the top leaders have to be really willing to bring the business forward.

Spot here Harry's inner capacity to 'View difficulty and disturbance not as obstacles or barriers but rather an important resource to learn from and be acknowledged so that the whole system gains strength'. I know – from outside of the research context – that Harry has had to close plants and exit many staff from his organisation. Many change leaders have to do that, that's nothing new. However, the way in which he has done that – acknowledging people's pain, honouring all contributions, not sweeping things under the carpet – has ensured that his departing employees feel recognised and that his remaining organisation stays committed.

This capacity to acknowledge that being in discomfort is a competency to be cultivated, and not a source of irritation or frustration, enables Harry to practise the first element of Container leadership with great poise, 'Is self-assured, confident and takes a stand for one's belief – is non-anxious in challenging conditions'.

Changing Meetings to Change Culture

Not only did Harry at the meta level calmly steward his organisation through major transition, he also turned to the power of the present moment to accomplish cultural change. He knew that by simply changing how meetings get run – especially in the senior leadership teams – you systemically change the whole company atmosphere. Management meetings are the most potent yet underutilised crucibles to effect change. How many do you attend where you just seem to rattle through the agenda, cramming the meeting full of content, not allowing the space for creativity or feelings to surface, and where the conversations seem to be going round in circles, with people not really listening or learning? Too many, I am sure.

Harry knew that his organisation did not have the time or money for inefficient and ineffective top team meetings. So he created well contained transforming meetings that had significant business and cultural impact. One very simple way in which he did that was to take the lessons of a leadership programme he had been on and adopt the practice of using meeting observers. These meeting observers were not outside consultants or facilitators, but team members who personally volunteered to take turns to observe their colleagues' behaviour and team meeting dynamics, intervene when they felt it could improve meeting quality and provide feedback at the meeting's end. Here's Harry describing what happened.

> The next step was how to set up a feedback culture more clearly; how to make meetings more interactive and nominate observers.

This was another step to change the mindset. But this also changed something in the way we are working together. It makes meetings more efficient; it shows also more emotional things so, for example, this morning at our board meeting we made a check in. And then also some personal things are coming on the table, not every meeting but it is an element that makes it easier to think about difficult decisions.

Fascinating. By providing a safe space to process feelings top leaders are able to take difficult decisions more easily. This is exemplary Edge and Tension alongside Container leadership. And let's not underestimate the inner capacities this required of Harry in a culture unused to accessing this kind of intelligence, the intelligence of emotions. While unnatural for him too, he learned that he needed to be able to tune into his own feelings in order to be able to get into better contact with the felt experience of his people. Here he is in action again, very aptly demonstrating the first inner capacity in Acknowledging the Whole, 'Notices and uses data about one's own feelings, impulses, and physical sensations as visible signs as to what is being felt and experienced in their team, organisation or wider society'.

So formally I would never have done this, but I then said, 'Okay, colleagues I feel I'm maybe today not in the situation to really be able to get in contact with you'. And then I asked them, 'What are the issues you have now and let's take a flip chart', I wrote them down and then we changed the agenda and we talked about them. So that's an example of how to invite people to be a little bit more emotionally present. Most of our people are engineers because we are technically driven. They are normally strong fact based or cost based, which sometimes hinders us to come to different solutions or to be open, or to be honest with people.

The wider cultural shift that occurred as a consequence of Harry using meetings as more open feedback spaces, where people could feel what they really wanted to feel, was that his organisation became more able to innovate and take risks. Again, this shift that Harry enabled is not to be underestimated in a culture in which any error could literally cost a human life. Here he is explaining what happened.

So if we do feedback and if we talk about meetings and about the top leaders and the feedback comes okay, such as, this topic went well, this was not very good because the preparation was missing, the mistake culture also changes. So I now more often hear that somebody says, 'Okay, understood, I could have done this better,' without them worrying about, 'It's my mistake now'.

The Art of Fierce Conversations

A final significant feature of Harry's Container leadership was his ability to confront the truth in a situation – not just speaking his truth, the authenticity I described earlier, but being able to create safe spaces to allow *others* to speak out. Here is one excerpt that reveals his truth-confronting skill.

> We have a proposal for a decision based on a commercial evalu-
> ation but this proposal did not include the impact on people.
> And when I went into the discussion I asked my team to take a
> wider perspective. So I proactively provided feedback; I don't do
> it generally in the meeting, I do it before or afterwards individu-
> ally. In that way they don't start explaining why. So if it is a
> conversation with some personal behavioural comments, I do
> this bilaterally and I tell them, 'Okay, there is something I want to
> share with you'.

Harry built an overall culture in this company where it was 'Safe to speak out and say risky things and have the hard-to-have conversations through empathy and high quality dialogue skills', the third essential practice of Container leadership. Places to simply let off steam were set up even deeper in his organisation, as one of his teams implemented what became to be known as the 'Anger Rooms' in the most negatively impacted plants. These rooms were dedicated meeting spaces where staff could show up to safely express all of their annoyance, rage and displeasure about what was happening to them. Again, not to take away the difficulty, but to create a culture in which the depth of people's feelings was given a place, where they could be seen. And the strength of this culture was very much influenced by Harry's leadership, what he encouraged in his team, and what he modelled to the entire organisation.

Container Summary: Arriving Where You Want to Be and Having People Know They Are Seen

Containment is the capacity of you and your organisation to internally manage the troubling thoughts, feelings and behaviours that arise as a consequence of anxiety. If these troubling elements are not managed the unprocessed anxiety will lead to defensive routines designed to reduce anxiety. Be that denial of necessary change or diffused accountability structures, these routines may make people feel more secure but they keep the system stuck. Which of course, in the end, will only create more anxiety!

Container leadership is acutely needed in any major change process. It can channel the troubling energy that will get stoked up by Edge and Tension and make people feel secure enough to venture into difficult and challenging experiences. The primary way to do this is to first manage your own inner state and become non-anxious. The task then becomes providing an affirming and encouraging presence for others, creating safe places for people to talk about difficulty and take risks. It's not a soft and easy practice, as it also requires the fierce upholding of boundaries and the inner capacity to see disturbance not as an obstacle but a resource to learn from.

At the very end of Harry's interview, we asked him for his definition of mindfulness. Without hesitation he told us, 'Really arriving where I want to be; whether it is a meeting or whether I'm at a site, *and making the people aware that I recognise them*.' Mindfulness is about really arriving where you want to be – a wonderful way of expressing how the inner state of leadership is about having your attention in the moment follow your intention. And more than that, it's about ensuring that others around you are seen, and recognised – giving others the sustained gift of your attention.

During my own restructuring story related in this chapter, my Container skills were also called upon in a role that I would never, ever, have wished for. And that was to help one of my best friends through the harrowing process of fighting, and eventually losing, her battle with cancer. She was a great business leader herself. We had many moving and painfully difficult conversations about her illness through-out this period where we processed what she was going through, and the role she was asking me to perform: guiding her through the medi-cal information and her choices at every stage, interfacing with her family, the medical staff and ultimately legal/financial professionals. At all times in her extreme anxiety she needed to know that she was seen and recognised. Indeed, that her whole life had been fully seen and recognised. When that occurred, she felt sufficiently strong and calm to face her ending.

The experience brought Container leadership all together for me. Acting as a non-anxious container for others, strong and secure enough to hold and guide them through difficult emotions and painful transition, while not taking over, is one of the most precious roles we can take on for another human being, or human system. It demands us to be present.

It calls on our compassion. It brings out our dignity. It can also bring out the depths in us as we learn to confront our own insecurity and darkest fears. It's a transforming and generous act. And, more generally, I believe our workplaces and society at large would become more enriching, secure and freer places if we could all build up the courage and selflessness to master it.

8

The Time for Emergence

I would love to live
Like a river flows,
Carried by the surprise
Of its own unfolding

John O'Donohue, Fluent

In the opening stanza to a poem I wrote following the reunion with my biological mother, I tried to capture that moment of sheer emergence about which John O'Donohue so beautifully writes:

I saw her coming through Herbert Park,
My hands stuck cold tight to a second gin
In the bar of that Dublin hotel.
How many more steps to go, I guessed,
Before what?

Emergence can be defined as the act of becoming known, or coming into view after being concealed – often with startling novelty. After 43 years, I was about to be seen once again by the parent who had had to give me away. And she was about to be seen by me, the child who had always roamed, and wondered.

While we both held this deepest of heartfelt intents – to experience truth, and in so doing, reconcile pain – neither of us had any idea what was going to happen, nor did we know whether we were even going to like each other. We had established some prior connection via writing and swapping photos, equipping ourselves for the journey, but beyond that, our burning intention and a few boundaries we had set for the reunion, primarily where and when to meet, on that day in Dublin it felt like 'press play and see what happens.'

Still Moving: How to Lead Mindful Change, First Edition. Deborah Rowland.
© 2017 John Wiley & Sons Ltd. Published 2017 by John Wiley & Sons Ltd.

Welcome to the unpredictable unfolding world of emergence, where much can result from a few well-chosen moves, and surprisingly new global patterns arise out of local-level chaos – as long as you can spot the ripest of issues that require attention, intentionally set up experimentation there, and then be prepared to take a leap into the dark, giving up any control over outcomes, moving step by step, just as sailors have to navigate the vast Mississippi river from bend to bend. In a sense, having set up these initial conditions for emergence, you have to let the change come towards you, not go chasing it.

What if we were to look on organisational life, and leading change, in the same way? In certain respects, it might feel more effortless. In this chapter I move beyond your personal leadership and *consider your role as the architect for the overall change approach in your system.* And I put forward the in-depth case for emergence as the most appropriate choice of change approach in today's unpredictable and uncontrollable world.

Put simply, the combination of my leadership experience, my understanding of the changing context and consistent research findings across 12 years all point to the same essential message: *in situations of high complexity, volatility and uncontrollability, leading change in an emergent way can bring about new results far more quickly and successfully than other change approaches.*

But, as emergent change works against the grain, it takes a certain kind of leadership. It requires us to address challenges in a fundamentally different way. And this demands effort. Doing change through a messier step-by-step, trial-and-error, bottom-up approach, when there is pressure on leaders to roll out high-profile, perfectly engineered, outcome-guaranteed and centrally governed corporate change programmes, takes both humility and guts. The humility to acknowledge that you don't have answers yourself, and the guts to trust the system to find its answers with you – and maybe even say *no* when external change consultants come knocking on your door with their latest transformation methodology.

But, stay with me, and prepare to be carried by the surprise of the unfolding of this chapter's journey, as emergence could be your most powerful, pre-existing – yet underutilised asset.

What is 'Emergence'?

Local Interactions Create Higher-Level Patterns

Let's continue with the river metaphor. Emergence, while self-organising, is not anarchy. It *is* governed by some underlying properties. Something arises at the higher level as a consequence of multiple interactions between the components of a system at the lower level.[1] In the case of O'Donohue's flowing river, its own unfolding might be governed by obvious elements such as the gradient of the river's fall, or the amount of rainfall in the previous month. Less obvious, yet still influential on the river's unfolding could be the number and shape of the rocks lying on the riverbed, how narrow or wide its basin, even how many otters have made their homes in the riverbank that year. All of these local elements, in their (unknowing and unintentional) interconnection, create the flowing river that we see.

So, it's hard to understand emergence when you examine parts in isolation, or attribute causality to just one factor. It's the interactions among the multiple parts that count. How many times while out driving have you encountered a traffic jam that seems to have arisen for no apparent reason? At one moment, the cars all start to slow down. And equally mystifying, after a while, the traffic jam just dissolves, and off you go again – and yet no accident, or roadworks.

Was it all down to just one idling driver at the front? Unlikely. Researchers in the science of what is called *complex adaptive systems* have modelled traffic jams as emergent phenomena and identified that they are a result of the interaction between the distance between the cars and how many times drivers swap lanes. These two tiny local rules govern how the whole fleet of cars behaves. Local interactions that appear random have resulted in discernible macro level order. And while we are wired to look for the pace makers, there is no single car, or driver, commanding the show. The system is a self-organising one.

The Self-Organising Power of Networks

As leaders we are often less in direct control of what is going on in our organisation than we would like to think, especially as we become more senior and thereby operationally distant from where results are produced. Moreover, as I have argued in Chapter 2, our world is becoming more interdependent and less unilaterally controllable. And even if top leaders *do* know what the answer is in today's fast changing landscape, which I contend is nigh on impossible, it is now far less easy in a world of crumbling hierarchies and snowballing peer-to-peer networks to change organisations, or wider society, from on high.

Just witness the emergence of The Anonymous group, a loosely associated international network of online entities. A website commonly associated with the group describes it as an internet gathering 'with a very loose and decentralised command structure that operates on ideas rather than directives'. Originated in 2003, the concept was adopted by a self-organising online community acting towards a loosely self-agreed goal, primarily focused on entertainment.

Over the years, the network has emerged and adapted into acts of collaborative hactivism, targeting groups such as the Church of Scientology, child pornography sites and corporations such as Sony, and also widespread activism – so-called Anons were early supporters of the global Occupy movement and the Arab Spring. While supporters call the group 'digital Robin Hoods' and critics have described them as a 'cyber lynchmob', their attempts to bring down extremists' websites and pro-ISIS (Islamic State of Iraq and Syria) Twitter accounts following the Charlie Hebdo shootings and the November 2015 Paris attacks, certainly had an impact.

Yet no Chief Executive, governing council or strategic grand plan. It has effortlessly evolved and innovated of its own collective accord.

Change is Always Here – You Don't Have To 'Bring' It

Just as flowing rivers, traffic jams and digital activist groups are self-directed complex adaptive systems, so too are organisations. Our workplaces are full of myriad interacting elements – teams, departments, resources, processes, buildings, structures (*complex*), loosely held together by a common purpose (*system*), and whose self-organising properties create patterns and outcomes (*adaptive*). Much of what happens on the ground is unplanned as people go about their daily work, bumping into colleagues in corridors, taking a risk and sticking your neck out in a meeting, having an inspiring chance conversation with a new joiner by the coffee machine, adopting a slight change to how you answer a call in a customer call centre.

And each chance conversation, each moment of encounter, each tiny experiment, while seemingly random on the ground, can have a surprising and changing impact on the overall outcome – as long as you have an open and richly interconnected culture. Change is, in fact, happening all the time. It's not something you have to *bring* to the system; it's an inherent property of organisational life.[2,3]

The question becomes, how do you make your naturally self-organising system more adaptive to changing environments? Can emergence be shaped? The component elements in a river system are unaware that they are interacting to create the global pattern. When a driver changes lanes they cannot see how this impacts the whole stretch of cars. But, as a leader, you can certainly help the different parts of your organisation connect across boundaries (be they vertical power distances or lateral peer-to-peer), in order that they see how they are systemically creating the whole. Imagine how adaptively powerful that single act of leadership could be.

So, while it is hard to control, this so-called emergent, unfolding, more ground-up and self-directed change *can* be harnessed. In fact, it can very quickly lead to new patterns and outcomes across large complex systems (this is why emergent change is *not*, as some people think, continuous improvement such as Six Sigma or Lean, which addresses lots of individually located process change). As long as the initial conditions are set, emergent change can rapidly go viral.

How You Do Change Determines Where You End Up

I have now highlighted the meaning of *emergence* – the formation of new global structures arising out of the unfolding and self-organising interaction between a system's component parts. Understanding emergence is central to understanding how complex systems form.

From the moment when Steven Johnson wrote his groundbreaking book, *Emergence* (1999), where he showed convincingly how complex organisms – including ant colonies, city neighbourhoods, Artificial Intelligence and the distributed networks in the human brain – could assemble and transform themselves without any master planner calling the shots, I became fascinated. Emergence just felt so natural, elegant and simple. And emergent systems can be brilliant innovators, as they tend to be more adaptive to sudden change than rigid hierarchical models. As a lifelong change theorist and practitioner, I felt this was a genuinely new avenue of inquiry.

And when asked by the Anglo-Dutch energy giant, Shell, to design and deliver a programme to develop their change skills during a significant period of transition, I introduced the notion of *emergent change* to their leaders. This was not without risk for me as it was such a radically new approach and it required me, in a rational logical culture, to ground emergent change in the science of complex adaptive systems (I told them about the need to give up control as a leader later...). What gave me the courage though was beyond science, I had a super client in Shell's change team who was prepared to be innovative and she partnered with me on this programme. But above all else, I had used it in my leadership and I had used it in my life, and *it just worked*.

At that time I characterised emergent change as: within a general overall goal, stimulating change at the periphery of a system around ripe local issues; using trial and error and experimentation; trusting and allowing people to self-organise; fostering lateral networks; and balancing out the goal of improving economic value *with* building organisational capability to cope with whatever arises. And I differentiated this emergent change approach from a *programmatic change* approach, which I characterised as: launching change and targets top-down or from the centre; moving in a linear fashion; assuming people are driven by inertia and require controlling; and with the sole goal of improving economic value.

We Try to Get to New Places Using Old Approaches

Teasing out the essential differences between these two approaches was illuminating. It's easy to deny you do the latter and claim prowess in the former. But that's not what I saw happening in practice, not just at Shell but across many organisations. The default standard operating procedure approach to change tended to be controlled and linear: create a vision, launch it, build alliances, roll out the roadmap, change behaviour, measure progress and align your systems. We have all grown up in this change model. Not only did leaders lead change that way, their organisations expected to be led in this way too: tell us where to go, assure us we will get there. And I saw the programmatic-type approach proving very costly, with at times pip-squeak return on investment (unless, of course, you were the supplier of these programmes). It's an excessively simple model for what are usually very messy circumstances.

This experience led me to a research study in my consultancy called, *Is Change Changing?*, from which we created a more nuanced set of four change approaches, two of which assumed that change was straightforward and linear – Directive and Self-Assembly change – and two of which assumed that change was in fact complex and non-linear – Masterful and Emergent change. These approaches, including the research findings, are written up in my first book, *Sustaining Change*. In a nutshell, Directive and Self-Assembly change lead to lots of busy action, and Masterful and Emergent Change are able to create movement. The former two layer change onto a system. The latter two change the system from its source.

This piece of work still feels fresh and alive when I consult with leaders today. Most are unaware that change *can* be approached in different ways, and they therefore unwittingly repeat the familiar. Time and attention is directed towards debating the *what* of the change, for example, the articulation of a new vision and set of values, working out a compelling story for the change, the design of a new organisational structure, the launch of an innovation platform, the remodelling of a business process, figuring out a new approach to delivering services to customers.

It is rare that I hear explicit talk about the *how* of the change, in other words, *how do we move our organisation towards this new future*, whatever the change and desired future happens to be. What process should we use to create the vision and values? Do we prototype the change in certain parts of the organisation, or do we roll it out everywhere? Do we ask for volunteers or do we assign people to project teams? Do we find solutions in the senior levels, or bring together a cross-section of the whole company. Do we build change skills and, if so, which ones are needed? Do we communicate via central messaging or via informal storytelling? How will we build in feedback as we go?

There are choices in the how. Do you discuss them with your colleagues? Most organisations I encounter only embark on change if they can travel in ways that reinforce existing patterns. So I see leaders attempting to get to a new place through methods they have always used. It is so hard to do new things differently! And yet my research points out how fateful is your choice of change approach. The way in which you travel fundamentally determines where you end up.

In both my original and most recent study, in contexts of high magnitude change, Masterful and Emergent change approaches are the most successful, accounting for around 40% of the variance between successful and less successful change. After your personal leadership, your choice of change approach is the second biggest swing factor influencing the change outcome. Conversely, Self-Assembly change (a euphemism for what I also call a *spray and pray*, lets-launch-a-lot-of-initiatives-and-hope-some-of-them-stick tool-kit change approach) and Directive change (lets-drive-a-one-look-change-from top-down-and-any-resistance-is-quashed change approach), lead to failure. These two approaches explained almost half of the reason as to why big change fails.

What is Emergent Change?

Over the years I have taken the science of studying emergence within complex adaptive systems, translated it into the messiness of leaders implementing change and identified six core practices that work.

Emergent Change Practice 1: Set an Overall Intention and Direction, Establish a Few Hard Rules to Guide Behaviour and then Allow Self-Organisation

Emergence does need well-bounded spaces. While the future might be unknowable and the strategy to get there fuzzy (indeed, Johnson claims that ignorance is useful when leading emergence), leading emergent change nonetheless requires you to set a loose direction, or intention, as purpose has a cohering presence. Another boundary that can be set to allow self-organisation to flourish is the guiding hand of a few hard rules that govern *how* you wish your organisation to work towards its purpose. These rules build the capacity of the system to cope with whatever arises – more than a little helpful in unpredictable dynamic environments where it is impossible for you to predict and control what happens.

And by *few hard rules* to govern how your people think and act I do *not* mean that you articulate a set of 30,000-feet-high noble sounding values. No. Remember the cars and traffic jams. You command self-organising complex systems by setting out the laws that govern *micro level* behaviour, as it is at this local level where interactions and decision rules make a difference to the whole. And this central tenet, that local rules create higher-level order, enabling your organisation to be self-assured, agile and adapt of its own accord, has been around for millennia.

The entire Viking culture, spread out across many successful trading routes that took them far beyond their Scandinavian homeland to places such as North Africa, Russia and even North America, was governed by just four laws: Be Brave and Aggressive (which included sub-clauses such as: use varying methods of attack; don't plan everything in detail); Be Prepared (with sub-clauses including: keep weapons in good condition; and keep in shape); Be a Good Merchant (which included: don't demand overpayment; arrange things so that you can return); and Keep the Camp in Order (which included: make sure everybody does useful work; arrange enjoyable activities that strengthen the group).

Just four laws – and you can see how concrete and specific they were – governed an entire group of people that lived from the late eighth to the early eleventh century, and who (as well as doing the odd spot of raping and pillaging) peacefully traded with almost every country of the then-known world. Emergent change is nothing new; it's something we have just forgotten. Perhaps bulldozed out over the past two centuries with the rise of the more top-down mechanistic controlling Industrial Age. Yet, today, we are returning to a less top-down controllable era.

The few hard rules that govern the decentralised network of the online Anonymous group include: not disclosing one's identity (in public places during protests members wear Guy Fawkes masks); not talking about the group; and not attacking media. Arguably the most successful rugby union team of all time – the New Zealand All Blacks – are governed by the ABC rules set by team coach Steve Hansen: assume something through analysis; believe nothing and go out and confirm it; change and adapt if the opposition have changed their pattern. His coaching style and ABC rules keep simplicity and clarity, so that the players can then repeatedly be in good places ready to make good calls – without him having to call the shots once the game is in play.

These kinds of hard rules can be set in the workplace. And they are *not* micro-management, far from it. Clear boundaries can be liberating. Once you have set the overall direction, for example, 'to move to upper quartile performance in our industry', and carefully chosen and articulated the few hard rules (and I counsel you to do that *with* the organisation, based on intelligence about the concrete behaviour that produces improved and sustained performance), for example, 'each month our refineries will share with each other three requests for help and three offers to help others', then, as I did in that Herbert Park hotel, you can simply *press play and see what happens.*

Emergent Change Practice 2: Start in a Small Way Around Ripe Issues or Hot Topics that Have Large Consequences

In emergent change you work with the belief that much comes from little. In the above oil refinery example, you wouldn't require that improved performance happens across all indicators, instead you would focus on the hot spots that seem to be most holding the organisation back; for example, a particular step in the crude oil distillation process. So you don't launch a grand change programme across all operations and all processes, but target where you go, creating and activating cells of change that might contain an answer that could help the whole.

And this type of approach to change requires good systemic observational skill. For example, consultants and medical staff at Great Ormond Street hospital identified that the greatest risk to child mortality lay in the very brief moment of time in which a child is taken out of the safety of the operating theatre and wheeled on a trolley into the Intensive Care Unit. That was their ripest issue, and they used creative ways to identify how to perform such a complex and dangerous manoeuvre at speed, including studying the pit stop teams at the McLaren Formula 1 team whose goal is to change all four tyres on a complex lethal driving machine in under 5 s.

In the business world, and via his book, *Small Data: The Tiny Clues That Uncover Huge Trends*, brand expert and organisational anthropologist Martin Lindstrom writes cogently about how by paying attention to small clues in your customer's world you can gain competitive advantage. Eschewing the increasing trend towards Big Data analysis, his approach to starting small and building momentum from there has seen him help turnaround the fortunes of the likes of Lego.

Lindstrom helped identify how Lego bricks could be cool again for the digitally obsessed younger generation, and just by noticing how an 11-year-old boy obsessed about his old scuffed pair of sneakers as a sign of his mastery at skateboarding. Apparently, all the Big Data assumptions about this generation moving totally towards the digital world were wrong. This single insight into the still current desire of young kids to proclaim mastery to their peers in the non-digital physical skill world, led Lego away from diversification into theme parks and video games and back to bricks basics.

Emergent Change Practice 3: Work Step-By-Step, Adjusting Plans As You Go, Using Trials and Experiments

Once you have your overall direction, and set of hard rules, and honed in on activating change in certain cells or around particular topics that could most unlock performance, you then go experimenting with end users, iterating the solution as you go. Emergent change is *not* about bringing a finished answer to the organisation – be that a turnaround strategy, a revised performance management process or a lean manufacturing efficiency methodology – beautifully designed and dreamt up by top management, external consultants or corporate staff groups. Instead, you test and iterate *a partially formed solution* with the target group for the change.

I find it confirming in this respect that the concept of Design Thinking is now coming of age in many corporations. Originally construed by Tim Brown at IDEO for the aesthetics of good product design,[4] this approach is now being applied to the way in which companies work and re-invent themselves. Its set of principles starts with empathy with users, and, from standing in the shoes of the so-called beneficiary of the change, you then move through a set of steps that includes the practice of prototyping – coming up with a *0.7*, or partially developed and imperfect solution, that you test and improve with your end users. At each stage, you have to be prepared to stop, learn, re-adjust your idea and even at times abort the effort if it is not going to work.

Not many corporate cultures I have worked with are naturally conducive to such a step-by-step, trial-and-error approach to change, as it values exploration and experimentation over perfection, predictability and rule following. In emergent change, however, doing what works is far more important than doing what is right. Are you able to prepare no more than the very first step, and then be entirely open to what might transpire? The push back to an emergent approach is mainly voiced along the lines of, 'Deborah, this kind of approach takes too long'. I suspect a desire to want to know and control the outcomes combined with a fear of looking like a failure is also usually in the mix. Hotbeds of innovation such as Silicon Valley are now showing us that *to fail early is to learn quickly*, and also less costly as you can 'pivot' your investment into an altered or new venture at speed.

Such lessons validate my original research finding that emergent change can get you faster, and not slower outcomes. I often muse on how much time, effort and money could be saved, and re-invested in more responsible places, if costly and perfectly engineered large-scale change programmes were aborted and diverted into more emergent-style, beneficiary-led rapid prototyping solutions instead. Simplicity is key; emergent systems can grow unwieldy when their component parts become excessively complicated.

**Emergent Change Practice 4: Build Skills in Changing
the Here-and-Now Moment, for, E.g., Effective Dialogue,
How to Run Meetings, The Art of Storytelling**

So, changing a culture to be more conducive to emergent change also requires some skill building. When you work in the unfolding flow of emergence it is crucial that you have the ability to hold off premature judgement, give up a desire to control the outcome and not rush into action (tricky in many cultures that I work in, yet rushing to action usually means you repeat what you've always done). In its place, you cultivate moment-to-moment awareness, sense-making skills, the approaching of experience with watchful curiosity, and then intervene to alter the flow when the time is right – usually when you can sense that you are on the edge of something new.

And as emergent change is about fostering local interaction and agility, building your organisation's capacity for devolved decision-taking also becomes vital. This can be tough in cultures that have learned to become dependent on the vertical hierarchy for direction, permission and approval. In these cultures I witness conversations stuck in opinions transmission, rigid cognitive debate, projective judgements and a fear of speaking out about risky topics or about what truly matters.

Nonetheless, many leadership and complexity theorists such as Johnson, but also Karl Weick, Meg Wheatley[5] and Patricia Shaw,[6] all point to the power of changing conversations as a lever to changing organisational routines and outcomes. A talent for speaking differently can be an instrument of cultural change. And the leaders I have worked with who are most able to catalyse emergent change and influence the quality of local interaction, do so primarily through the exquisite and transforming power of inquiry, the skill of asking the right questions.

Simply by building the skills to tip your organisation's conversations away from convincing-driven advocacy, and towards learning-led inquiry, you unlock your culture's capacity to shift its repeating patterns.[7,8] And please don't think of inquiry as the soft option to tough advocacy. We can find it very challenging to ask the big systemic questions that get to the underlying causes of how today's repeating patterns are formed. The skill is how to ask the big questions without provoking a defensive response from others.

The other significant capacity I have seen leaders use in emergent change is to transform the nature of their organisation's meetings. Meetings are like collapsed microcosms of the overall culture. What gets revealed in meetings – how they are structured, how they are set up, the nature of the discourse and, in particular, decision-making – is a fractal of the wider system. In emergent change, you pay close attention to what happens in meetings, and know that, by making even a small change to how meetings get run, you can de facto change the wider culture.

I once coached a Chief Executive in the UK's National Health Service, who, by simply changing how her board meetings were set up – in this instance, having no pre-set outcomes or agendas, and removing the need for her organisation to produce lengthy pre-read reports – completely transformed her organisation's culture, leading to breakthrough changes in how patient care was delivered. While her agenda-free meetings were described to me by one of her direct reports as 'explosive', the space it provided allowed all the right topics and troubling issues to come out. I say, 'simply', above. This Chief Executive had to summon up courage and rip up her past attachment to routines to take this one tiny step. Going against the grain took much effort but once in place, the change flowed with far less effort than before.

Another organisation I am working with simply uses the power of observers to transform the quality of their meeting conversations and interactions. And, as the observers are volunteers from the participating team members (no need for external coaches or consultants) this client has now created its own internal capacity for providing clear and direct feedback, one of the main fuels of emergent change. We are all adults; we know, intellectually, how to have good conversations. And if all it takes is to have volunteer meeting observers to put this into action, there is no need to roll out at best expensive, and at worst patronising, corporate training programmes on the art of effective dialogue.

Emergent Change Practice 5: Use Informal Volunteer Networks to Build Change Understanding, Energy and Novel Connections – In Particular Tune into the Periphery

Emergent change is about stimulating the natural energy of a system to do its own changing. The role of senior management is less concerned with setting direction and more involved with encouraging distributed networks of cells to generate their best ideas. And when these cells leave behind trails isolated ideas coalesce into wider movements. Working across boundaries is catalytic. This can be as simple as inviting leaders on one wave of a leadership programme to volunteer to buddy up with leaders on another wave to pass on their knowledge, a device I have used to impressive effect (our original, more directive idea in this instance was for the programme's senior management sponsors to coordinate the learning between the waves!).

Indeed, asking for volunteers is a very powerful way to tap into the latent energy of an organisation. People support what they create. More conventional-style change approaches tend to appoint people to key change roles, in emergent change you do the opposite. Now, sometimes more set-piece types of change are best served through making appointments, for example, when you are implementing an acquisition you need to ensure you have subject matter experts in corporate financing on the team. However, when you are working with a change challenge that is not about going from A to B, and is one that necessitates tapping into new ideas and creativity, then asking for volunteers could be your best route.

In particular, seek out the opinions of people beyond your comfort zone. New perspectives can arise from unexpected sources. Back to the National Health Service example, when the CEO opened up her organisation to an approach called Open Space Technology to improve performance, a process in which, within a loosely held frame, anyone can volunteer ideas for how to move performance forward, she found that a hospital porter, called Chris, came up with the most creative and practical solution for improving the accuracy of how drugs were administered to the wards' patients.

I have used this approach with another client who was seeking to move their organisation to a new state of performance, and, where again, the circumstances were such that there was no easy solution. Simply by switching Day 2 of their 2-day top leadership conference away from prescribing which topics people were going to work on, and dictating who was going to go into what topic, and by moving towards an open space volunteer-led approach, they came up with new solutions for accelerating the change. And, as importantly, it unleashed an enormous amount of energy in their leadership team, who for the first time had been trusted to come up with their own solutions.

So, emergent change is governed by the power of lateral networks and connections, paying attention to your neighbours. It is not commanded and controlled by an all-knowing organisational centre or hierarchy. As a leader, you therefore need to believe and trust that there *is* a distributed intelligence inherent in your organisational system, and acknowledge that your task is to break down barriers to organisational collaboration, setting up the conditions for rich, innovative, networked relationships.

Research into complex adaptive systems shows us that most change happens at the periphery, and not the centre of a system, as diversity stimulates innovation. For example, species in the living world adapted most rapidly when they came out of the forest and onto the savannah. So, important in this regard is your task to create the spaces for your people to go to the edge of your system, and stimulate interest in the periphery. That might be visiting frontline operations in your own business, your customers, or going to meet the groups of people in society who somehow are already living the future you are trying to create.

Emergent Change Practice 6: At all Times, Cultivate the Emergent Conditions of Connectivity, Diversity and Rapid Feedback Loops

In summary, while the process of emergence cannot be controlled, it can be guided, a leadership process I call *fanning the flames.* The skill is to at all times cultivate the three conditions that most enable emergent change to flourish: the amount of *connectivity* and high quality interaction across the system you lead; the degree to which this connectivity contains rich *diversity*, or, a cross section of the whole system; and, finally, the absolute insistence that your system has access to open, transparent and *rapid feedback* loops, so that your people can know how they are doing and make adjustments as necessary, without the need for a central controlling intelligence centre. When patterns are fed back to a community, small shifts in behaviour can rapidly escalate into larger movements.

I hope through this explanation of emergence I have dispelled the myths I have most often heard about this approach to change: that emergent change is slow, ungovernable and too full of risk. Emergent change is not anything-goes free-for-all corporate anarchy. Neither is it the last-resort approach you turn to when you have run out of ideas. It *is* governed by a loose intention and set of hard rules. It *does* require that you build new capacities to equip your organisation for agility. And, by modelling inquiry and the capacity to be in a state of not-knowing yourself, it can unleash boundless creativity.

Quite frankly, in today's world where today's solution quickly looks outdated, and where leaders cannot easily know or control what is going on in their organisations, emergent change could be the only answer to move your organisation to a new state of change agility and performance. It's there anyway. Harness it.

But it also takes a certain quality of Still Moving leadership to accompany emergent change. Maybe you have already picked up a clue or two. Our new research threw some light on this. *Where emergent change was successful, its leaders were significantly more able to use the Attractor leadership practice* – pulling people towards a new purpose, without the need to impose change from on high, or from the outside. *They were also differentiated from the rest of the sample by their skill in two of the inner capacities – Staying Present and Acknowledging the Whole.* Clearly, the successful unfolding of emergent change requires leaders who are focused and adaptive in the here-and-now moment, and able to integrate all of experience, even the difficult bits, into a coherent narrative.

Emergent Change in Action – Much Comes from Little

I now turn to a story of a business leader who made this happen, let's call him Vincent. Through his personal leadership style and conscious adoption of an emergent change approach, he dramatically transformed the change agility and performance of one small market in his company's global pharmaceutical company. So much so that the innovative formula from this small part of the company has now become the gold standard for realising growth and innovation across the world. It's a story that proves just how catalytic for the whole system stimulating change in one part of the organisation can be, using a bottom-up self-organising change approach.

Amplify Positive Deviance

In the technical language of complexity theory it is a story of *positive deviance*: one cell's radically countercultural act has improved the adaptive capacity of the whole system. A £15 m market in sales (and now £40 m) has woken up a £28bn giant. So, it is a story not just of Vincent's ability to lead dramatic change in one part of the system, it is also a story of how he helped the whole company to tune into an outlier in their system. Emergent change requires that the traditional command and control centre becomes a listening and learning organisation, picking up examples of positive deviance and amplifying their success code for the rest of the system. It is such a different change approach to one that starts by rolling out one-look change programmes from the centre (where change starts large and often ends up small).

To help interpret what made a difference to Vincent's success I will be using four lenses onto his leadership that you can refer to in Figure 8.1. Alongside the six central tenets of *emergent change* are the three elements of Still Moving leadership our research found to be pivotal to emergent change success: the two inner capacities of *Staying Present* and *Acknowledging the Whole*, and the external practice of *Attractor* leadership. I have already described the practices of Staying Present and Acknowledging the Whole in earlier chapters. As Vincent's story unfolds I will therefore offer particular commentary on his Attractor leadership, as it appears so crucial in your ability to stimulate radical change from the ground up.

When Vincent arrived in this country (the eighth largest populated country in the world), he found a £15 m revenue one-segment business that had been losing market share for 10 years. A traditional style hierarchical general manager who micro-managed his kingdom led the business. And he ran a defeatist management team who believed that, in the highly regulated and protectionist local environment, no further growth from a multinational company would be possible.

By the time we interviewed Vincent, just 18 months after his arrival, sales had grown by over 100% to £40 m, the business had rapidly diversified into new segments, the general manager had converted from a die-hard stability agent into a 'Mr Energy' and the dramatically upgraded leadership team had only the previous week in London been ecstatically proud to present their country's success story to the Head of Emerging Markets (one step down from the Group CEO). And this accomplishment was no flash in the pan. The team is predicting 90% growth this

EMERGENT CHANGE
I can only create the conditions
for change to happen

Sets an overall intention and direction,
establishes a few hard rules to guide
behaviour, and then allows self-organisation

Starts in a small way around ripe issues or
hot topics that have large consequences

Works step-by-step, adjusting plans as you
go, using trails and experiments

Builds skills in changing the here-and-now moment,
for e.g. effective dialogue, how to run meetings,
the art of storytelling

Uses informal volunteer networks
to build change understanding,
energy and novel connections-
in particular tunes into the
periphery

At all times cultivates the
emergent conditions of
connectivity, diversity, and rapid
feedback loops

Figure 8.1 How to lead emergent change.

year and then 70–80% in forthcoming years. Emergent change can have lasting impact not just quick results.

Here's how he managed this remarkable turnaround.

Ignorance is Useful

Vincent's previous role had been Head of Corporate Strategy, reporting directly to the company's Group CEO, a position he held for 6 years. Given that this role, and his tenure, had provided Vincent with a unique vantage point from which to understand the performance and business models of all of his company's markets, you might imagine that he would have come to his new assignment – General Manager of a cluster of Emerging Markets – with quite a few fixed ideas already in his head about what should be done.

Not in this case. Vincent chose instead to first deeply tune into day-to-day reality, to get beneath the skin of the local market, at all times inquiring into how the management team and the rest of the organisation saw the situation. And from this ground truth, he started to shape a loose intention and story for the change. This is classic Attractor leadership, co-creating a shared intention. Moreover, he reached out beyond hierarchy to the layers beneath the management team to do this. This is a very skilful move when you are wishing to work emergently, as high levels of power differential can be an inhibitor of emergence. So, via town hall meetings and dinners, he went to figure out what the 'young next generation think'. Here he is colourfully describing his approach.

> So my general leadership style is to not pretend that I know more than anyone else, I assume everyone else knows more than me, I tried to learn, I showed people I wanted to find out about their challenges. I didn't prepare myself at all for their briefing meetings, I just sat there being really focused in the moment, listening and asking questions. I often describe it as being the Shakespearian fool.

Clearly Vincent was a leader not afraid to look ignorant, and he was calm and confident enough to simply show up and be present. How much more effortless this kind of leadership style can be! So his Attractor leadership was fuelled by the inner capacity of Staying Present – not getting distracted, and paying attention to what is happening with a positive, generous and appreciative frame of mind. Far from leaping to judgement, he stayed intentionally open-minded and curious. Here he is further describing his empathic leadership style and intent.

> The challenge was there had never ever been any real focus on this market, and the general manager had never had any kind of management or strategic support. So I would say the first 12 months were a struggle; what I was trying to do was to have the leadership team recognise they had a problem, and to see if they could, through their own leadership, change their ways of working.

Tap into Purpose

By tuning into ground-level reality and also his own felt experience of the local struggle, Vincent sensed that this team, with some changes in the direct reports to the general manager, *could* indeed through their own leadership transform the business. His task was to help them believe in that growth possibility too. And he did this by attending to all of the difficulty of their experience, not sweeping it under the carpet, demonstrating his capacity to Acknowledge the Whole. And he connected with them at an emotional level. Just hear how his Attractor leadership created a pull towards purpose during one particular meeting.

> So I went out in September last year, and I said, 'Look guys, we could be the beacon, we could be the example that's held up by the rest of the local operating companies in our business unit, we could be the gold standard, and, you know, why shouldn't we be that, this will help us get the investment, it will help raise your profile. Look, you know, we're 17th in the market, why aren't we third, and what would you do to get to third, what's growing, what's not growing, where are there partnerships, let's be ambitious and take some risks here.' And they said, 'We are really up for the challenge, we want to do this'.

Vincent's ripest issue was making a call on the local General Manager. Could he switch to become a visionary leader of growth? He could have easily arrived at premature judgement here. The General Manager had been there for 10 years and had let this market decline. Vincent's first tactic was to keep asking him about the business problems, but that got them nowhere as he simply became defensive. So, he intentionally and mindfully decided to change plan. Listen to how in this pivotal encounter he used curious intention and Attractor leadership to tap into the well of the General Manager's inner purpose, which unlocked his natural energy and subsequently the spirit of the entire organisation.

> He was being defensive about it, so I changed, I remember deliberately changing tacks. I'm going to use our Personal Development Plan process to ask about where does he want to go in his career. So, not how his performance was in the last month but really talk about where did he want to be in 5 years' time? And suddenly he switched. He said, 'Nobody has ever talked to me about this, I want to go on a global assignment'. And I said to him, 'Okay, tell me how we are going to get there and I can help you with this'. And then all of a sudden, it was like he was night and day. It all became a different dynamic and level of energy. He became Mr Energy and Mr Can Do, and then he brought people into the team that were exactly like that.

This is your Problem

In all the dialogue to date you can notice Vincent's use of inquiry, the art of asking big questions, to build the capacity of this country's management team to believe in themselves and solve the issues. He could have come into this market and either solved the problem himself and told them the solution, or got in a firm of external consultants to do the market analysis and propose routes to growth. That kind of leadership though is constraining with regards to creativity and it also requires that you the leader be around all the time to make things happen.

Instead, having created an inspiring alignment around purpose, both with the General Manager and his team, Vincent now put the big bold challenge about how to realise that purpose back to the management team, enabling him to leave them to come up with the growth plan, while he attended to the other markets in his portfolio. Here's how emergent change needs to be nudged along by Edge and Tension and Container leadership from time to time.

> The challenge was to basically point out that this was serious and that we needed to do something about it and that actually it was their problem, so I made it very clear, 'This is your problem and the challenge for you is to fix this problem and what I'm going to do is to help you both in terms of thinking through the problem, thinking through your level of ambition and then get you the resources you need to implement it'. I said to them, 'I will support you, I will get the investment, and you have to trust me on this stuff', and I threw the problem at them.

Notice how calm and objective Vincent remained during what could have been a tense encounter – this was such a new management style compared to what the team had been used to. But he stayed present and held his nerve. And in true emergent change style, he didn't just give them a long rope and leave them to it. That is a style that could be called irresponsible abdication.

Hard Rules that can Liberate

Vincent very skilfully gave them a set of hard rules that were to govern *how* they reached the goal. In that way he built the capacity of the organisation to do its own changing without him needing to be around all the time to call the shots. The few hard rules he set for them were: work across boundaries; release energy in the organisation; the plan has to be owned by the whole team; and be positive and requiring (to the centre) about investment and growth. He amplified this final rule with the exhortation, 'be very thorough, robust and quick'.

These were skilful hard rules in that they were countercultural to how the organisation had been used to working. Without helping them build the capacity for new routines, they would have likely come up with old solutions. This was a culture that had always looked to their sole leader to tell them the way forward and offer the assurance of predictability. And, more than that, this market had systemically been caught up in a wider corporate culture of extreme cost control and budget compliance. Getting on was achieved by hitting your numbers, not asking for investment. Sometimes building capacity in your organisation is about removing barriers and constraints. Here he is liberating them from the shackles of the wider culture with his fourth hard rule.

> So, the first thing we should think about this is in terms of not using our normal business planning process, which, like all companies, is to have a budget review cycle, updates, and then we'll be told to get target and blah blah blah. So I said to them, 'What we really need to do is to think through where do we want to be in 5 years' time and what does that mean in terms of additional investment and resources that we could ask for?' This is a very unusual thing for anyone to do here because we're used to managing for cost versus manage for growth, so we end up in a cutting mode and we starve our business.

Nudging the System and Staying Out of the Way

While Vincent was away attending to his other markets, this country's team came up with an ambitious growth plan. In essence, the plan was to turn a highly vulnerable business focused on sales in just one or two therapeutic areas, carrying a lot of cost with a fixed manufacturing facility, into a diversified business targeting four to five areas of high market growth. This plan required an investment in people, manufacturing and a doubling of the sales team. They set a bold 5-year target to reach £100 m in sales by 2020, all from a base of just £15 m. And this sales growth was to be at a pace greater than the market, stealing market share from their competitors.

It is testimony to the success and speed of this emergent change approach that when we interviewed Vincent, just 12 months into the plan, the team had already reached £40 m in sales.

His style during this phase is also illustrative, he recounted to us, 'I would come in every 6 weeks or so for an update on progress, and I would challenge them a bit, ask a few questions here and there'. Even when the key number two position to the General Manager, the Finance Director, was recruited, he decided to not get involved. He had left them inspired with a clear purpose and guided by a set of hard rules, and then he trusted them to get on with the task. In his words, 'From there on in,

my job was almost done. We agreed on the four key areas and then they
went away to implement their brilliant plan.'

Listen to his recounting of his style during these market visits, and you
can literally feel the free flow of an emergent leader in action.

> I enjoy being the outlier in meetings, I definitely don't do it in a
> directive way. I do it by asking, 'Can we explain this? Have you
> thought about that? Let me just play back what you've said. Let me
> give you some context of why I think this.' So it is very informal
> discussion, with a lot of give and take. I would say, 'That is a really
> good point, so if you can't do that because of that why don't you
> think about this?' So it was a free-flowing discussion back and
> forth, and if we got bogged down in detail we would step back
> and say, 'What are we trying to achieve here? Can we be just 80%
> and be comfortable with that?'

Vincent could nudge movement along by gently encouraging his team to
embrace uncertainty and feel okay with not needing to know, or perfect
everything, as, 'Lots of stuff can happen in the next 5 years and we need
to divorce ourselves from the finance planning process, which is really
challenging their mindset and the culture of the company'. His ability to
work within a dynamic, unpredictable environment, and feel perfectly
fine to operate with just 80% certainty, was founded upon the inner
capacity to Acknowledge the Whole. He was able to view obstacles as
resources, and to model to others non-reactivity in the face of difficulty,
a capacity that shines through in this statement.

> That was really the big challenge, it was not that people didn't
> want to grow the business, it was more the culture and our
> processes don't allow us to think like that, and I was saying, 'Look,
> trust me, let's ignore those things and let's think like this'.

Testimony to Vincent's skill in being able to work across a whole system,
and nudge forward change on many levels, is the fact that the top leaders
of his company took the unprecedented step to sign off their approval to
a doubling of the sales team in this market 'despite that we hadn't yet got
the plan signed off'. His side stepping of the constraining financial planning process had clearly not produced enemies in the wider system. They
were inspired by this local market's spirit and ambition. And this allowed
Vincent and the local team to move forward at a pace unheard of in their
company. Within months 50 new sales reps were recruited, trained and
had started operating in the field. In his recount of the London review
with the Head of Emerging Markets, the week before we interviewed

Vincent, I share a final example of his fine Attractor leadership in action – clearly, he had pulled this organisation towards its own purpose, and not towards himself (a big trap that a more ego-led leader would have fallen into).

> I flew four of the local leadership team to London, and we had 4 hours with the Head of Emerging Markets, which, by the way, I did no presenting at whatsoever, as they did all the work. And he said, 'This is amazing, the team are fantastic and I can't believe we have not been investing more in this market'. So, that's another good boost for the team. Oh, and then the final thing is, it looks like the General Manager is going to get the bigger market job.

To which our interviewer, swept up in the inspiring capability-building people-centred swirl of this leader spontaneously proclaimed, 'Oh, how wonderful!'

Leading Emergent Change: Helping the System 'See'

A very gifted emergent change leader I once worked with summed up his role to me thus, 'To help the whole see what the parts are doing, and to help the parts see the whole'. Rich feedback loops between the parts and the whole, a cornerstone of emergent change. And note that this leader described his role as to *help see*. An emergent change leader's task is not to induce change from on high but instead to author interpretations, to catalyse a noticing process across their organisation. How different is this style to one that holds information for the benefit of a central intelligence centre?

Vincent continually connected his local team with the rest of the organisation to give them access to resources but also to help them see and act differently. And at the same time he helped other parts of the organisation to see and acknowledge what was happening in this newly entrepreneurial unit. This stimulated change across the board, without him having to lead it all. In a sense, he didn't create change, he simply certified it. When you lead change in a more emergent style, you not only empower the organisation, you can free yourself up too. It really does take away the pressure and the burden (not least the cost) of launching and implementing enterprise-wide change initiatives.

Once the loose intention and hard rules are set, you end up running the business through outcomes, not programmes, at all times equipping the organisation to see and notice the world differently. I am often asked,

'What is the single biggest thing you would do in my situation to accelerate change?' and I tend to respond, 'Build the skills in your organisation for greater systemic perceiving.' Feedback, neighbour interaction and pattern recognition are the hallmarks of self-organising and adaptive systems. In a sense, once you crack the process of emergence, you just simply lead in this style all the time – it's no longer about using an emergent approach for a particular change challenge, as the essence of emergence is that it has no beginning or end point.

Vincent at the end of his interview summarised the benefits that leading change in this way had brought him, 'So I try not to work too hard. By that I mean I don't spend hours every day sitting at my computer trying to do lots of emails, or rewriting others people's work. I try to really think, I try to sit back, I find the time to reflect on my work and think about the big interventions, not just jump in and do stuff.'

If, as a leader, you would love to live your life as a river flows, then try out a more emergent approach. Get out of busy acting and make a few choice-ful interventions. It not only makes your life flow more effortlessly, it also brings quicker and more sustainable outcomes. But remember, the treasure will only come to those who have built both their inner capacities and external practices. How to do that is the subject of the next chapter.

9

A Tale of Still Moving and Business Transformation

The necessity of an ending
now and here
a surprising sense of belonging
who will be us and them?
To be kind we slow down
don't you see it?
We become paralysed
Can we carry the spirit of this?
Stay with it long enough...
the change in me already
small stones in a river
that alter the flow

Sytske Casimir,
Now and Here

We were about to do something we had never done before. That's not quite accurate, as the faculty team and I had previously tested this exercise during a week's design event. But, in the now and here moment, and with 36 of the top executives of our client organisation seated expectantly around us, this was a major first.

Calming my nerves (breathing deeply), I made a concerted effort to stay present, not worry about what will happen next, nor even imagine what *should* happen next, and instead trust in the power of self-organising chaos. I invited the group of leaders to stand, and walk slowly in silence through a physical map of their organisation and its dramatically changing context.

A few moments earlier, their CEO – also a pioneering participant on this new leadership development programme – had courageously built up this physical map. He had picked up 30 large white cubes and placed them one by one on the ground in the middle of the circle of participants. Each of the cubes represented either an internal element of the

Still Moving: How to Lead Mindful Change, First Edition. Deborah Rowland.
© 2017 John Wiley & Sons Ltd. Published 2017 by John Wiley & Sons Ltd.

organisation, such as one of the business units, its leadership culture or the board, or they represented an external influencing element, such as climate change, politicians, customers and the media. The CEO's task had been to place these cubes on the ground, in relationship to each other, as a representation of the complex interconnected energy system he and his top leaders needed to help transform.

Building a physical map of an organisation over a large floor space was a very different kind of activity to presenting a PowerPoint organogram chart. The goal of the exercise, however, was not to see who reported to whom or where the change journey fitted into the strategic plan, it was for the leaders present to be able to really *see, touch and feel* the dynamic complexity of the system they needed to lead into a radically new future – Tuning into the System, in Still Moving language.

As the leaders walked around the cubes, visiting each one, closing their eyes, trying to register in their bodies what was being *felt* in this experience, and not just cognitively processing (and silently judging) where their CEO had placed the elements, I was trying to sense what was going on in the room. Were people lost and checking out of the exercise, was *anyone* 'getting it', had I given clear enough instructions, what was my stomach saying, how and where were the rest of my faculty team?

Some of the group moved the cubes slightly, as they felt that the actual system was a little messier on the ground than their CEO would like them to think. That was fine, the goal was not accuracy and precision, the objective was to develop the sensibilities of leaders to tune into a large complex system that was currently under much stress and uncertainty. And this tuning in capacity was suddenly demonstrated very forcibly and memorably by one participant who did something that was for him – and his colleagues – quite out of the ordinary.

This leader, who happened to also be the tallest, dropped to the floor and sat slumped next to the cube representing the organisational unit that was facing the starkest future. This business unit was facing decline and closure – at significant human cost. Some of this leader's colleagues noticed his distress, some shuffled past his seated figure, others ended the activity simply not noticing this had happened at all.

But this leader had given a great gift to the group. He had (in the moment, unknowingly) pointed out the price that was going to have to be paid to grant this organisation a future. This price, of decommissioning the very entity whose generations of leaders had for decades built this company's success, was rationally understood in the business but, until this point, the necessity of this ending had never been so openly felt and collectively faced.

A Fateful Opening to a Story of Business Transformation

This remarkable, disturbing and unplanned moment – indeed a Transforming Space – was much talked about in this, the first pioneering wave of participants on a new leadership development experience, whose story is the subject of this chapter (and inspiration for its opening poem, written by one of my faculty colleagues).

And this opening incident on the very first wave, this dramatic facing of an ending, was a small stone in the river bed that set the tone for all that was to follow. Not only did the incident help them – a bunch of independent leaders running their own separate parts of the system – to see the whole complexity and enormity of the change task their CEO was facing, it also, in the room (and later, in the business), enabled them to voice their personal fears in the face of uncertainty.

The leader who had slowly come down to the floor in a heap of grief had felt safe enough to show emotion. As we sat debriefing the experience he described his moment of deep sadness as like being at someone's funeral. Such heartfelt disclosure – in a business setting – was an unprecedented feat in the rational, logical, engineering-dominated culture of energy production and supply. But the deeper connection that this emotional contact brought within the group built trust, openness, courage and a far deeper appreciation of the human cost of their change.

And all of these skills that this single moment began to tease out – tuning into self and others, seeing the multiple interconnected impacts in a system, taking risks, putting your head (and heart) above the parapet, showing public vulnerability, building rapid trust in a group of relative strangers, acknowledging a difficult reality – were going to be vital leadership resources to ensure this company's survival.

So, in this chapter, I tell a story of how a pioneering organisation put in place an innovative leadership development programme to cultivate Still Moving skills, which ultimately contributed to them being able to achieve radical change. At the time of writing, the jury is still out on whether this change will be a success. But they managed to take the first step on a historical transition for the company. Moreover, it is also a tale that shines light on the cultural conditions and (non-conventional) type of development intervention required to cultivate Still Moving leadership – as the programme certainly impacted individuals and has left the organisation in a forever-changed place.

I will not relate the whole story of their business transformation. You can imagine there was a lot more to it than just this top leadership development programme. Nonetheless, the organisation's leaders now say that they could not have taken the major strategic decision that is aimed to rescue their company without it.

Here's what it took.

Facing the Conundrum

Imagine this scenario. You have recently been appointed Group CEO of a 100-year-old company facing unprecedented disruptive change, where there will be no revival of the business model that has built its success. The market is going to remain volatile and demanding so that whatever change you bring in needs to have both immediate impact but also an on-going sustainable character. And the solution is going to be a bit tricky, as there are multiple external stakeholders – including national governments and politicians – who are making decisions and taking actions that influence your company's trajectory, so you are not entirely in control of its direction and likely success.

Moreover, attracting confidence and capital is not going to be easy. With activists threatening your power plants and spraying graffiti on the entrance to your headquarters building, you have lost the trust of the society you have long served. And, given the lower profit levels ahead and current high net debt to EBITDA (earnings before interest, taxes, depreciation and amortisation) ratio you have no available cash to buy your way out of the problem. You know that your company's performance is going to get worse before it gets better, and the only pathway to get out of the hole is going to be a long, stony, uncertain and perilous one.

At the same time, your organisation and its shareholders are relying on you to find an instant answer to fix the crisis. After 100 years of control, certainty and a regulated marketplace surely this company's right to exist is not under challenge. There is significant, high-profile and vocal pressure on you to come up with a rescue plan that will provide future certainty and continued financial returns. Not only that, the rescue plan has to be one that will cause no discomfort, sacrifice or betrayal to what has come before.

When you turn to your organisation you find you have inherited a leadership culture that looks to the hierarchy to provide the answers and, unused as it is to providing any form of upward challenging feedback, is scared to speak up about what truly matters. Not only that, you are trying to steer an organisation that has horizontal silos, multiple management layers and, via historical mergers and acquisitions, is governed by a panoply of boards and legal entities whose sense of independent entitlement makes it impossible for you to get aligned and speedy decision-making.

This is no imaginary scenario, but the very real situation 3 years ago that faced my client, a Group CEO of the major European energy provider featured in the opening of this chapter. Let's call the CEO, Pat. Pat not only had a strategic and structural crisis, he had a cultural and leadership one. His response to this scenario, while not perfect (and under the above circumstances, whose would be?), is a vital part of this story. Together with his board colleagues, he built the leadership skills of his organisation to come to terms with a radically new world.

So, what did he do and how?

A Visionary and Courageous Leader

Pat embarked on this change journey via, in my experience at least, an unprecedented upfront investment in building the capability of his most senior leaders to be flexible, resilient and open to whatever they needed to face. He did not succumb to the enormous projected pressure on him as CEO to come up with a quick fix solution. For sure, he and his board took some tough short-term tactical measures that were necessary to keep the company afloat, such as disposals and cost cutting. Yet this was not enough to save the company.

While the situation sounds somewhat dire, he knew he was not powerless to act. Overriding all of it he knew that in such a volatile and uncertain environment, the best single response he *could* make at the start of this change was to invest in the how, creating a new culture and the capacity of his company to walk into the unknown. And these new capabilities would, over time, help his company find the innovative and responsible answer to the what, the strategic solution to get to the future.

When not only his organisation, but also pressure from the external world and media were calling out for a defining strategy, this was pretty courageous. See how, in this excerpt from his interview with us, he used the inner capacity of Curious and Intentional Responding to make a conscious choice on how to respond to the pressure.

> People say, 'Holy smoke, you're the CEO; tell this joint where to go!' And it's tempting to step into that and say, 'I've given it some thought; here we go', but you need to be very careful with that because it's like a plexus that people are asking for in a direct control environment that they're used to working in.

So we have here a CEO wishing to break with routine and create *collective* responsibility to find a direction, building a place from which all of his leaders would start to operate differently. This was a sensible move in a dynamic and unpredictable environment where no single individual could ever know, let alone control what to do (remember traffic jams, the Anonymous group). And he knew that this would need to be accompanied by the building of new capacities and a different approach to how the company operated (remember, emergence can be shaped).

Investing in the How When You Don't (Yet) Know the What

To build these new emergent capacities he used subtlety, and not a top-down directive style. He was a CEO who could let things flow. He told us, 'The first thing is if, as a new CEO coming in, you try to convince your top leadership about the ideal change approach you get a lot of theoretical discussion and you get a lot of opposition. So I started to create pull, instead of me pushing.'

He created the pull by getting his top leaders to see the benefit of approaching their challenge in new ways. This started with his board colleagues, where I joined him and their team to explore together their lessons in the *how* of leading change. He set up the frame for this using skilful Edge and Tension, 'At our first offsite I carefully said, "Well, we can talk about what we need to do, the agenda settings, but we have been doing that for quite a number of years and it doesn't work. So obviously we need to talk about how we do things as well as what we do, because that is what radiates into the organisation."'

After rich conversation at this meeting (nudged by my research findings into the relative success of different change approaches), the board agreed to move from what had been a top-down 'leaders know best' directive change approach to one that engaged the whole organisation more fully in finding the answers – from dictate to co-create. To do this, they knew that they would have to create a common change language and build new change skills in their senior leaders to, again subtly, radiate new ways of working into the culture. Here's what the board did.

> The next step was that we established change leadership workshops, where we started working on the topics of the management agenda and just because we changed the format in which we work, we suddenly got results that nobody could have imagined before. That's when the pull started. What is this? So it's obviously not the what we defined that made the difference; *it is how we work on the what.*

Here's a leader who knew he had to work on the underlying system that produced the results, not try and drive new results through keeping the current system and its routines intact. Simple new formats, such as dropping PowerPoint presentations and moving to working visually on large meta plan boards, signalled this shift from 'advocacy-led convincing' to 'inquiry-led collaboration'. With his organisation now warming up to a new way of working, achieved not through directives, but by creating different experiences that yielded better outcomes (note, Transforming Space leadership in action), he then turned his attention to the top leadership programme.

Building a Living Laboratory for Change

In the opening to this story I gave you a flavour of the novelty of the leadership development experience we created. When I accepted Pat's invitation to become its Programme Director, I did so on the basis that this CEO was up for doing something bold and different. Not as an end in itself, but I now knew in my career just how important it was for any change intervention to dynamically model where it is you are trying to head. It's so easy to attempt to get to new places by doing things in old ways.

The CEO and I had worked together in a previous assignment, so there was an existing basis of trust and respect, and this served us well through the turbulence of what was to come.

The core intent of this programme was *not* to solve all the business issues, as he and his board colleagues had put other interventions in place to do that. The aim of this particular programme was to take his most senior 360 leaders (in a 65,000 strong organisation) to a new level in their leadership, a level that was able to face into disturbance and navigate a large complex organisation through major transition. A task described by him to me early on as, 'Deborah, I'm sending them into the woods'. Critically, his overall vision for *how* best to develop these skills was to, 'Guide our people through a living laboratory, not a theoretical concept, but in a real, company-based pressure-cooker laboratory approach'.

I, and the faculty team that we were to select, clearly had the licence from this CEO to use the intervention as a Transforming Space journey for participants. Indeed, it was not to be a taught 'programme' in the conventional sense at all, but rather a challenging in-the-moment *experience* in which learning and change came from the leaders themselves and the group dynamics created in the room, not from lectures, case studies, tool kits and theoretical leadership models.

The intervention therefore was to *model the unpredictable and disturbing nature of their business environment*, and invite leaders to master the ability to notice, *own* and regulate their response to this experience, which is the only thing you *can* do in uncontrollable dynamic systems. As you can imagine, this novel format was going to provoke anxiety in participants (maybe coming onto this programme for some brief respite from the fray), and it also took extraordinary resilience and skill in the faculty team – more of that later.

Let's stay here with Pat, as this 'living laboratory' format decision was not without its consequences for him either. Eschewing the more conventional business school-type leadership programme was a brave move. His company had used those in the past; he felt now that this format would be unable to provide the holistic solution needed. And this new step into the unknown required his *own* inner leadership game to be at its best, in his words.

> It was seen as being willing to step, you know, out of your comfort zone and into a risk position, because if it wouldn't work out then it clearly would have been my, I wouldn't say failure, but at least, you know, it would have clearly linked back to me. So I was clearly nervous, there was an element of tension. It was, most of all, a feeling of making myself vulnerable.

Systemically speaking, Pat's reflection on his inner experience is a beautiful holographic expression from a Group CEO of what his whole *company* needed to learn. Unless this company could commit itself to go out of its comfort zone, take a risk position, endure the ensuing tension and make itself vulnerable in the society that it served, it would simply not survive. As CEO, he was creating the stage upon which others had to walk.

A Development Programme *That* Changes, Not a Programme *About* Change

With this challenging vision for the programme in place, the next step was to build it. Pat and I, and his HR team assembled for this challenge, knew we had to select a faculty who could hold such a changing experience. And we did, assembling a 12-strong team largely comprising independent change coaches and facilitators. This worked well, as we knew we had to get not only the very best individuals able to moderate the experience, we also needed to design a holistic experience that no single supplier could provide.

Together, our mission was to design and deliver a culturally changing experiential journey that would invite participants both individually and collectively to walk into their emerging future. Let's start with the journey design.

A Container to Help People Move Through Change

We knew we needed to create a Container structure that would enable transition and channel its anticipated turbulence. In Figure 9.1 you can see what we came up with. The high-level programme design had three formal modules over a 6-month journey with activities before and after each module. We created and tested this design and its core content with a cross section of leaders who were going to be participants on the programme – modelling working from the beneficiary back. The two biggest leadership shifts *they* expressed were needed to unstick their organisation were how to have controversial conversations and how to build the courage to take initiative. This was certainly going to be on the menu.

The overall programme architecture stood the test of time in that it did not change across the course of 2.5 years and 10 separate waves of 36 participants, despite the change and market context for this organisation going through all kinds of twists and turns along the way. While we did make quite radical design shifts within and between the modules to accommodate present group dynamics and the wider changing context, the programme structure could accommodate whatever got thrown at it. So it seemed to be a container, indeed, crucible, able to hold an organisation and its leaders through transition; it was not just an elegant design for a leadership development programme.

In that respect it helps validate the work of Otto Scharmer and his Theory U methodology,[1] a major contribution to the field of how to lead in disruptive change when you can no longer learn, or lead, from the lessons of the past. This approach is very difficult to do, and it fundamentally changes the nature of the learning experience. This programme was going to challenge leaders who were used to showing up on a training programme in which learning was evaluated by the quality of its guest speakers and the tangibility of its *takeaways*. This time, success meant the quality of their *contribution to a journey*, and their live leadership learning within a temporary micro-community of their business – their wave of 36 leaders.

An Attractor Frame for 'Leading From the Future'

As this was to be a transforming experience *that* changes, modelling the disruptive business environment, and not an experience *about* change, we needed to have the settling power of a description of the loose direction and capacities required for this journey. So, with the theory of Theory U aside, we positioned for participants what *leading from the*

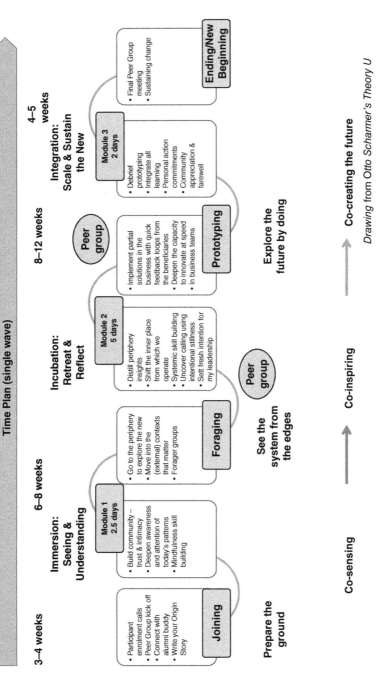

Time Plan (single wave)

3–4 weeks	6–8 weeks		8–12 weeks	4–5 weeks

Immersion: Seeing & Understanding

Incubation: Retreat & Reflect

Integration: Scale & Sustain the New

Joining
- Participant enrolment calls
- Peer Group kick off
- Connect with alumni buddy
- Write your Origin Story

Module 1 2.5 days
- Build community – trust & intimacy
- Deepen awareness and attention of today's patterns
- Mindfulness skill building

Foraging
- Go to the periphery to explore the new
- Move into the (external) contexts that matter
- Forager groups

Module 2 5 days
- Distill periphery insights
- Shift the inner place from which we operate
- Systemic skill building
- Uncover calling using intentional stillness
- Sett fresh intention for my leadership

Peer group

Prototyping
- Implement partial solutions in the business with quick feedback loops from the beneficiaries
- Deepen the capacity to innovate at speed in business teams

Module 3 2 days
- Debrief prototyping
- Integrate all learning
- Personal action commitments
- Community appreciation & farewell

Ending/New Beginning
- Final Peer Group meeting
- Sustaining change

Peer group

Prepare the ground

See the system from the edges

Explore the future by doing

Co-sensing   Co-inspiring   Co-creating the future

Drawing from Otto Scharmer's Theory U

Figure 9.1 Cultivating Still Moving leadership: development programme architecture.

emerging future meant for their company, and this programme's journey. Here's what we came up with.

- *Operate at the edge of what is known*: in an energy world that was transitioning fast and moving into unprecedented territory, could we invite participants on this programme to practise walking into a space of not knowing, building their capacity to deal with whatever arises with curiosity, not judgement – even if the experience felt disturbing, different or uncomfortable?
- *Connect in a hyper connected world*: as this organisation had to shift from an *ego*-system world of centralised energy production and supply, to an *eco*-system world of decentralised and networked energy production and consumption, could this programme provide an opportunity for participants to walk more empathetically in the shoes of others? Could the programme model that the nature of relationships is as dependent on feelings, emotions and impulses as it is on rational exchange?
- *Act at pace using trial-and-error*: in the fast-moving dynamic energy world, where disruptive technology and new competitors were now part of daily life, could *we* offer participants an experience that modelled how to keep adjusting in the moment to changing times? Building the capacity to be present, creative and resourceful, working step-by-step, and admitting that some things just have not worked, or are no longer useful?

In Appendix 2 you will find a more detailed description of the development journey. What I will do here is focus on the design elements that had the greatest impact on participant learning and change. But before I do that, as this is a chapter as much about how to lead business change as it is about how to design a development programme, I will signal the systemic consequences of putting in place something so totally new. It helps picture the environment within which this programme had to deliver – and which it would, in turn, turn out to influence.

The Systemic Consequences of a Counter-Cultural Design

One key to understanding how to work systemically is to acknowledge that every change intervention has a consequence – and that the unbalancing will be both welcoming and rejecting. It's so important for leaders embarking on a major transition experience to realise this, and to have the robust and allowing capacity to handle all that comes your way, because to get movement *both these welcoming and rejecting energies need integrating* (Acknowledging the Whole). In this story, the consequences panned out as follows.

The Light Side – It Made the Business Change More Able to Be Faced

Relatively soon into the implementation of this programme we realised that, aside from its official objectives, the experience was acting as a parallel change container to the one in the business, where, given the deeply woven cultural fabric and power politics in change, many things felt unable to be faced and shifted. On the programme, however, things were able to *move*. So I use the four change leadership practices as my lens:

- *Attractor*: by putting together senior leaders from across all reaches of the organisation into a non-agenda filled and emotionally charged space, and, in particular, with external world exposure through the 'foraging' visits (more later), the experience tapped into a collective and heart-felt desire to move more in tune with the times (which no manner of mission statements and compelling story documents in the wider system could elicit with the same degree of heart-felt pulling power).
- *Edge and Tension*: by making it permissible in the learning experience, indeed, expected, to voice what was difficult, to amplify disturbance and be comfortable with not being comfortable, the experience did what one participant eloquently articulated as, 'put the finger on the pain'. Given the anxiety and uncertainty in the wider system such truth telling was almost impossible to do outside the safer space of this learning environment.
- *Container*: by working with a skilled faculty team, able to individually and collectively hold their own anxiety in disturbance and seek its systemic source, the programme modelled to participants a capacity for non-reactivity and a staying open to all of experience, which powerfully channelled what often arrived as participant scepticism and doubt into open-mindedness, curiosity and full engagement with the learning. Moreover, the participant networks set up in this programme helped the top leadership team of this organisation stay united under fire.
- *Transforming Space*: as 90% of the programme was experiential and not taught, visceral activities such as the Peer Groups, (power lab) business simulation, systemic constellations work and external foraging visits to more future facing contexts (e.g., innovation hubs, renewable energy providers) gave participants greater depth of insight into their own repeating patterns and it provoked a real stimulus to do something about them (which circulating slides about stuck repeating cultural patterns in the business usually failed to do).

Through time, the programme became a place to evolve the collective attention of this organisation on what the change deeply required of their leadership. It gave them the skill, licence and courage to challenge the stuck internal society of their business culture. In the words of one participant, 'this programme is giving the permission to exercise Edge and Tension and Transforming Space leadership in the business.'

The Dark Side – Working With and Integrating the Shadow

At the same time, and as its participants built in critical mass and increasingly became 'forceful mirrors' back in the wider system, the programme became a lightning rod for organisational projection. By this I mean that the unprocessed anxiety, all the difficult emotions that could not be owned or vented publically in the wider organisation, had to spill out somewhere. And in times of change what appears to be new and out of the ordinary can become the target (indeed perceived source) for the difficulty that cannot be owned elsewhere. Here's what the programme evoked.

- *Rumours spread* like wildfire through the organisation that this programme was about playing silly games, which, as the waves progressed, impacted the open-mindedness of leaders arriving on the programme to be available for learning. They often left positively bemused – and more than pleasantly surprised – as the experience turned out to be so *not* what the rumours were saying.
- *Leaks appeared in the press* that the company was going into crazy land (and with a British woman acting as change coach to one of our national treasures!). Stories were spun that, as the company struggled to find an answer to a go forward strategy, it had resorted to desperate attempts to go for silent walks in the woods or meditate their way out of a crisis.
- *Leaders in the organisation too junior to join the programme felt like an 'out crowd'* and (at times very justifiably) would claim that they saw no difference at all when their bosses came back to the workplace. Participants saying to me that the programme was helpful would turn out to say something very different back in the business.
- *Unrealistically high expectations* were put onto this programme to address all of the business issues and save the company. Which, of course, it could only ever fail at as no single programme would be able to solve such a complex challenge. However, by projecting too high an ambition – and then shooting it down – it could keep people safe in not needing to fully engage with the learning.

Give Difficulty a Place

Here's my point. Change leaders need to be able to hold the whole mix of feelings within the frame, and give all of experience a respectful place as the normal and to-be-expected turbulence of transition. Engage with the difficulty as much as the opportunity, be curious about the shadow as well as the light, and let it all be able to be talked about. Indeed, difficulty can be a resource not an obstacle as it is in the shadow where we find clues as to what a system holds most dear and is scared of losing. This is important information.

In this story, the programme emerged as a place in the system where the shadow of the change could be examined. Far from pretending it wasn't there, or casting judgements (tempting to do), as faculty we learned to Acknowledge the Whole and bring the difficulty in: be that inviting participants to voice the most scary thing they felt they could say in this group, or by posting up on a bulletin board all of the journalists' commentary on the company, or through me as Programme Director non-defensively asking people in front of the whole group to talk about what they were finding difficult with the programme. Such interventions led to what I call the 'squirmy' conversations, but it was always in these conversations that we felt most present and alive.

Make no mistake this is – and was – hard to do, especially when you are the visible leader who is championing the new. I, and in no small part due to my faculty colleagues' robust yet empathic feedback, could often catch myself denying what was proving difficult in this programme and only eulogising the positive. Yet, I always knew that at the meta level *our task was to model the handling of disturbance, the approaching and not the avoidance of difficulty, and the ability to experiment and learn*, accepting that not everything was going to be liked or work. In this culture of engineered perfection participants were often startled that the faculty adopted a trial-and-error approach, able to simply be with what is, and at times admit that certain exercises needed scrapping or changing.

When participants left the programme, their newfound capacity to non-reactively allow whatever shows up to 'be the case', looking on it with systemic curiosity rather than personal frustration, led them to no longer grumble that 'it should have been like that', or, wish that 'if only it could have turned out differently'. Moreover, this (Curious and Intentional Responding) capacity rubbed off on others, making the non-judgemental approaching of difficulty a far less dangerous thing to do – as difficulty *has* to be faced in change. Over time, this built greater coping skills, resilience and the capacity to address the tough stuff.

The Design Elements That Created Most Movement

While it was the programme's holistic nature that left its mark on participants (and faculty), here are the experiences that in particular could integrate the shadow as well as the upside of the organisation's turbulent change journey – creating most insight, learning and movement.

Peer Groups and Origin Stories

This programme would not have achieved what it did without the intimacy and containing holding space of the Peer Group process. They became small crucibles of cross-company networking, change journey sense making, personal feedback and change, stress relief and reflection on learning. I would advise any company now going through major change to set up a similar process. You don't need a formal leadership development programme to do so. But here's how they helped on this one.

Each of the separate 10 waves of 36 participants was broken down into Peer Groups of five to seven leaders. As with the whole wave we aimed to have maximum diversity of nationality, business unit, length of service and gender. The Peer Groups met before, during and after each of the three modules. On the modules themselves they met daily, usually at the end of the day to process what had occurred through the day in the large group. Between the modules, they acted as a vital sustaining force to keep the spirit and practice of the learning alive in the day-to-day environment (that often felt very stuck and different to that which had been created in the programme). Indeed, many of the Peer Groups continued to meet way beyond the programme's formal ending date. Each of the Peer Groups was assigned a faculty member who stayed their constant guide – call it, 'sherpa' – through the journey.

What accelerated trust, connection and openness in the Peer Group at the very outset was their first (and only, set) task in which each Peer Group member was invited to share their *Origin Story*. The purpose of the Origin Story was to have participants reflect on how they had been 'formed' as a leader, in order to deepen their understanding of how they now showed up as a leader today. Once you accept your fate you can make best use of it. When you learn how to notice your impulses and habitual responses (Staying Present), and understand the history that brought them here, then you can learn how to regulate and if necessary change them (Continuous and Intentional Responding). You do have choice and personal responsibility to be who you want to be.

The format for the Origin Story was a written narrative, guided by such questions as: What have been the two or three big life experiences that have shaped who you are as a leader today? In what way do the experiences still impact you as you lead? Who have been your guardian angels along the way? In what way are they still with you as you lead?

You may have noticed that I have used this book to share much of my Origin Story with you.

On this programme, the sharing of the Origin Stories was designed to build rapid trust and intimacy among Peer Group members; it built the courage to be authentic and vulnerable when disclosing to others what could be quite personal matters, and it built deep empathy and compassion in those listening. All of these are essential skills in leading change. It is very difficult to change a system that you have no emotional resonance with. Participants learned how to do this rapidly.

> I was initially sceptical about the peer groups – you expect five meetings to get intimate, on this programme it happened in the first 30 minutes! There was huge trust present through the Origin Story, we were no longer worried about what people thought of us.

We are all on our individual journeys, and the Peer Group (and Origin Story) process helped ensure that this leadership programme did not coldly assume that all participants were equal and in the same place. Behind each participant is a unique life, and behind that life there is a multitude of experiences and impacts that are there to be honoured and understood in order to be able to see the world as another sees and experiences it. And once these empathic connections are formed the field is forever changed. In the words of one participant reflecting on the process, 'The Peer Groups were a break with the past culture – with emotions now being okay. If we could connect like this every day, we could change the company!'

Aside from being a crucible for connection, and a place to build the courage to change habitual responses, the Peer Groups, systemically, acted as a holding space (note, Container) at the boundary between the small group and the larger plenary group. They were not just a sum of their individual members – they were also a cross-section and an importer of the dynamics that were being experienced in the whole group. And what happens in small groups is often a signal as to what can't be held in the large group. In that respect, the Peer Groups became a lens through which to look at the whole system that was being acted out. This was helpful for the faculty's capacity to Tune into the System, and each night we met to debrief the Peer Group meetings as they very often had quite different experiences (showing how dangerous it is to generalise about a system just by seeing it from one or two angles…).

But it also brought great benefit for participants when the events and experiences of the day were debriefed. In large groups deflection is a friend and we lower the intensity of our language. And in this organisation's culture it was particularly hard for participants to speak out about what they truly felt in the large group (especially with hierarchy present).

However, rather than these non-discussables going underground, or staying as fixed views in people's minds, they could be openly talked about in the Peer Group that had now created a safe place to take inter-personal risk. And so the larger group dynamics were processed in the smaller groups, at times having Peer Group members challenge their colleagues, who held a very fixed view about the larger group, or the programme (building Acknowledging the Whole capacity). The Peer Group space also prepped people to speak out in the next large group session. So, these intense, yet transforming conversations enabled the larger group to shift when it next convened. Again, in the words of participants.

> I would like to emphasise the merit of the Peer Group as kind of 'safe haven' to re-calibrate whenever something weird or 'pittoresque' happened in the plenum.
>
> Reflections in the peer group helps to settle down the plenary learning and experience, make it more sustainable and bring it to another level and thus prepare for next round of learning in the whole of the group.

Last, but by no means least, was the role of the faculty member acting as the Peer Group's coach. The role of the faculty coach was not to simply convene a nice chat. It was to remind the group throughout the journey of the programme's intention, to deepen understanding of the capacities being taught on the programme, and, critically, to act as a firm yet compassionate agent provocateur to help the group see and hence shift its own processes and defence routines.

While each Peer Group coach had a different personality and style, they were all clear on the intention of the role, and used three consistent *hard rules* that were shared with participants to enable that: keep steer-ing towards the edge (let's not stay in our routines); constantly scan the room (be present for all of what's here); and ensure equal airtime for all (give each other the same amount of space). Here is how two participants described the role.

> Strong moderation was crucial. At certain points you need some-one who can observe the actions/statements and the emotional development of the group members and their interaction and who can intervene by asking the right questions at the right time.
>
> The Peer Group facilitation was important to get things going, to promote contracting between group members and to challenge each of us when we were being cautious and diplomatic with the truth, our motivations and behaviours. I would describe this as encouraging people to explore and take best advantage of the good intentions of their colleagues and the safe environment.

Cultivating Mindfulness

While Pat had given us carte blanche with the design of the programme, his only key request was that *mindfulness* become, in his words, the 'tent pole' for the curriculum. He had the foresight to realise that if he was asking leaders to take his business through major disruptive change (and compressed into an experience on this programme), then they needed to be fit, healthy and alert, and in the best place personally to be able to do that. By best place this meant the holistic care of themselves in body, mind and spirit. This was another exposing risk for him as the Group CEO of a publicly listed company – what had mindfulness to do with the boardroom?

He was reassured by its scientific rigour and described it to me as being about achieving mental fitness that was as equally important for executive functioning as physical fitness (we also had a hugely popular and impactful doctor on the programme, giving advice on how to build and sustain physical energy and fitness). In Chapter 4 I have described how we found mindfulness to be the essential foundational capacity in leading change. Here is how the CEO described its read across into business leadership.

> First of all, it enhances your working memory capacity, which means that more of your attention is available to address the things you have on your plate and you're less preoccupied by things that were yesterday's issue or tomorrow's problem. So the stress generated by that is released. It is very much a conscious getting out of autopilot and being present and aware in the moment, and that is of utmost importance because that is the only moment when you can make changes, which might be a precondition for things for tomorrow.
>
> So I think that all of that allows you to be much more noticing of what goes on. You don't have a filter in between the signals that come in. There's a, kind of, non-judgemental, curious way of looking at things, and then you suddenly see a lot more than when you don't have that.

You suddenly see a lot more than when you don't have it. Remember in the previous chapter the voice of the emergent change leader who described his task as being able to 'help people see'. For this CEO, his mindfulness practice – in his case 12 years of daily meditation – had helped him through the difficult and burdensome parts of this role. He described its benefits as, 'Allowing things just to happen, and I feel myself in flow, and that's what people notice. It's a natural way of doing things, I feel so comfortable with it because, you know, this is what it is, and this is how he is.'

So, how did we train the capacity to be mindful on this programme? It was certainly a big hit with participants, and, more than that, we frequently heard reports from others that their bosses and colleagues had become more calm, self-aware, attentive, less controlling and judgemental – able to deal with whatever was being thrown at them during this period of unprecedented change (we also heard it had improved the quality of family relationships).

First, we had the great advantage of Michael Chaskalson as a faculty team member. A recognised and expert mindfulness practitioner for over 40 years, he brought the core concepts of the subject to life through three mini lectures and one in-depth tutorial (the very few in the total of 10 days across the formal programme). While I have heard it said, 'mindfulness is caught, not taught', nonetheless a new subject for business leaders merited explanation and grounding in theory. These worked well.

But, as importantly, we introduced participants to a range of practices across the programme that could cultivate their capacity for greater mindfulness. This began with the most classical method of meditation, which we built up during the programme starting with the well-known 'mindful raisin-eating' exercise through to breathing meditation, body scans and, helpful for building in mindfulness through a busy day, a mindful minute meditation.

But we emphasised to participants that there are many routes to becoming more mindful. The two key criteria are: use a practice that makes you more aware of the present moment – your thoughts, emotions, sounds, touch, taste, smell and physiological state; and make sure this practice is a regular, and preferably, daily one! And so each day on the programme before breakfast, we offered participants a choice between several guided mindful activities: meditation, yoga, walking in nature, running and swimming.

Throughout the day we also built in mindful moments and at times simply the space of taking a walk outside together as a group. This was a very popular activity on Day 4 of Module 2 – a quiet contemplative day of choice where participants let the eventful learning of the week (see next section) settle and knit together for them personally. These guided walks entailed walking in silence with a colleague alongside you for 30 minutes. This is something I enjoy very much, and yet I was pleasantly surprised to learn how much participants got from this simple activity. It not only helped them tune into self, it also formed a precious and noticing bond with another. In silence with another there is so much that can be experienced.

Finally, we aimed to run the whole development experience in a mindful way.[2] Mindfulness, ultimately, is not a technique or a tool but a way to live your life. At all times we as faculty aimed to keep participants' attention in the direct present moment experience of the living laboratory. And when, as we are wont to do, the group's attention moved away from direct experience and into narrative mode, getting caught up in stories about the 'world out there', we gently brought them back to what was happening, now, in the room. There is nothing wrong with narratives but they can take leave of reality, and comfortably cushion you from facing what is being acted out in the present moment, which is wasteful if not dangerous when leading change as you miss the only moment available *to* change things.

So the entire programme had an aim of increasing participants' attention and awareness on the present moment, taking a look at what their minds were habitually up to, in order that they might hear themselves and notice their defensive routines more deeply ('Gosh, I never realised how much I use sarcasm to distance myself from others!' or, 'Now I can see how much my own self-judgement is holding me back!'). And, once they had developed the capacity to notice, they had the power to choose how they wished to lead and live their life.

But there was another reason why we kept participants' attention on the present moment. And that was to help them learn to see that what was happening in their minds, and that of the group, was also a property of the wider system. The 'system in the room' was but a fractal of the wider culture, not just about the individual personalities and group dynamics present. Once you are more mindful you have the capacity to see this.

Developing Systemic Skill

I learned greatly through this experience about how to position the importance of systemic capacities for leadership. It is not an easily explainable skill. Here's the frame that I found helped most. The operating model that had brought the company success in the past was defunct. A whole system had been built up over time perfectly designed to run that model, including visible structures and management processes, but also less visible hierarchies, loyalties, professional allegiances and ways of working. As the world had now forever changed and the operating model needed reinventing so, too, did its underlying nested system. It was no good trying to get new results from an old place. The source needed attending to.

We therefore positioned this development experience not as a programme to *solve* the business issues; it was an experience to develop the new underlying capacities required *to* solve the business issues. Our task was to work *on* the system in the room, not *in* it. In the words of one participant, 'My big "aha!" was that this programme is not about solving things but drawing things out in novel and insightful ways'.

This core intent became very important to how the faculty held and ran the programme. Given the urgency and pressure to change, participants understandably would want to move quickly into *doing* and solving issues (staying *in* the system), 'Let's grab a flip chart and create our new mission statement!' This often happened as a rebellion at the start of an experiential process in which we were inviting participants to do something new, changing and uncomfortable (working *on* the system). In times such as this we would simply highlight what we saw happening in the room, and invite them to explore the choice they had – to rush into standard-operating-procedure action to feel more task-y and comfortable, or, to stay in what was feeling very awkward for them and find out if this could build new capacities for approaching their tough business situation in a very different way.

We found the systemic capacity almost impossible to teach via lectures. Almost all of the systemic learning (how what is happening here in the room is also a microcosm of the wider organisational culture outside this room, so, let's try and change it here in order to learn how to change it there) started in experience and we worked back from there. Being able to drop into another level of reality and see the underlying system at work can only come via felt experience, guided by real-time systemic observational interventions from the faculty.

We ran three key experiential learning activities that were most able to cultivate systemic skills: a *business simulation* (learning about power dynamics and how you take up your role in an organisational hierarchy, both of which fundamentally influence the quality of the system's performance); *systemic constellations work* (creating living maps of complex systemic issues that brought phenomenological intelligence to bear on seeing and resolving stuck problems, leaving both leaders and the whole system deeply moved); and a *'spiral' large group dialogue process* (a pressure cooker of a process that involved a novel seating format and self-directed dialogue to enable participants to see how they co-created the system in the room).

These three activities stirred up the most participant disturbance on this programme, 'You have stolen a day of my life!' was just one extreme version of the feedback. This could easily have thrown us as faculty, and we took responsibility when at times the experience could have been better. But, mainly, the disturbance was a positive sign. It showed us that the underlying system was pushing back against something new. So, we kept going – as these experiences always stirred up a new way of being in experience, a radically altered perception of reality, a more emotionally intelligent way of relating to others and a capacity to collectively walk through difficulty – system changing capacities that this company acutely needed in its business, and in its relationship with society.

In the wise words of a participant, 'I now know that it's more satisfying to have both comfort and discomfort.'

Foraging Groups and Prototyping

Foraging and prototyping afforded participants valuable opportunities to step into something that is not yet known. While they also led to tangible outcomes – innovations in how to lead the company and run the business – it was the *experience* of doing something new and different that powerfully created most insight and learning ('So, *that's* what it takes to listen to and learn from the outside world!' 'Now I can *feel* what it takes to act like an innovator!').

Again we were drawing on inspiration from the work of Otto Scharmer and his Theory U process, which contends that the route to being able to *lead from the emerging future* entails: immersing yourself in future pointing contexts on the periphery of your system; going to source and deeply sensing what is now being called for; and putting in place experimentation to explore this emerging future by doing. To broadly follow that journey we set up foraging visits to the external world between Modules 1 and 2, and rapid prototyping experiments between Modules 2 and 3.

The *foraging visits* had participants self-organising into small groups and then setting up and entering a new context either outside, or on the periphery of the organisation. The stated aim was to move into the contexts in which they could experience the future. As faculty, we would make sure that participants did not just go to the seductive exciting places (Google, Amazon, Berlin Innovation hub) but also contexts that would be challenging and confronting (politicians and environmental NGOs).

These experiences provided Transforming Spaces for learning, especially as they shone light not just on what the outside world was up to, but also on the character of their own company – nothing beats visiting another culture in order to better understand your own. In the words of one participant, 'I feel more open and connected to the outside world; it has opened my eyes and stimulated new insights about my business. I am now recreating the atmosphere from the Forager Groups in my teams.'

Drawing on these external foraging visits, and all the systemic learning about what needed to change in the internal culture, participants then ventured into rapid prototyping. Part of the overall process of Design Thinking,[3] rapid prototyping is a human-centred approach to implementing innovation around big ripe issues that starts with a half-baked (0.7 complete) idea that you test and get beneficiary feedback on in a small context (it's not a big idea planned out in all detail in advance). Participants created prototypes ranging from new decentralised energy solutions for housing associations, leaner business planning processes and even an 'Anger Room' staff engagement process in the business unit most facing a difficult future.

This rapid experimentation approach was an extremely *system changing* one for this organisation and had great impact in the wider culture. Again, the programme was not expected to produce prototypes that would necessarily save the company, but the *experience* of prototyping built radically new capacities in the leaders and their business that *felt* the change they were planning to do. In the words of participants.

> We have already started testing things out through prototyping. We realised we fell back into old programme management habit! We have now moved to a more open and iterative approach.
>
> The idea of the 70%/0.7 solution for prototyping is very difficult here, we are always trying to be perfect, in 100% mode!
>
> The prototyping is great, we have put it into action today. It is reducing the power distance. The frontline staff thought it was great – but what about the hierarchy?

While it was the learning experience more than the outputs that mattered, nonetheless prototyping did lead to operational impact that helped improve credibility for the programme, 'Following the prototyping someone came to me and said, "Can you do this in my OpCo?" There was an overpayment/invoicing problem in the team. We did it, and it was a success. My colleague then said to me, "You are not wasting your time on this programme".

Still Moving and Business Transformation – Final Reflections

I hope the chapter has shone light on both how Still Moving skills can act in service of business transformation, and how those skills can be developed. It's a story of how important it is to first attend to the *Still* inner capacities when you are facing disturbance and uncertainty. In this situation it is so easy for leaders to want to rush into action and not consider the very source of how they act. The quality of this source, or how you *be* as a leader, fundamentally determines the quality of how you *act* and the results you create. In times of big change ignore this inner state at your peril.

We learned through this experience how important it was for leaders to Stay Present and notice their autopilot impulses, in order to invite in the new: to cultivate Curious and Intentional Responding in order to approach, and not avoid difficulty; to learn to more deeply Tune into the System in order to lead a system that was stuck and under stress; and to be open enough to Acknowledge the Whole so that they could sense and respond to what society was now asking of them. And I, myself, learned what these inner capacities truly meant, and how they connected to my *Moving* outer game.

In particular, I had to up my game in Acknowledging the Whole in order to provide strong Containment in and around the programme. As you can imagine a lot of my attention was not just on the faculty team and participants, I also needed to help channel the curiosity and, at times, anxiety in the wider system. I therefore spent time with various leadership teams in the business helping them to have the difficult conversations about the change.

My second biggest personal development was to learn how to cultivate the calmness and detachment so essential in Staying Present, in order that I could place Edge and Tension back into the wider system when I needed to. There were several times when I wrote quite confronting email messages to the CEO and his board colleagues when I felt that they needed to up their game in how they led the change. This was in response to what I had experienced on the programme (once I had decluttered that from projections, as very often I became the 'kicking horse' for top management).

As I said at the beginning of this tale, the jury is still out on whether or not the big strategic move that this programme helped generate will be a success. However, its leaders have said that the decision to take this bold step (splitting the company and launching an initial public offering (IPO) for one of the parts) could not have been made without this programme. While, in its pioneering novelty, the programme was not for every individual seen as helpful, I *can* say that at the level of the whole it has built the skills of this organisation's leaders to face an ending and create a new beginning – this is movement, not just action.

Here's one participant summing up what for me was the most critical capacity created in this programme that enabled the company to endure the stomach-churning nature of major transition, 'In meetings we now share our emotional journeys and personal experience, using more feelings-based language. One leader did that recently and it completely changed the impact in the large group, it positively changed the space.'

And neither is it just the participating leaders making positive claims. A recent pulse survey of the company's top 1,600 leaders revealed a positive attitude and vote of confidence in the radical structural solution, despite its major uncertainty. This is an organisation prepared and ready for change. Not only that, external hard-nosed bankers and other professional advisers supporting the move have said they have never experienced a group of senior leaders so able to quickly and collaboratively put big change into place.

One reason for this could be explained by the comment of a recent new joiner from their major competitor. He said to me how much more informal, open and emotionally connected this culture felt to his previous one. He said people make strong eye contact here. They hug each other. And as they connect they are stronger.

Those words meant a lot to me. As I sit here in the Cornish tranquility of Portloe, writing this book, I am reflecting on all that this experience required of me, and, in turn, what I took from it.

Without it, you would not have this book. It inspired me to do the latest research into the impact of mindfulness on leading big change. Around me on my writing desk sit the faces of all the 360 leaders I met – and laughed and learned and cried with – along the way. Without them, and their visionary CEO, I would not have formed such an unimaginably close and committed faculty team. Who, in addition to the many trials and tribulations of running over 100 days' worth of living laboratory development together, helped five of its members grieve the loss of a parent.

The experience was a window into the importance of connections, and connecting. Of simple truths such as acknowledgement of reality, respect for what is and gratitude for what can be so freely given.

Experience is a generous teacher. And it's the best way to learn Still Moving leadership. Let's now turn to that.

10

Still Moving and Your Leadership

> *Do I dare*
> *Disturb the universe?*
>
> T.S. Eliot, The Lovesong of J Alfred Prufrock

'You are not born with this chart', sagely observed one of our research participants. He and I were poring over the bar graph that showed his Still Moving leadership profile, the relative strengths of how the four inner capacities and four external practices had showed up in his Behavioural Event Interview. Here was a CEO of one of the largest North American cable TV companies in deep reflection. He continued with a confession, 'At 29, I was a controlling micromanager'. I probed a bit, 'So what happened between then and now?'

His response helps illuminate what it takes to become the kind of leader that made his change story one of the highest scoring in our study – containing rich evidence of both the inner and outer skills and with zero incidences of non-mindful controlling behaviour (one of the very few leaders out of the 65 research participants who achieved that). He clearly had come a long way: Still Moving leadership can be developed, but it doesn't happen overnight. Working on the self is slow, deep and never-ending work, and it requires you to be open to unknown and potentially confronting territory.

Pause and notice: before you read on, what have you done to this point in your life in your development as a leader?

Here's what the CEO said about what it had taken him. His response to my question was all about experience, but here was a leader who could *learn from* and not just *be* his experience. He talked about two leaders he had particularly admired in his early career and how he had watched them both pull off major turnarounds of their companies. He then described how he had put those lessons into practice in his first international assignment, also a turnaround. I had worked with him at that time,

Still Moving: How to Lead Mindful Change, First Edition. Deborah Rowland.
© 2017 John Wiley & Sons Ltd. Published 2017 by John Wiley & Sons Ltd.

and knew just how much that assignment had required him to handle significant pressure while working in uncertain and unfamiliar territory – a 'dark alley' experience, in his words.

Throughout his career he had worked with the same coach, who helped him with 'savviness and street smarts'. And it was street smarts that he had to learn, as this leader was extremely bright in IQ terms. Indeed, he explained that one of the biggest things he had to learn as he matured and rose in the ranks was, 'How to create ownership when you're really smart'. I heard this as a genuine conundrum for him, not a boast. I have worked alongside many leaders like him – exceptionally bright people whose temptation is to always have the smartest answers before others can get there. The problem is that theirs might not be the complete answer, and this *shaping* style is profoundly disempowering and leads to failure in large complex change (not least executive burn out).

As we continued our conversation, he began to talk about his life experience. In particular, learning as a parent how to handle a teenage son with addiction issues. He had had to look at himself in the mirror and handle difficulty in contexts way beyond the boardroom. Recalling him from 20 years ago I was struck by my memory of his leadership humanity when under fire. I was now starting to understand where this came from as the whole person behind the leader emerged.

Bringing it back to the present I asked him how he cultivated the ability to be mindful as a leader. While he had no formal mindfulness practice he observed.

> I think a lot about stuff, as in today's world where things are constantly changing you need to be constantly reflecting, checking for a change in the winds. And I have a lot of plane time as I'm doing bi-coastal commuting and I use that time to reflect. Or when I'm getting ready for a board presentation I stop for a moment and pull my thoughts together. I strongly believe that self-awareness and reflectiveness is an integral part of leadership.

This is a leader who had in just 2 years transformed the customer experience journey of a complacent organisation, doubled its net promoter score, had management buy-in move from 22 to 84% and in doing all the above saved his company $100 m per year.

He concluded our conversation with an in-character reflection that *what* to change is usually pretty obvious; it's *how* you lead the change that is far more problematic. He had spent 30 years in personal development figuring out how to crack this nut. A life-long learner, watching others and learning from his own experience in handling change – be that in business or in life. He was able to reflect on both what worked and what had not worked for him. This leader's investment in his development, and his journey into darker places, had certainly paid off. Yet even now he has his fears and insecurities as he left me saying, 'Am I too nice a guy? Will people take advantage of me?' I for one wish him to remain exactly as he is, as our world needs more leaders like him.

Pause and notice: what, if anything, has this CEO's story stirred up for you?

How Can Still Moving Leadership Be Cultivated?

My conversation with this CEO (and other research participants) got me thinking. How *do* you develop the depth and range of skills in Still Moving? My research proved Still Moving leadership led to successful change but how do you become good at it? I have seen (and personally experienced) just how tough it is for leaders to shift ingrained habits, especially Still Moving's prime enemies – inattention, self-protection and the ego's instinct to control experience. We learn to operate in auto-pilot, defend and shape mode because it can be effective for our survival not just our day-to-day functioning.

Before I close this book I want to share some reflections on how to learn to cultivate and sustain a Still Moving leadership approach – a style of leadership that could be so much more conscious, expansive and able to deal with today's disruptive and interconnected world.

As I set out in Chapter 2, we have had decades of leadership development investment yet still see institutional leadership around the world that frankly isn't cutting it for today's challenges. Maybe it's the leadership frameworks that are misguided. Perhaps. But I also believe it's the *leadership development approach* that is responsible.

So, my focus in this chapter is on *how you develop your inner state*, the mindfulness and systemic capacities. Still Moving leadership and hence its development has to start on the inside. Our research showed that these inner capacities *antecede* the practices when you lead change successfully. You've got to get your self into the right place first. The quality of all your action comes from this inner place. Yet, irksomely, the inner capacities are by far the more challenging to learn and master! They are not tools and techniques, as I learned while trying to get to grips with the still movement flow of Qigong. They are about *intentionally and open-mindedly working on the self* in order to operate from a different mode of awareness, consciousness and being.

An evolving self is therefore central to Still Moving leadership development. Now, I don't know about you – but for me this can be a little challenging, so:

Don't Be Prepared to Go Past Go, Unless…

You *are* genuinely open for the journey, as here's the catch-22. You have to already contain an element of mindfulness and systemic awareness to have the capacity to learn it. In order to learn about your mind and how its responses might not always serve you well, you first need an open and curious mind and be able to be gentle with yourself (beating yourself up is not the way to learn these deeper, more challenging skills). To be open to a systemic lens and a wider frame within which to view reality you need to be prepared to see the unique, magical unfolding of the here-and-now experience and have let go a little of your past, and your own judgements. If these conditions are not present, this type of leadership cannot be learned and fully embraced.

When I entered as a participant on the challenging 2-week Tavistock Institute's Leicester Group Relations conference last year, I was a little sceptical and standing in judgement. My defences were on the alert – this was going to be purely for professional and not personal development, so if I wasn't finding it useful to my change practice after 2 days I had my get-out-of-jail card prepared. I had sharpened my intellect for the fray – proudly in the conference opening I had already begun to (silently) disagree with some of the statements of the faculty, and found myself eyeing up the other participants to assess if I could learn from anyone here.

I caught myself in these routines, thankfully, and switched them. This was not easy to do. It took a whole 2 days to trowel away my routines, as the defences (to stay on the edge and not jump in – remember, adoption!) ran deep. However, if I had not switched them not only would I have wasted a lot of money, I would have missed what was for me one of the greatest learning experiences in my last decade. But, in order to switch these self-protecting routines into an open learner's stance I had to get up on Day 3, ditch my 27 years of experience in the field (which until that point had served me well), and simply enter the conference as me, here, now, Deborah, bringing to you my fears, imperfections, desires and still unmet needs. The conference wasn't going to change unless I changed my response to it.

Here's the good news. If you *do* want to pass go and be open to doing something differently, stepping into this field of greater self-awareness and systemic perception, whatever you pick up and incorporate into your leadership will be of high leverage. The nature of adult learning is hard, but any little change is very important. By shifting just a little of how you perceive reality, by adjusting a tiny fragment of how you sit with experience, you will show up to that moment and your life a whole lot differently and your leadership practice will flow. And who knows what immediate and wider impact that could bring.

At the Leicester conference when I gave up the professional Deborah persona (ouch), stopped trying to moderate and guide others (what do I do now?!) and saw the whole conference, its participants and its strange activities as a river to flow in and not a field to impress in (re-lax!), I accessed the core of myself that had been dormant for a very long while. And that's when my leadership started to flow and I could be a more valuable learning resource to the whole community. But first I had to put aside my skilfully constructed professional defences.

Pause and notice: what's going on for you now? Ever had a 'Leicester moment' too? If yes, what did it take of you?

In the previous chapter I told the tale of working with 360 such leaders and I feel them, and the faculty, alongside me as I write. The experience gave me great insight into how to develop Still Moving skills. A bit like myself at Leicester, without that CEO's courage to personally show up in the first wave of that programme with his whole self, struggles and all, not just 'playing to the crowd' as their leader supporting a new programme, it would have got in the way of his and other people's learning and the programme would not have been nearly as impactful.

How you learn as a leader will be noticed by your team and spoken about in the wider organisation. But it doesn't come without personal risk, as doing anything new or strange risks failing. As I was reminded in Leicester, the only way to learn is the willingness to look ignorant. It requires openness to vulnerability.

How to Cultivate Still Moving Leadership – Overall Principles

I have already firmly put out *principle number one – be fully prepared to invite in the new.* Enough said. But it leads me to the overarching must-have to cultivating Still Moving leadership, which is that your approach has to *live* the Still Moving construct. If learning experiences are not mindfully designed and delivered, the outcome could be mind*less*ness.[1] The best way to learn Still Moving is therefore to have a Still Moving type experience. So as well as being fully prepared to invite in the new (i.e. Curious and Intentional Responding), I'd suggest that your learning needs the following features: make it experience based; impact being before doing; don't go it alone; and pick a regular practice.

Principle Number Two: Make It Experience Based

In the entire 2 weeks of the Leicester conference there was not one single lecture or input of theory. Recall again the CEO from the previous chapter's story. In order to build new capacities in his organisation he first put people into Transforming Space experiences that looked and felt different. When people were pleasantly surprised at the outcome they were then ready to theorise as to why that was the case (it was not until the penultimate day at Leicester that we were allowed to buy books related to what we had been learning). Experiences prompt you to notice things – the essence of becoming mindful. You become curious. Not just about what you see and experience but how you respond on the inside to what you see and experience (and perhaps even what you do about that!). But you have to have the lived experience first.

If you begin in the head you will only stay in the head. We can't simply think our way out of a habit. When our habitual mind is involved we can struggle to understand why we do what we do, as habits largely function outside of our awareness. Whereas, in experience our intentional mind can be more engaged as we make conscious decisions about our behaviour.

Remember from the previous chapter how we built mindful systemic capacities – we did so by first providing (carefully structured) experiences that required participants to *function* in a new type of system. At times that system changing move was as simple as changing the seating arrangements in the room and our role as faculty. The spiral seating format and non-faculty directed dialogue was so unusual for participants that the experience often began in several minutes of silence. This was agonisingly uncomfortable for most leaders. With 36 pairs of eyes boring into me I sat still and did nothing.

And I did so because this totally visceral experience – if participants were open to it fully, see principle number one – built all four of the inner capacities. It cultivated the capacity to tune into their inner experience, even to hot flushes, backaches and a yearning to get up and *do* something (Staying Present – what's going on for me now?). Participants learned how to be with something new and strange, in approach and not avoidance mode, gingerly trying out new ways to respond to such an experience, 'I'm used to only leading when I can see people's faces, let me now get over my discomfort and experiment with how to do this when I can't' (Curious and Intentional Responding – how do I consciously want to show up with what is going on for me?).

If participants had invested effort in reaching this more mindful place, and not checked out, this newfound capacity enabled them to notice more empathically what was happening in the group. For example, they noticed where and how were we all sitting in this spiral and what that said about how we took up our leadership roles in this organisation more generally (Tuning into the System – can I interpret what's going on here for all of us)? And as this dialogue process developed through the week and participants were prepared to stick with it and experiment, it enabled them to experience the transforming power of discomfort and difficulty. Each time they continued with what felt strange they broke through into a radically deeper and more connected place (Acknowledge the Whole – can I give all that we have experienced a respectful place?).

I contend that this form of lived collective experience brought far more powerful learning than a lecture on brain chemistry, or an explanation of Bion's basic assumption groups, could have ever achieved.

This is why I intentionally use the word *cultivate* for developing Still Moving, and not train. The capacities are not straightforward tools that can be taught, but deep sensibilities, ways of perceiving and experiencing the self in a system that need to be felt and nurtured within a context (either a real or simulated one). This is hard to do *offline* and in a classroom, where the temptation to teach absolutes only brings stability, not movement. It can only be done *online* in real time, where you can be open to the unfolding nature of experience, getting feedback and adjusting as you go. Mindfulness is not about *thinking* more clearly; it is about *experiencing* more clearly. And that is exactly what Still Moving leadership is about – changing the *now* of experience. I'm not saying that classroom learning and training are not effective; I just don't believe the results are sustainable enough for deep leadership work.

What do I mean by *experience*, as development does not always happen in the workplace? It can mean so-called real life experience (like we did with the foraging and prototyping activities in the development programme in the previous chapter) but it also means offering an experiential activity that replicates working situations (such as the large group dialogues and business simulations). Both, however, are about learning and change *in real time*, not sitting around a flip chart writing up behaviours about what is to be done – the very activity *itself* is designed to live what has to be done. In Still Moving language, make sure that your Still Moving development happens within a Transforming Space.

Pause and notice: how are you currently trying to develop yourself as a leader? Does anything you do reflect this principle of making it experience based? What does this mode bring you that other modes cannot? What might you risk by doing it?

Principle Number Three: Impact Being Before Doing

The next principle relates to the *quality* of the experience you set up. Learning experiences can be hyperactive, fizzy and noisy, or they can be more tranquil, still and spacious. As we know that effective change leadership starts in your *being* and not your *doing*, attending to the quality of how you *stand* before you *move*, it's important that the learning experience offers space for intentional, non-obstructed inner contemplation.

Without space there is no movement.

A personal example of this kind of experience is the *silent working retreat* I referred to at the start of Chapter 3. This was a 5-day experience with six other participants, held by Anjet van Linge and Sytske Casimir (two experienced group relations conference faculty), set in a magical environment in nature. Between 9:00 a.m. and 5:00 p.m. each day we spent the time by ourselves in silence, gathering together just for lunch – which was held in silence. Some of us brought a task to create a work of art, some came to write, some arrived to figure out how to start up a new business venture. Others showed up to contemplate what the next phase of their life was going to be about. At 5:00 p.m. each day we would gather for a guided meditation followed by supper when we caught up with each other's days – often finding magical connections between what we imagined were separate personal journeys. Without these annual retreats I would never stop, notice and reset myself in a different way. I see them as a bit like an annual leadership checkup.

My faculty colleagues from the development programme in the last chapter brought much imagination to the spaces within which their Peer Groups met. Sitting around in an office type environment was one way of doing it, but what brought greater learning impact at the *being* level was inviting their Peer Groups to their homes – one of my colleagues is a stone sculptor and her Peer Group members got to spend a day in her studio trying to (calmly!) carve letters in a piece of stone. Another colleague runs leadership workshops with her horses, and her Peer Group members had the very challenging yet joyful experience of learning just how much the quality of their inner self impacted their ability to work with them. One Peer Group met at the top of a Bavarian mountain, another in the stunning modern art gallery that is the Museum Folkwang in Essen.

This perspective-altering source-level being-impacting development approach is not the norm in most corporate leadership development settings. My colleagues and I are working with a company that knows it needs to lead change in a different way. One that is based more in transforming co-creating dialogue and less in transmitting centrally led programmes (mirroring how in the business they need to relate more humbly and collaboratively with their rapidly changing customer base). In our design conversations with our client the pull is always towards, 'Train us in the tools of effective dialogue', despite our gentle invitation to 'Set up an open space in which we can *feel and notice* our inner responses to participating in an unstructured conversation that we create together in real time'.

Training in tools and holding a space to *be with being* mindfully are two quite different learning approaches.

Here's another example – the more traditional leadership development method of 360-degree feedback doesn't cut it for me – at least not for cultivating Still Moving capacities. Three hundred and sixty-degree feedback is an approach done offline; it is not a lived embodied experience that changes the nature of the field. It is a task to complete with an analysis and feedback that then moves on to a development plan and hopefully implementation. This is a *doing* type energy, that does not impact the *being* of the learner and their leadership field. It does not change the very source from which a leader and their team operate (and is often a long laborious process to administer and complete).

As an alternative, I prefer to use *live real-time feedback* processes. Imagine a process in which you sit down with your team, in a circle, and invite each one of them to provide you with feedback on how they have experienced your leadership. This usually raises the hair on necks (you do of course give them a frame and a chance to prep in advance). As your team provides you with feedback, practise sitting still, in silence throughout, listening to them and journaling both what they are saying, *and*, your thoughts, feelings, sensations and impulses *as you take in* what they are saying (Staying Present). When they provide the feedback you move your chair slightly out of the circle so that they speak to each other about you as if you are not in the room. This provides you with a degree of detachment, like acting as an impartial observer to your leadership (leading to a more Curious and Intentional response).

Note down themes and patterns in the feedback, and when you rejoin your team have a conversation with them about how that process felt for you as you were listening and what you picked up about the emotional climate in the room when they were speaking about your leadership (Tuning into the System). In that debrief process appreciate what each individual has said about you – even if the messages were contradictory, and in particular highlight the points of their feedback that might have felt most dangerous for them to say, or were the most difficult for you to hear (Acknowledging the Whole).

Each time I have run this process, either for others, or myself, it has always led to deep goose bump kind of moments that shift the system in the room. In that respect it is a powerful way to develop Still Moving capacities in teams. When a leader can sit with this kind of experience, intentionally working on their inner game throughout, the quality of the intervention takes the team to a new place of trust, mutual support and connection. And the individual leader, after such a moving public experience, more often than not puts the feedback into action.

Pause and notice: is your leadership learning more in being or doing mode? Which development experiences have most shifted you on the inside? What conditions were present to enable that?

Principle Number Four: Don't Go It Alone

When you are learning through live embodied experiences that impact the nature of your being, it's helpful to have wise mentors who can create the psychological safety to hold you through the experience and help you (re)perceive its nature. Psychological safety allows you to take personal (and, in groups, interpersonal) risk. And good guides build a sense of confidence that you will not embarrass yourself, or be rejected or punished for speaking up or doing something new. This is deep work. You need to feel well held. You can (feel like you) look a little silly when learning something new.

Have you reached out as a leader to find good guides? Especially guides who invite you to look inside your self and become more personally and systemically aware? Remember my story with Chris at the start of Chapter 5. While change can only operate from within the self that doesn't mean the learning to provoke it has to be only with the self (which would be tempting for me, as a Myers–Briggs Introvert – just send me out in nature or give me lots of books to read please!).

So it helps to have encouraging and supportive guides whose role is to work with you in real time (not reported) experience, and intervene *in the moment.* And by intervene in the moment I don't mean pointing out a theory that might help you, or, being the process time manager, or offering you 'If I were you I'd do this' type of advice. Guides who help build Still Moving capacity best act as acute observers of present moment emotional and behavioural dynamics (including their own felt experience) and are able to use that noticing awareness either as a source of inquiry or a confronting mirror. This might be a facilitator moderating a group, or a coach working with an individual. *The principle here is that they use what shows up in the live interaction as the learning material.* This kind of learning plummets from the cognitive head right down into the toes of your being, acting as a powerful gateway to movement.

And it takes a certain set of skills to do this that spring from a *deep helping place.* Critically, the guide's presence and practice aim to model Still Moving leadership. I used Still Moving type skills (in their then nascent state) when selecting the faculty for the development programme in the previous chapter. I looked for critical qualities that included: being able to stay present and work with what arises from moment to moment;

being able to intentionally approach what arises with curiosity and not judgement; being able to tune into and systemically interpret the emotional undercurrent of a group; can work with and integrate difficulty (including their own) as fertile learning material; and has the ability to bring all of these inner capacities to bear in providing both challenging and supportive in-the-moment interventions.

Pause and notice: how do any guides that you use in your leadership development check out against this role and these qualities?

The don't go it alone principle doesn't mean you always have to have an external coach guiding you. Recall in previous chapters how leaders ask for volunteers from their teams to act as meeting observers. A further example: while it helps at the outset to have strong moderators to set up a Peer Group process I have seen these groups able to take the learning along alone. *What is critical to learning in teams, however, is that there is enough psychological safety for learning to occur.* Most teams are set up to (at times competitively) deliver results, not intentionally learn from each other and the experience, which takes interpersonal risk. But when I work with leaders wishing to create a so-called 'high performance team' (which, I would contend, is a very wise move when the team is having to pull off big change together), then they are for sure teams who need to be able to learn together, giving each other honest feedback and adjusting in the moment, rapidly.

Pause and notice: are you well resourced with guides along your leadership journey? Who might you have missed as a teacher? Feel their presence with you now.

Principle Number Five: Pick a Regular Practice

The quality of your being is not something you switch on and off. Even if out of awareness your inner state is your constant companion. Your mind and your mental state are always there in the background whirring like an operating system on a computer. It therefore helps to find a reflective practice that you can use to regularly tune into your inner state. We know from the observer effect that the very act of observation changes what is being observed. So, by regularly observing your inner state you become adept at changing your response to experience *in all of experience.* This is a magical skill, and an essential one in the hurly burly of leading change (and dare I say it all forms of human relationships).

Whatever formal practice you select to become more present-moment aware, the key is to do it regularly. Neuroscience imaging shows us that the regular practice of mindfulness meditation correlates with changes to the physical structure and patterns of activation in your brain, leading, for example, to enhanced left prefrontal cortex activation and reduced right prefrontal activation, thickening of the cortex, and reduced activation of the amygdala.[2] And these changes, in turn, can result in greater non-reactivity, empathy and enhanced cognitive functioning. Over time, therefore, with regular practice, mindfulness can start to become an enduring character *trait*, not just a *state* of being stressed or otherwise in one particular moment. You *remain* alert, emotionally regulated, curious and able to handle whatever comes your way.

This is a real prize. Your leadership presence and character become enduring assets. Being kicks in. You ditch the leadership tools you might have learned at business school. While the situation around you might remain challenging, you become a leader who as one CEO described to me is like 'the eye in the storm'. Of course, as humans we can still act out in impulsive ways and get caught up by experience. 'Regression' is what my therapist calls it. I prefer saying that I can 'lose it' from time to time. But as Michael Chaskalson says, 'Practice is what this is all about and, if you commit to your stream of practice and do it with whatever regularity you can muster, real change will follow.'[3]

A mindfulness practice is an activity in which you intentionally bring your attention to your present moment state (your thoughts, stories, feelings, any bodily sensations, impulses), in a welcoming and non-judgemental way. The object of the exercise is not to *change* your state, it's purely to bring greater attentiveness *to* your inner state, and notice whatever shows up – be that joy or sadness, ease or discomfort, alertness or fatigue. What you are doing is developing the *capacity* for non-reactive and intentional noticing in the present moment, learning how to get in direct contact with that experience, so you can be at ease with your life more generally.

Mindfulness practices can be either formal or informal. Formal practices include mindfulness meditation (such as breathing and body-scan meditation), yoga (especially hatha style or those with an emphasis on breath awareness) or mindful journaling (regular noting down of your thoughts, feelings, sensations, impulses). Informal practices are essentially going about your existing activities in intentionally mindful ways, paying full attention to what you are doing and bringing your mind back when it wanders. My formal practice is hatha yoga. My informal practice is walking in nature, which I aim to do daily, even if it's just a 30-minute walk in a park at lunchtime.

When we asked research participants whether they had a regular practice to intentionally cultivate mindfulness, we got a range of responses. There were some meditators, but people also cited regular yoga, rowing, weight lifting, running or simply contemplating the flowers in their garden and not thinking about work. All though were about intentionally bringing their attention, in the present moment, to their inner state (not just running to get fit) – and simply noticing non-judgementally what was there, even the negative and difficult emotions.

But you don't have to add activities to your schedule. It's surprising how opportunities to practise the art of still contemplation are around you all the time. Just take routine activities. How do you eat your meals? By slowly and single-mindedly focusing on the experience of eating, taste, texture sensation and digestion, or by watching TV and having a call with your friend at the same time? How do you brush your teeth? By focusing on exploring the sensation of touch, taste and freshness, or by clearing up the bathroom and mentally rehearsing your to-do list as you're brushing? How do you drive to work? Do you get to the office not being able to recall how you got there, or do you drive mindfully, paying attention to the whole experience of your journey? We take, on average, 18,000 breaths a day. Allowing for sleep time, how many of the 10,000 remaining do you consciously notice?

I recently met a leader who had to pull off the turnaround of a major bank in the US that was under Securities and Exchange Commission (SEC) scrutiny – a very challenging and stressful time for her. Here's what she did every morning. When she got out of the shower and the bathroom mirror was all steamed up, she drew on it with her finger little faces that expressed the mood she was in. A routine she said that helped her greatly with how she entered the office that morning. As my therapist once memorably said to me, 'Deborah, when you can enjoy the moment of washing your dishes you know you've arrived.' That might take a little longer for me...

Pause and notice: do you have a (daily) practice that you intentionally use to get in contact with your inner state? Is there more that you could do? What would it take to commit to a more regular practice?

Developing Still Moving – Summary of Principles

So, in short, if you wish to cultivate Still Moving (inner) skills: be fully prepared to invite in the new; make sure you ground the development in a lived experience; create a learning space that can impact being before doing; don't go it alone; and pick a regular reflective practice that enables you to tune into your self.

Before I close this chapter I wish to comment on two frequently asked questions I get around this work, and which relate to how to learn it. What is the impact of personality type on a leader's ability to learn Still Moving? And, what cultural conditions need to be in place to encourage Still Moving leadership to flourish?

Still Moving Leadership – Do Individual Personality Differences Count?

Will some people find it naturally easier to learn Still Moving leadership than others? While not strictly a personality tool but a contextual preference type framework, people often try and associate their Myers–Briggs Type Indicator (MBTI) profile with Still Moving inner skills. Can people who hold an 'S' (sensing) MBTI preference more readily take up mindfulness as they enjoy getting in contact with direct sensory experience, and are less likely to take leave of reality into narrative? Are 'N' (intuitive) MBTI preferences more able to see beneath the surface of experience and learn systemic skills?

The other frequent comparator is with a leader's capacity for emotional intelligence. Studies have indeed shown that emotional intelligence and mindfulness are interrelated. Mindfulness helps build personal resilience and greater empathy, and makes people less likely to act defensively when they feel threatened – all indicators of someone who has high emotional intelligence. At the same time, emotional intelligence traits of self-awareness and the appropriate labelling of feelings help you become more aware of your inner state and able to de-centre yourself from troubling thoughts – in other words, emotional intelligence helps you to cultivate mindfulness.

Mindfulness is a radical shift in the way we pay attention (on the present moment, and without judgement). Systemic skill involves a shift in how we read and interpret what we are paying attention to (dropping down to see an invisible structure beneath reality). While in my research I did not explicitly investigate the relationship between personality and these inner capacities, my experience guides me to say that personality traits more naturally predisposed to these skills include: an openness to experience and learning; high self-awareness and authenticity; being self-secure, relaxed and at ease – low neuroticism; conscientiousness and application; a predisposition to work for the whole and not just seek to optimise the parts; and a sensitivity to a world beyond the concrete and the immediate.

Here's my take though on this question. Across almost three decades I have now worked with hundreds if not thousands of leaders helping them to learn about how to lead change. And their personalities cast a beautiful rainbow of colours across my mind. I do not believe that anyone's personality precludes him or her from being able to learn Still Moving leadership. Some find it easier, but all are able as it is a set of capacities and practices that can be learned. So ultimately, going back to my principle number one, it is the mindset to be fully prepared to invite in the new that is the vital precondition: being open to experience, able to show up to life expectantly and with genuine curiosity about what might unfold in the present moment. We are born with this instinct. While I acknowledge that our Origin Stories might have knocked us around a bit, leading to the construction of inner defences, I believe we *can* make a choice as to how we want to show up for our lives.

Still Moving Leadership – Does Culture Eat It for Breakfast?

There is, of course, a strong correlation between leadership and culture. You need a culture that is conducive to mindful and systemic leadership to give leaders an incentive to learn it. At the same time, by leaders learning it you will alter the culture around them. It can become a positive and mutually amplifying feedback loop. And yet sometimes it can feel like it is not enough for a leader, or even a leadership team, to be able to impact an organisation that is itself systemically wired to stay stuck.

Just as autopilot, self-protection and the ego's need to control what happens are the individual enemies of Still Moving, so too do you find its collective opponent. Organisations sleepwalking their way into the future, defending themselves against any external challenge and fixating on the self-deluding belief that they are in charge of their destiny. If these enemies are at your gates, learning Still Moving capacities could prove challenging.

Yet I am of the firm belief that leaders can and do make a difference to an organisation's culture, and that even tiny small changes in leadership style in one part of the system can get picked up and escalate to the rest. From my early days in this field with Dr George New, applying the pioneering and quite brilliant work of social psychologist David McClelland and his Harvard colleagues into leader motivation, style, organisational climate and outcomes,[4,5] I saw how just a tiny switch in the leader's mind could generate different results.

Here's my advice if you are a senior leader wishing to both learn Still Moving type leadership, and in turn, shape organisational culture: start small and build momentum from there. Take some of what you have learned from this book and try things out in your immediate team. Develop greater noticing skills in your team as to what is being experienced in the present moment – especially during difficult encounters. Have them become more conscious of their inner state as you approach a moment of significant decision-making, so you make wiser choices on how to respond to what is being experienced. Go out as a team into your organisation and the wider world to tune into the emotional climate of your system. Use this to anticipate the impact of your decisions and action.

Make sure you bring in a rich diversity of perspectives when you are sensing what direction you need to take. Make it safe for the team and your organisation to raise difficult subjects. And, from time to time, simply hang out together as a leadership team in a still and spacious setting and find out what most matters to each person and you all.

I have seen how more leaders in a culture collectively practising Still Moving leadership make a difference. It becomes a bit contagious. It's a much more appealing form of leadership. They start to build webs of relationships that can ease the strain of what feels like a non-mindful and non-systemically aware context. Over time, the fabric of the internal society starts to shift. The organisation as a whole becomes more conscious of the gap between its intent and its action. It stays attuned to its shadow and indeed encourages its exposure. It gets in greater contact with itself. And all of this can bring benefit to the wider world.

So, as an individual learner – please keep learning. And if you happen to be in a senior leadership role, please encourage your whole organisation to do so too.

11

The Sense of an Ending

*The golden moments in the stream of life rush past us and we see
nothing but sand; the angels come to visit us, and we only know them
when they are gone.*

George Eliot, English novelist (1819–1880)

Reported in Josiah Hotchkiss Gilbert, *Dictionary of Burning Words of
Brilliant Writers* (1895)

My life – as stated in the book opening – began in an ending and now
I face one here. I feel a touch sad as I write this final chapter and bring
a close to a writing process that has been my guiding companion for
6 months. An at times challenging and frustrating companion, but nonetheless a stimulating and enlarging one. Maybe you have felt similar
emotions in the reading experience. If this book has resonated then the
mirror neurons firing in my mind will have ignited a similar response in
yours. I am curious. What will have become present and precious for you?

Ultimately, we are all in some way connected in our messy, unpredictable
and disruptive world. It is, of course, our choice as to how we wish to take
up leadership in this context. But what we each individually choose to do
(and I hope it *is* a conscious choice as intentional leadership has been a
central tenet of this book) will impact others' lives. Leadership is increasingly a systemic act and a collective accountability. I set out at the start of
this book how I believe that *change is changing* since when I wrote *Sustaining
Change*. One salient feature in today's geopolitically and digitally joined up
world is interconnection. We cannot tackle systemic challenges such as
climate change, terrorism, refugee crises or joint economic prosperity
through the isolated acts of individual governments or CEOs.

A further feature of today's landscape is that *change* has ceased to be
about one-off set piece events and has morphed into an ongoing endemic
phenomenon – we now live in an extremely present *changing* world.
As digital and technological innovation continues at pace and the power

Still Moving: How to Lead Mindful Change, First Edition. Deborah Rowland.
© 2017 John Wiley & Sons Ltd. Published 2017 by John Wiley & Sons Ltd.

of ever-demanding and savvy consumers rises, today's business solutions can fast look outdated. Within such interconnected and dynamic contexts, a premium is now placed on leaders who are able to both connect and find common ground across traditional boundaries, and build their own system's capacity for continuous rapid change. Leadership today has to place change as its core competence.

However, just as the stakes for being able to lead change well within and across institutions are rising, so is it becoming increasingly impossible to implement change through traditional methods.

A collapse of trust in centrally commanded vertical authority and the powerful elite has been accompanied by growth in the power and authority of local communities and virtual peer-to-peer networks. It is now increasingly the periphery of a system, and not its centre, that instigates change. And as our organisations grow, become more complex and interconnected within their environments, it becomes a set of networks and relationships, not centrally provided programmes, which sustain change. So how do you now lead change in a world that is unknowable, interconnected and rapidly changing but also uncontrollable in the traditional sense? Has our environment outstripped our ability to lead it?

I believe not. However, I have argued throughout this book that leaders will not be able to lead change in today's world unless they sharpen their attention to its process. The simple fact is that *how* you do change fundamentally determines where you end up. Old ways of doing change in new contexts will no longer get us different futures. We will be busily acting but not still moving. So what are the fewest things you can do – as there can be so many elements to consider when implementing change – that will make the greatest difference?

I am asking that we become more conscious as leaders about three things: our overall approach to change; how we personally lead it; and how we develop the skills to lead change in others. Backed up not only by personal change leadership experience but also rigorous research, here is my summary of what I believe matters most.

Overall, Adopt a More Emergent Approach to Change

In our less top-down, controllable and knowable world, I believe that a change approach that is open to the dynamism and unfolding nature of experience is our best bet. Emergent change is based on the premise that all leaders *can* do in complex distributed and fast-moving contexts is shape the conditions within which a system can govern its own change. While this more bottom-up and self-organising approach to change assumes a relinquishment of control, we do know from the study of complex adaptive systems that emergent change can be shaped. We can in some way influence how local-level behaviour unfolds in order to create an aligned, coherent and innovative system at the level of the whole. And here's how.

First, set a loose intention or overall direction for your organisation. In emergent change, there is no need for fixed and detailed visions and plans. Second, create a set of hard rules that govern the micro-level behaviour of your system, rules that will ensure that people can act independently when in the heat of the fray, without any need to constantly check back with you. Third, identify where the ripest issues are in your organisation, the hot spots that most need attention, and focus innovation there first. Take the learnings from that experiment and transfer them elsewhere through networks and enthusiastic volunteers. In emergent change there is no need to roll out large-scale programmes across the whole system. And from there on in, work step by step, adjusting as you go. Your ongoing role as a leader of emergent change is to stay present, fan the flames, build new capacities and encourage multiple feedback loops so that the system as a whole becomes more joined up, intelligent and adaptive.

All of my research points to the compelling fact that emergent change is the most successful approach to change in contexts characterised by pace, uncertainty and complexity. However, as it goes against the grain of so much traditional change it will require a fundamental change in mindset. A mindset that not only relinquishes control but that is also able to quiet the ego's need to launch (expensive) high profile change initiatives. I am saddened when I see so much wasteful effort in change, and skip each time I witness the courage and wisdom of leaders to trust in the transforming power of localised adaptive behaviour.

For Yourself, Cultivate the Skills of Still Moving Leadership

Your personal leadership remains the single highest leverage change tool. I have created a new change leadership framework – *Still Moving* – that explains over half of the reason why big complex change can be led well. Put simply, by not consciously cultivating its skills you halve your chances of achieving successful change outcomes. I have contrasted *Still Moving* leadership with *busily acting* leadership. The former is conscious, mindful and systemic leadership that uncovers and shifts the source of today's routines through a few choice interventions. The latter is impulsive, habitual and shaping leadership that through multiple events and initiatives keeps a system spinning in its repeating patterns.

Still Moving leadership requires the mastery of eight interconnected skills. The four *Still* skills are *inner* capacities, qualities of *being*; the four *Moving* skills are *external* practices, qualities of *doing*. My research showed convincingly that the inner capacities antecede the external practices. Stillness is first required in order to move well. Change leaders therefore need to work on their own source of behaviour before they can begin to work on the source of their system's routines. So when I define change as the *disturbance of repeating patterns* this applies equally to your own way of perceiving and acting as it does to the system you are seeking to change.

Here is a summary of all eight skills (see Figure 11.1).

The Still Inner Capacities – How to 'Be' as a Change Leader

The first two inner capacities draw deeply from mindfulness practice and my research showed that they are the foundation for all that follows. If leaders are not inherently mindful, they will be unable to lead big challenging change.

Staying Present: leaders who have this capacity pay close and continual attention to the here-and-now moment without getting distracted or thrown by experience. They can observe what is going on for them (inner thoughts, feelings, sensations and impulses) calmly and objectively. The key skill is a *noticing* skill – what is here now. By being able to bring focused and non-judgemental attention to the present moment leaders build a keener awareness of reality, they don't miss the vital signs occurring in current experience that point to where change is needed.

Curious and Intentional Responding: leaders who have this capacity use deep awareness and personal intention to slow down the period between experience and reaction, staying curious and open-minded to what arises. They switch their minds from impulsive habitual reaction to creative intentional response. The key skill is a *choosing* skill. By being able to notice and regulate their emotional and cognitive response to experience, especially troubling experience, they move off autopilot and through resourceful responding can powerfully shape new contexts for themselves and others.

The next two inner capacities shift the attention from how you show up in experience to your capacity to interpret that experience through a systemic lens. Mindful leaders are alert clean tuning forks to wider systemic dynamics.

Tuning into the System: we are wired since birth to tune into others and leaders who sustain this capacity, free of personal projection, can

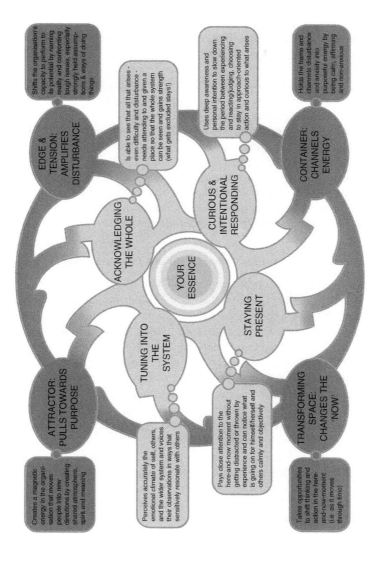

Figure 11.1 Still Moving: summary definitions.

tune into the emotional climate of self, others and the wider system, and put this into an interpretation that accurately and sensitively resonates with others. The key skill is a *perceiving* skill. By being able to drop into a deeper level of seeing reality they are able to interpret what is being directly experienced as a property of the system, not just the individuals present, leading to powerful diagnosis of what needs changing. *This skill was the inner capacity most correlated with successful change leadership.*

Acknowledging the Whole: leaders with this capacity are able to see that all that arises in experience – and in particular difficulty and disturbance – needs attending to and being given a place so that the whole system can be seen and gain strength. The key skill is an *integrating* skill. When leaders find the wisdom and capacity to sit with all of experience – including being open to what is not wanted – they can sense and shape the system's intentionality. By incorporating wobbles as revelatory and developmental material they can powerfully guide a system across dangerous yet transforming threshold experiences. This skill was in particular associated with successful top leaders of large complex systems.

The Moving External Practices – What to 'Do' as a Change Leader

The next four skills in combination enable you to create the capacity in your system for ongoing adaptive change – without you having to shoulder all the effort. They are contrasted with a leader-centric shaping style that, by personally controlling all of what gets done, leads to failure in large complex change. Here is what *to* do.

Attractor: leaders who have Attractor skill create a magnetic energy in the organisation that moves people into new directions by creating shared atmosphere, spirit and meaning. This skill creates a *pull towards purpose.* Leaders do this by getting out and about to tune into ground-level stories from which they shape a compelling change narrative. Without Attractor leadership change feels aimless and uninspiring. With it, change deeply matters. Importantly, people can see and feel that their leaders hold the entire purpose for the change effort as their own; it matters to them, and is in their hearts.

Edge and Tension: leaders who have Edge and Tension skill shift the organisation's capacity to perform to its potential by naming reality and confronting tough issues, especially strongly held assumptions that are acting as a handbrake on the change. This skill is about *amplifying disturbance.* Leaders do this by speaking plainly about difficulty, holding up the mirror to show a system its repeating patterns, holding the course when things get rocky, and ruthlessly focusing on the few priorities and performance indicators that most matter. Ultimately, this skill is predicated on the belief that systems get stronger and not weaker when reality is seen and squarely faced, and *it was the external practice most correlated with successful change leadership.*

Container: leaders who have Container skill can take the anxiety stoked up through Edge and Tension and channel it into productive energy by holding a clear frame for the change, staying non-anxious themselves and creating the psychological safety for people to speak out about difficult topics. This skill is about *channelling energy*. It's a key accompaniment to Edge and Tension and ensures that people's anxiety does not turn into defensive routines such as change denial or blaming upwards. Instead, by being clear, calm and affirming, leaders who practise Container skills create secure and felt safe workplaces that can move towards the new.

Transforming Space: leaders who have Transforming Space skill make and take opportunities to shift thinking and action in the here-and-now moment and this is based on the assumption that the only thing you *can* change *is* the present moment. This skill is about *changing the now*. Leaders who do this are able to make interventions that draw attention to current repeating patterns, they pay attention to the physical environment for transforming encounters, and they put together novel and diverse mixes of people. With this leadership skill, your change process moves that much faster and ensures that you are genuinely moving, not just making your organisation busy.

The inner capacities and the external practices are intimately connected. And the way into developing the external practices is through working on your internal capacities first. If you are not in the right place personally, it becomes impossible to lead change well.

How to Develop Still Moving Skills

I have also paid attention in this book to the leadership development processes that best cultivate these skills. I have put forward the proposition that Still Moving leadership cannot be developed in the conventional sense through *offline* taught models and programmes. Instead, the skills need to be incubated and nurtured via *online* experiential approaches that immerse leaders in a living laboratory style setting. Importantly, the development experience has to *be* a Still Moving experience.

In addition to development needing to be experience based, I set out four other key principles: be fully prepared to invite in the new – you cannot learn Still Moving leadership unless you are already mindfully open and systemically alert; impact being before doing – it's important that the learning experience offers space for intentional, non-obstructed inner contemplation; don't go it alone – have wise mentors who can create the psychological safety to hold you through a challenging development experience and help you (re)perceive its nature; and pick a regular practice – find a reflective mindfulness practice that you can use to regularly tune into your inner state.

I contend that the majority of the annual $45bn spend on leadership development could be saved if we moved away from expensively provided training courses towards live, experience-led development. This kind of leadership development though requires a different role and skill set for the faculty, one that is focused on holding difficulty not teaching models, one that can help participants recognise and regulate their inner state, not just hand out change tool kits, and one that importantly looks to their own inner experience to systemically diagnose the participants' experience, not just show up to give lectures or moderate exercises. Such mentors act like 'sherpas', guiding leaders across dangerous developmental thresholds.

We need to crack the code of how to design and deliver transforming leadership development interventions as well as understand the model of leadership that they are predicated on.

The Contextual Requirements for Still Moving

This leads me, in concluding this book, to pull together the broader contextual factors that need to be present in order that Still Moving leadership and a more emergent approach to change can flourish in today's world. We can't just plop these elements into a systemic context that is not conducive to their essence. Whether the focus is societies in transformation, institutions adjusting to continuous change or individuals adapting their leadership to today's disruptive world, I believe there are several essential preconditions for Still Moving leadership. I have hinted at them throughout but now articulate them as a final provocation to their consequences for how we run our communities, institutions and, ultimately, our lives.

First, a Preparedness to Uncover the Deep Sources that Create Today's Reality

It is nigh on impossible to practise Still Moving leadership, or adopt an emergent change approach, unless we are willing to open to depth. This requires us to sharpen our perception and cultivate a supreme noticing ability – can we pause and reflect in the heat of experience, look inward at the deep structures and assumptions that are creating our beliefs and acts *before* we seek to project onto, speculate on or judge the situation around us? Can we uncover our individual and collective blind spots?

This preparedness is a challenge. Could we imagine having an observer role in our parliaments and governmental institutions that would spot dysfunctional patterns, provide feedback and coach our politicians on how to examine and be open to their true motives and intentions? This would certainly help to eradicate narcissistic political leadership. Could we have a world in which multi-stakeholder groups gather – across conflicting boundaries – to tackle systemic issues such as child poverty, giving each other mutual feedback on how their assumptions and beliefs are conspiring to keep the whole system stuck? Could we envisage a collectively stewarded process that would coach the main boards of publically listed companies to root out the sources of corporate corruption and greed? Would the leadership development profession be prepared to replace their 360-degree feedback tools with in-depth live feedback processes that uncover and develop a leader's inner mental state?

I do wish for a more self-aware world that is courageous enough to create spaces for deeper observation and reflection.

Second, a Genuine Desire to Find Collaborative Solutions

Just as the physicist Henry Stapp describes elementary particles as, 'in essence, a set of relationships that reaches outward to other things', so do we live our lives in networks of connections. In today's systemically inter-connected world leadership is a collective act. In today's fast moving world we need trust and collaboration, not control and separation, to govern our institutions. The ego is clever in seeking its own reinforce-ment. Being in connection to others forces us to grow and move beyond being a clone of our own values.

Collaboration takes effort. Could we imagine more all-party initiatives such as that in the UK parliament that produced the Mindful Nation report, a truly collaborative effort that transcended political divides in order to put in place practices to build a happier, better-educated and healthier population? Could we envisage organisational structures designed more flexibly around projects and lateral networks that pool together skills when and where they are needed, and are less focused on fixed vertical hierarchies and business unit silos that divide and protect their own resources? Would we have the guts to tear apart divisive and controlling reporting structures that separate our corporate headquarter staff from their operational colleagues and put in their place more trust-ing and collaborative structures? Could we envisage companies' annual leadership events, that self-seal their 100 or so expensive executives in a fancy hotel for 2 days, instead sending leaders out into society to become more alert to their external beneficiaries?

I do dream of a more outer-reaching world that could transcend fixed, rigid, partial solutions.

Third, The Courage to Run Towards, and not Away from Difficulty

Can we learn to function more adroitly while at our edge? Both Still Moving leadership and emergent change call us to be fully alert and alive to the unfolding messiness that is life. They invite us to explore and not deny anxiety. They draw on sources of intelligence – such as feelings and emotions – that we are not trained to handle through conventional education. They both acknowledge that what we most seek to avoid could in fact be the source of greatest revelation and movement. We are most alive when we feel insecure.

Approaching difficulty is not our default setting. Can we imagine corporate cultures though that dispel muddy language in their communications and instead speak more plainly and truthfully? How about more CEOs being able to convey bad news to their staff, analysts and investors? Could we envisage politicians with the guts to fess up when errors have been made, not fearing that this will lead to a victory for their opponents and a decline in voter confidence in the population? Can we see a world where all managers give tough performance feedback, no longer shielding their staff from difficult personal truths? What would we liberate for thousands, if not millions of people's lives, if organisations in difficulty could remove the gilded prisons that are the employment contracts that make it seemingly impossible for staff to simply up sticks and leave? What greater innovation would we unleash in our institutions if leaders could open up their cultures to mistakes, trial and error, and the at times humility of learning?

I do long for a braver world in which difficulty is given a more respectful place.

Ultimately, Still Moving requires that we operate from our highest and most conscious self. The inner capacities in particular are all bad news for the ego. Just sitting with experience as it is confronts our need for things to be something else. Being curious about all that arises challenges our inbuilt wiring to make instant judgement. Interpreting experience through a systemic lens disputes the validity of our carefully crafted personal narratives. And the radical allowing of all experience rubs up against our worldview that we are in charge.

The upside, however, is that Still Moving is a style of leadership that allows us to be part of something bigger. Who and what are we ultimately serving? This is not only a key question for our leadership; it is a question for our lives. My task of examining my story of origin and my life's journey was not an exercise in narcissism but a task to serve what my deepest nature asks of me. Can we all find the story that serves our life? And can we then allow ourselves to live this core?

Writing this book has helped me uncover mine – to sit alongside human communities, and, by joining up various energy fields, enable them to transform. And sometimes examining the fruits of your work enables you to discover your life's work. I notice I have become more provocative and barnstorming in this book, compared to *Sustaining Change*. Perhaps we all become less cautious and careful in the second half of life. But I also know that, through my adoptive parents' containing love, meeting my biological parents enabled me to integrate a part of myself that had been missing, and that I needed to feel complete. It enabled me to leave behind my old identity of being unwanted and unlovable. I am now less fearful of causing offence. I hope I can now bring a larger person to the world.

Join me.

Appendix 1

Detailed Still Moving Research Methodology from Chapter 3

To date studies in mindfulness and leadership have been predominantly quantitative, self-assessment based, experimental (interventions enhance an individual's mindfulness state in a laboratory setting), single faceted in their measures and individual outcomes focused (see Chiesa, 2013[1]; Good et al., 2016[2]). We responded to the expressed limitations of these studies and ours used both quantitative and qualitative methods, had multi-assessor ratings, was situated within work contexts, and studied the inter-relationship between several facets including individual leadership behaviour and inner state (both classic present-moment attention mindfulness *and* its broader systemic perception dimensions), change contexts and organisational outcomes.

We started by building multi-faceted dimensions, to measure a leader's inner state. We took the widely known *Five Factor Analysis (FFMQ)* mindfulness survey instrument (developed by Baer et al., 2006[3]) and adapted its items for a leadership assessment questionnaire. We added items relating to systemic skills into this questionnaire felt to be important in leading change (see Weick & Putnam, 2006[4]). We tested our questionnaire with 150 respondents and the factor analysis from these data enabled us to refine the inner state mindfulness and systemic elements that were most related to change success. From this we created the four inner capacities coding framework (which contains elements of the FFMQ but substantially reconfigured).

We then conducted interviews with leaders in 56 organisations (65 leaders interviewed, leading to 88 separate stories of leading change). The sample comprised leaders drawn from private sector, public sector and 'third sector' organisations (NGOs, charities, etc.). All were at a senior level in their organisation and had played a major role in the implementation of change. We adopted a Behavioural Event Interview approach to the interviews to ameliorate the limitations of retrospective recollection and self-report methods. Each interviewee was asked to

Still Moving: How to Lead Mindful Change, First Edition. Deborah Rowland.
© 2017 John Wiley & Sons Ltd. Published 2017 by John Wiley & Sons Ltd.

recollect in detail (examples of behaviours and responses) one or two stories relating to a change in which he or she had been involved and played a significant leadership role. By probing for multiple examples, the problems associated with interviewees' 'smoothing' the data were ameliorated if not eliminated. Each interview lasted for between 1 and 1.5 h. The interviews were recorded and transcribed.

The interview transcripts were coded using a coding frame that comprised: the leaders' inner capacities – including non-mindfulness; the leaders' external behaviours from our original study; contextual data (e.g., magnitude and timescale for the change, history of change); and degree of change success. To obtain an indication of the degree of change success, a panel assessment was employed. This entailed the interviewee's self-assessment, the coder rating and ratings from three members of an independent expert panel. To establish a higher level of reliability in the coding process, a 10% sample of transcripts was double-coded. Where a degree of coder alignment of less than 90% arose, the transcript went to a third coder for adjudication of differences. Finally, summaries of coding from each coder were reviewed by a separate researcher to check for any apparent consistent biases in their use of codes.

The data analysis was then conducted employing the following steps. Each change story was used as the basis for analysis (88 in total). As we were interested in the role of mindfulness and leadership behaviours in significant change implementation we computed a score that combined change success with the magnitude of the change. This created four categories of stories: 'top tier' – top 10 success × magnitude ratings; 'up there' – next 31 success × magnitude; 'just about okay' – lower 37 success × magnitude; 'unsuccessful' – bottom 10 success × magnitude. We then turned the coded data into a numeric format, using percentages of responses in each code. Using these converted data we undertook various statistical analyses of the data. A rigorous test of significance was applied – significant findings are those that represented a 5% possibility of occurring by chance (or lower). We ran various correlational (factor relationships, hierarchical regressions, partial correlations and t-tests) analyses between the inner capacities and external leadership practices and the change contexts within the four story categories above.

The research was closely supervised by Professor Malcolm Higgs, Professor of Organisational Behaviour and HRM, Southampton Business School, University of Southampton, and Michael Chaskalson of Open Mind, a four-decade long expert mindfulness practitioner.

Appendix 2

Detailed Leadership Development Programme Description from Chapter 9

The participant journey comprised three formal modules, with activity before and after each one. The design itself was *co-created*. Both the overall architecture and certain of its concepts and exercises were tested before the programme was launched with a cross section of the participant leaders, modelling how to work from the beneficiary back. This gave the design team valuable insights into how to adjust and position what was to be a very different style development experience for this organisation. *Modelling the need to start with the beneficiary in any change journey.*

Participants began their journey in enrolment calls with me, the Executive Sponsor and the Programme Manager – sometimes there were up to around 25 participants on one phone call. These calls were a first for this organisation, and it provided an early signal to participants of the importance we were to place on building a trustful and open community across this senior leadership group. Each wave of 36 participants was divided into smaller Peer Groups, of around five to seven participants each. Importantly, each Peer Group also met to get to know each other before the first formal programme module – another intervention to form contact and relationships before the main development task began. *Modelling the need to build community as you embark on major change.*

The primary aim of Module 1 (2.5 days), which we called *Immersion*, was to jump together into an experience to build seeing and noticing skills, leading to greater awareness of today's patterns – at the level of the participant's personal leadership style, their collective culture, and their organisation's relationship to its history and society. At this stage in the journey we were seeking to *model that all major change begins in noticing where you are today, what brought you here, and why.*

Between Module 1 and 2 participants journeyed to the periphery of their system in what were called *Forager Groups*. These had been formed by participants in a self-organised process at the end of Module 1, and

Still Moving: How to Lead Mindful Change, First Edition. Deborah Rowland.
© 2017 John Wiley & Sons Ltd. Published 2017 by John Wiley & Sons Ltd.

their purpose was to have participants step out of their own system and visit the contexts that they felt most mattered to their organisation's future. These contexts included customer groups, politicians, environmental activists, innovation hubs, other companies who had been on similar transformation journeys and also employee groups in their own organisation who directly interfaced with customers and society. *Modelling the need to sense what the external world is calling for so that change is led through the wider context and not the at-times narrowly perceiving ego.*

All of these external insights and inspirations were then brought into a 5-day *Incubation* Module 2, which was an intense and challenging week designed to have participants transition from an old reality to a new one. The week offered a special retreat-type space for participants to move beyond awareness and to deep dive into the very source of today's repeating patterns, and, in particular, to help each participant see their own responsibility for creating them (don't blame 'the system'!).

As the week progressed they put together both the external foraging inspiration and the deep dive into their own patterns, and, through an intense mid-week re-ordering day (using organisational *constellations* methodology), followed by a (much needed by this stage) reflective personal contemplation Day 4, set an intention for what needed to emerge for the future – both in their own leadership and the wider organisational system. Having set clear intention for what leading from the future meant, we then set up a process of rapid prototyping – having participants build experiments for how they wished to lead their business differently that they would test between Modules 2 and 3.

Overall, this essential module in the learning journey *modelled the need in any big change to create challenging yet safe spaces to confront today's routine and allow a new inner knowing to emerge.*

Between Modules 2 and 3 participants tested their prototypes in the wider system, to, in Scharmer's words, *explore the future through doing.* These prototypes ranged from new customer product and service offerings, streamlined business processes and empowering plant operations procedures, to new ways to run meetings and more open ways to engage the emotions of staff going through major change. The primary aim was not to have every prototype 'succeed'; indeed, the very essence of prototyping is to fail early to learn quickly, but to have this organisation learn how to more rapidly bring innovation into the business, working with partial solutions and iterating those solutions with the end beneficiaries. *Modelling that big change has to build in experimentation and the risk of failure.*

Participants brought their prototyping lessons back to a 2-day *Integration* Module 3 whose main aim was to *consolidate* all the lessons

of the entire development journey into a commitment to sustain mainte-
nance of the new sensibilities in day-to-day reality – at the level of the
wider culture, the participants' business units and their personal leadership. Also, and no less importantly, this module was designed to bring
closure to the formal programme, acknowledging and honouring all that
had been experienced – even the struggles and the difficulty. After a
6-month intense and challenging journey together, in which we had got
to know each other at a level not often experienced in a business setting,
facing this ending was not always an easy thing to do, and we gave the
space for this to be felt and processed. *Modelling that intense change is
about managing endings, not just creating new beginnings.*

Notes

Chapter 1: Introduction

1 Higgs, M., & Rowland, D. (2010). Emperors with clothes on: The role of self-awareness in developing effective change leadership. *Journal of Change Management, 10*(4), 369–385.

2 Gelles, D. (2015). *Mindful work: How meditation is changing business from the inside out.* Boston, MA: Houghton Mifflin Harcourt.

3 Chaskalson, M. (2011). *The mindful workplace: Developing resilient individuals and resonant organizations with MBSR.* Oxford, UK: Wiley-Blackwell.

4 Shapiro, S. L., & Carlson, L. E. (2009). *The art and science of mindfulness: Integrating mindfulness into psychology and the helping professions.* Washington, DC: American Psychological Association.

5 Killingsworth, M. A., & Gilbert, D. T. (2010). A wandering mind is an unhappy mind. *Science, 330*(6006), 932.

6 Roche, M., Haar, J. M., & Luthans, F. (2014). The role of mindfulness and psychological capital on the well-being of leaders. *Journal of Occupational Health Psychology, 19,* 476–489.

7 Reb, J., Sim, S., Chintakananda, K., & Bhave, D. P. (2013). *Leading with mindfulness: Exploring the relation of mindfulness with leadership behaviours, styles and development.* New York, NY: Jossey-Bass.

8 Dane, E. (2011). Paying attention to mindfulness and its effects on task performance in the workplace. *Journal of Management, 37,* 997–1018.

9 Aviles, P. R., & Dent, E. B. (2015). The role of mindfulness in leading organisational transformation: A systematic review. *Journal of Applied Management and Entrepreneurship, 20*(3), 31–55.

10 Gärtner, C. (2013). Enhancing readiness for change by enhancing mindfulness. *Journal of Change Management, 13*(1), 52–68.

Still Moving: How to Lead Mindful Change, First Edition. Deborah Rowland.
© 2017 John Wiley & Sons Ltd. Published 2017 by John Wiley & Sons Ltd.

11 Glomb, T. M., Duffy, M. K., Bono, J. E., & Yang, T. (2011). Mindfulness at work. *Research in Personnel and Human Resources Management, 30*, 115–157.

12 O'Leonard, K. author of Bersin by Deloitte (2014), *Corporate Learning Factbook.*

Chapter 2: Is Change Changing?

1 Pew Research Center (November 23, 2015). *Trust in government: 1958–2015.* Washington, DC: Pew Research Center.

2 Tett, G. (October 23, 2015). Why we trust the cyber crowd. *Financial Times.*

3 Boynton, A., & Barchan, M. (July 2015). *Unilever's Paul Polman: CEOs can't be 'slaves' to shareholders.* Forbes.com. Retrieved 2016, September 9 from:http://www.forbes.com/sites/andyboynton/2015/07/20/unilevers-paul-polman-ceos-cant-be-slaves-to-shareholders/#3384afc540b5

4 Microsoft (Spring 2015). *Attention spans.* Consumer Insights, Microsoft Canada.

5 Scharmer, O., & Kaufer, K. (2013). *Leading from the emerging future: From ego-system to eco-system economies.* San Francisco, CA: Berrett-Koehler Publishers.

6 Kuper, S. (November 20, 2015). Paris attacks: Notes from a wounded city. *Financial Times.*

Chapter 3: Still Moving – The Inner and Outer Skills

1 Waldrop, M. M. (1993). *Complexity.* New York, NY: Simon & Schuster.

2 Kabat-Zinn, J. (2005). *Coming to our senses: Healing ourselves and the world through mindfulness.* New York, NY: Hyperion.

3 Killingsworth, M. A., & Gilbert, D. T. (2010). A wandering mind is an unhappy mind. *Science, 330*(6006), 932.

4 Siegel, D. (2011). *Mindsight: Transform your brain with the new science of kindness.* New York, NY: One World Publications.

5 Langer, E. J. (1989). *Mindfulness.* Cambridge, MA: Perseus Publishing.

Chapter 4: It All Starts in Mindfulness

1 Kabat-Zinn, J. (2005). *Coming to our senses: Healing ourselves and the world through mindfulness.* New York, NY: Hyperion.

2 Weick, K. E., & Sutcliffe, K. M. (2006). Mindfulness and the quality of organisational attention. *Organisational Science, 17*(4), 514–524.

3 Shapiro, S. L., Carlson, L. E., Astin, J. A., & Freedman, B. (2006). Mechanisms of mindfulness. *Journal of Clinical Psychology, 62*(3), 373–386.

4 Killingsworth, M. A., & Gilbert, D. T. (2010). A wandering mind is an unhappy mind. *Science, 330*(6006), 932.

5 Langer, E. (2014). *Mindfulness, 25th anniversary edition*. Boston, MA: Da Capo Lifelong Books; 25th edition.

6 Riggio, R. E., & Reichard, R. J. (2008). The emotional and social intelligences of effective leadership: An emotional and social skill approach. *Journal of Managerial Psychology, 23*(2), 169–185.

Chapter 5: The Power of the Systemic

1 Oshry, B. (2007). *Seeing systems: Unlocking the mysteries of organizational life*. San Francisco, CA: Berrett-Koehler.

2 Weick, K. E., Sutcliffe, K. M., & Obstfeld, D. (1999). Organising for high reliability: Processes of collective mindfulness. *Research in Organisational Behaviour, 21*, 81–123.

3 Weick, K. E., & Sutcliffe, K. M. (2007). *Managing the unexpected: Resilient performance in an age of uncertainty*. San Francisco, CA: Jossey-Bass.

4 Jacob Stam, J. (2006). *Fields of connection: The practice of organisational constellations*. Avenhorn, the Netherlands: Uitgeverij Het Noorderlicht.

5 Whittington, J. (2012). *Systemic coaching and constellations: An introduction to the principles, practices and application*. London, UK: Kogan Page.

Chapter 6: Make Disturbance Your Friend

1 Heron, J. (2001). *Helping the client: A creative practical guide*. Fifth Edition. London, UK: Sage Publications.

2 Conner, D. (1993). *Managing at the speed of change*. New York, NY: Villard Books.

Chapter 7: Holding the Fire

1 Menzies Lyth, I. (1988). *Containing anxiety in institutions: Selected essays volume 1*. London, UK: Free Association Books.

2 Armstrong, D. (2004). *Organization in the mind: Psychoanalysis, group relations and organizational consultancy (The Tavistock Clinic Series)*. London, UK: Karnac Books.

Chapter 8: The Time for Emergence

1 Seel, R. (2003). *Emergence in organisations*. New Paradigm Consulting.
2 Mihata, K. (1997). The persistence of emergence. In R. A. Eve, S. Horsfall, & M. E. Lee (Eds.), *Chaos, complexity and sociology: Myths, models and theories* (pp. 30–38). Thousand Oaks, CA: Sage Publications.
3 Mihata, K., & Weick, K. (1997). Emergent change as a universal in organizations. In M. Beer, & N. Nohria (Eds.) (2000). *Breaking the code of change* (pp. 223–224). Boston, MA: Harvard Business School Press.
4 Brown, T. (2008). Design thinking. *Harvard Business Review, June*, 84.
5 Wheatley, M. (1994). *Leadership and the new science: Learning about organization from an orderly universe*. San Francisco, CA: Berrett-Koehler.
6 Shaw, P. (2002). *Changing conversations in organisations: A complexity approach to change (complexity and emergence in organizations)*. Didcot, UK: Routledge.
7 Berger, W. (2014). *A more beautiful question: The power of inquiry to spark breakthrough ideas*. New York, NY: Bloomsbury USA.
8 Schein, E. (2013). *Humble inquiry: The gentle art of asking instead of telling*. San Francisco, CA: Berrett-Koehler Publishers.

Chapter 9: A Tale of Still Moving and Business Transformation

1 Scharmer, O. (2009). *Theory U: Learning from the future as it emerges*. San Francisco, CA: Berrett-Koehler Publishers.
2 Langer, E. J. (1998). *The power of mindful learning*. Boston, MA: Da Capo Press Inc.
3 Kolko, J. (2015). Design thinking comes of age. *Harvard Business Review, September*, 66.

Chapter 10: Still Moving and Your Leadership

1 Langer, E. J. (1997). *The power of mindful learning*. Cambridge, MA: Perseus Books.
2 Davidson, R. J., & Begley, S. (2012). *The emotional life of your brain: How its unique patterns affect the way you think, feel, and live – and how you can change them*. New York, NY: Plume.
3 Chaskalson, M. (2014). *Mindfulness in eight weeks: The revolutionary 8 week plan to clear your mind and calm your life*. London, UK: Harper Thorsons.

4 McClelland, D. C. (1953). *The achievement motive.* Eastford, CT: Martino Fine Books.
5 McClelland, D. C., & Burnham, D. H. (1995). *Power is the great motivator.* Boston, MA: Harvard Business Review Press.

Appendix 1: Detailed Still Moving Research Methodology from Chapter 3

1 Chiesa, A. (2013). The difficulty of defining mindfulness: Current thought and critical issues. *Mindfulness, 4,* 255–268.
2 Good, D. J., Lyddy, C. J., Glomb, T. M., Bono, J. E., Brown, K. W., Duffy, M. K., Baer, R., Brewer, J. A., & Lazar, S. W. (2016). Contemplating mindfulness at work: An integrative review. *Journal of Management, 42*(1), 114–142.
3 Baer, R. A., Smith, G. T., Hopkins, J., Krietemeyer, J., & Toney, L. (2006). Using self-report assessment methods to explore facets of mindfulness. *Assessment, 13,* 27–45.
4 Weick, K. E., & Putnam, T. (2006). Organizing for mindfulness: Eastern wisdom and Western knowledge. *Journal of Management Inquiry, 15,* 275–287.

Bibliography and General Recommended Reading

Brown, P., & Brown V. (2012). *Neuropsychology for coaches: Understanding the basics (coaching in practice)*. Milton Keynes, UK: Open University Press.

Chase, R. (2015). *Peers Inc.: How people and platforms are inventing the collaborative economy and reinventing capitalism*. New York, NY: PublicAffairs.

Collins, J. (2001). *Good to great*. London, UK: Random House Business.

Coupland, D. (2016). *Our brains rewired*. London, UK: FT.com

Frankl, V. (2004). *Man's search for meaning: The classic tribute to hope from the Holocaust*. London, UK: Rider.

Grosz, S. (2014). *The examined life: How we lose and find ourselves*. London, UK: Vintage.

Harris, S. (2014). *Waking up: A guide to spirituality without religion*. New York, NY: Simon & Schuster.

Hollis, J. (2000). *Creating a life: Finding your individual path*. London, UK: Inner City Books.

Johnson, S. A. (2001). *Emergence: The connected lives of ants, brains, cities and software*. London, UK: Allen Lane.

Kline, N. (2002). *Time to think: Listening to ignite the human mind*. London, UK: Cassell.

Lindstrom, M. (2016). *Small data: The tiny clues that uncover huge trends*. New York, NY: St Martins Press.

Marturano, J. (2015). *Finding the space to lead: A practical guide to mindful leadership*. London, UK: Bloomsbury Press.

McLaren, K. (2010). *The language of emotions: What your feelings are trying to tell you*. Boulder, CO: Sounds True Inc.

Morris, D. (1977). *Manwatching: A field guide to human behaviour*. London, UK: Triad Books.

O'Donohue, J. (2008). *To bless the space between us: A book of blessings*. New York, NY: Doubleday Books.

Still Moving: How to Lead Mindful Change, First Edition. Deborah Rowland.
© 2017 John Wiley & Sons Ltd. Published 2017 by John Wiley & Sons Ltd.

Reb, J., & Atkins, P. (Eds.) (2015). *Mindfulness in organizations: Foundations, research, and applications.* Cambridge, UK: Cambridge University Press.

Rowland, D., & Higgs, M. (2008). *Sustaining change: Leadership that works.* Oxford, UK: John Wiley & Sons.

Siegel, R. D. (2010). *The mindful solution: Everyday practices for everyday problems.* New York, NY: Guildford Press.

Tan, C.-M. (2012). *Search inside yourself: The unexpected path to achieving success, happiness (and world peace).* New York, NY: Harper One.

Turkle, S. (2015). *Reclaiming conversation.* London: Penguin Press.

Watson, G., Batchelor, S., & Claxton, G. (2000). *The psychology of awakening: buddhism, science, and our day-to-day lives.* Newburyport, MA: Red Wheel/Weiser.

Index

Page numbers in *italics* denote illustrations, tables or figures.

Still Moving: How to Lead Mindful Change, First Edition. Deborah Rowland.
© 2017 John Wiley & Sons Ltd. Published 2017 by John Wiley & Sons Ltd.